COURSE TECHNOLOGY
CENGAGE Learning™

Professional • Technical • Reference

More Than One Way to
SKIN A CAT

Create Eye-Popping Effects Using Aviary
(Without Paying for Photoshop!)

Aviary

Meowza Katz

COURSE TECHNOLOGY
CENGAGE Learning™

**More Than One Way to Skin a Cat:
Create Eye-Popping Effects Using Aviary
(Without Paying for Photoshop®!)
Meowza Katz**

**Publisher and General Manager, Course
Technology PTR:**
Stacy L. Hiquet

Associate Director of Marketing:
Sarah Panella

Manager of Editorial Services:
Heather Talbot

Marketing Manager:
Jordan Casey

Acquisitions Editor:
Megan Belanger

Development/Technical Editor:
Lisa Bucki

Project/Copy Editor:
Jenny Davidson

PTR Editorial Services Coordinator:
Jennifer Blaney

Interior Layout Tech:
Bill Hartman

Cover Designer:
Mike Tanamachi

CD-ROM Producer:
Brandon Penticuff

Indexer:
Larry Sweazy

Proofreader:
Heather Urschel

For product information and technology assistance, contact us at
Cengage Learning Customer & Sales Support, 1-800-354-9706

For permission to use material from this text or product,
submit all requests online at **cengage.com/permissions**
Further permissions questions can be e-mailed to
permissionrequest@cengage.com.

Photoshop is a registered trademark of Adobe Systems Incorporated in
the United States or other countries.

All other trademarks are the property of their respective owners.

Library of Congress Control Number: 2008902392

ISBN-13: 978-1-59863-472-3

ISBN-10: 1-59863-472-0

Course Technology
25 Thomson Place
Boston, MA 02210
USA

Cengage Learning is a leading provider of customized learning solutions
with office locations around the globe, including Singapore, the United
Kingdom, Australia, Mexico, Brazil, and Japan. Locate your local office at:
international.cengage.com/region.

Cengage Learning products are represented in Canada by Nelson
Education, Ltd.

For your lifelong learning solutions, visit **courseptr.com**.

Visit our corporate Web site at **cengage.com**.

Printed in the United States of America
1 2 3 4 5 6 7 11 10 09

Dedication

A special thanks to my family: Shaena, Mama, Didi, Obs, Sach, Steve, Akemi, and Panda.

Thank you, Mama and Obs, for everything you've given me growing up.

Especially flower okaki.

Thank you, Didi, for being the first to support me when I decided to quit my old job and go for art.

I'd like to dedicate this book to my sweetii, Brandi, whom I met just as I began writing this. Whenever I'm standing in a store and see this book on a shelf, I'll be thinking of the first time I saw you and how my whole life changed from the moment I saw just the top of your head at the grand court. Love you! Muah!

Acknowledgments

To the Aviary staff: Avi, Iz, Michael G., Ari, Mario, Mo, Gabriele, Andrea, Alessandro, Maudie, Sumul, Gila, Amira, and the rest of the wonderful folks, advisors, partners, and birds at Aviary. It goes without saying that this book would not have existed without the megalomaniacal dedication of every single one of you.

To the book staff: Lisa, Jenny, Megan, and all those at Course Technology. A huge thanks (in English this time, Lisa!) for giving us at Aviary a chance to spread our voice.

To friends who have dealt with my increasing descent into insanity while I wrote this book: Tammy "Nickname Still Pending" V., Chris "The Nigerian Nightmare" G., David "David Lopez" Lopez.

To the Aviary community. Aviary wouldn't be what it is today without the help and enthusiasm of every member constantly testing, creating, and pushing the suite to its absolute limits. And then pushing it some more.

To those people I failed to mention, your name was just too hard to spell!

About the Author

Meowza Katz is a self-taught graphic artist, illustrator, and popcorn eater from Vancouver, BC, Canada, who went full-time as a freelance artist in 2004. After finding success in greeting card design, he had his first public art show in Spokane, Washington, where a number of his multimedia pieces were exhibited before going full-time as Artist in Residence for Aviary, Inc. His work has been featured in media all over the world, ranging from greeting card illustration, to company branding, to magazine cover art. He's won numerous awards and accolades (including the "Grand Jury" award) on the highly popular Photoshop contest website, Worth1000.com. His personal work can be found on his website, www.meowza.org. And he also likes colorful pants.

Contents

Introduction x

1 Phoenix Basics 1
Phoenix Tools 2
Understanding Layers 6
Making Selections..10

2 Basic Tutorials 15
Casting Shadows...16
Matching Shadows 20
Matching Lighting 24
Background Cloning...28
Layer Masks 32
Three Ways of Color Replacement 36
Precision Selection 40
Lighting Effects..44
Surface Reflections 48
Motion Blur 52
Perspective Sign..56
Changing Skin Color 60
Creating Lightning..64

Foggy Day 68

Snowy Day 72

Rainy Day 76

Flood 80

Day to Night 84

In the Clouds 90

Behind Glass 94

Tattoo Art 98

Graffiti 102

Face Swap 106

Liquify—Melting 110

Liquify—Displacement 114

Liquify—Texturizing 118

Clowning Around 122

Coloring Line Art 126

3 Sprucing Up Photography 131

Enhancing Saturation 132

Borders..134

Dodge & Burn 140

Compositional Cropping..144

Cross Processing 148

Selective Desaturation 152

Selective Inversion...156

Aging a Photo 160

Photo Retouching 164

Coloring Hair 170

Enhancing Eyes 174

Warhol-izing 178

Turning a Photo into a Comic Book Panel.................182

Miniaturizing..186

4

Fun with Phoenix 191

Lemon Car 192
Chocolate 198
Aliens! 202
Aging a Person 208
Animal Hybrids 214
Edible Architecture 218
Gender Bending 224
Flying Cars 230
Toiletbot 236
Inanimate Objects 242
Unzipped 246
Fire! 252
Water 256
S-s-smokin' 260
Chrome 264
Stone 268
Canvas Earth 272
Robot Frog 278
Animal Dress-Up 282
Creating an MP3 Player 288
Anatomy Scramble 294
Creating a Sea Monster 298
Cyborg 304
Dragons 310

Index 317

Introduction

For years, as a digital artist, I felt almost as if I belonged to an exclusive, secret club.

In this club, we all watched each others' backs (as long as we weren't vying for the same design jobs). We felt smug in the sense that we'd overcome the barrier to entry, and laughed as our non-art savvy friends were impressed with our three-minute image manipulation of their head imposed on a lingerie model's body. We loved creating and altering images as we saw fit, and in a sense, changed the course of history to our liking. We loved making you laugh, making you cry, and making you angry with the images we created. We loved that you didn't know what we knew.

With this club came thousands of dollars in membership costs in the name of software prices.

When I first heard of the plans for the Aviary suite, I was immediately floored by the sheer ambition of the project. As an avid enthusiast of Adobe Photoshop, I was very interested to see how the idea of a browser-based image editor, which costs a fraction of its desktop predecessor, would come to fruition, and what the benefits would actually be.

Not only Aviary's affordability, but the stripped-down nature of the program, with the software including just the most important tools and features commonly used by artists compared to its desktop predecessor, created an unparalleled low barrier to entry for the casual creator and the new artist who wants to dive into this world without the demanding initial investment. All of a sudden, the world finally had a place where anyone with an internet connection could create. When I saw the community and collaborative aspect for the suite, I began realizing the future for this piece of software. In essence, the door to our secret club was opened.

When I was asked to write Aviary's first tutorial book, I was honored, to say the least. I was given this powerful new toy and set out to create images that I felt anyone can follow along and do just as well. As much as I loved being a part of the exclusive club, I get an enormous sense of pride watching a new artist take a technique I taught him and apply it to his own images. And I'm left to wonder where I would be in art had I had the opportunity to dissect works of digital art I admired during my days starting off in the industry.

So with that said, welcome to Aviary's first book, *More Than One Way to Skin a Cat.*

The book is divided into four parts, plus a CD. The first section deals with "Phoenix Basics," explaining the various tools, layering system, and features you'll need to familiarize yourself with to execute the tutorials.

The second section is full of "Basic Tutorials" that a beginner could easily pick up and follow. These tutorials include simple effects such as colorizing, face swapping, creating lighting and shadows, and more. They illustrate a sample of the basic effects one can create within Aviary.

The third section is "Sprucing Up Photography." From helpful tips involving retouching skin and cross-processing your images, to more fun effects such as turning a photograph into a comic book panel or a Warhol image, this chapter deals with all sorts of neat ideas to enhance that old picture in the shoebox gathering dust in the back of your... harddrive!

And finally, the last section, "Fun with Phoenix," is chock full of tutorials that show just a fraction of the kind of work you can create by putting together all the knowledge gathered within the early chapters of the book.

The included CD has all the source images needed to complete all the tutorials within the book. But for added fun, try applying the same techniques to your own personal photographs and show them to your family and friends. The CD also comes packed with a coupon for a free one-year membership to Aviary, allowing unlimited use of Phoenix, and also access to all the layered image files online to dissect at your whim through the Tutorials section on the site.

So whatever your skill level is in art, I hope there's something to learn in this book for everyone. And everyone finally has somewhere where they can let their potential soar. Because when the world is creating, we do some amazing things.

So welcome to the book. And more importantly, welcome to the club.

Just remember to take your shoes off at the door.

Meowza Katz
proud member of the Earth

Phoenix Basics

If you've used photo editing programs before, working with Phoenix will feel familiar. If you don't have experience, no worries. This section introduces you to the Phoenix tools and key features used in nearly every photo editing technique. Take a quick tour of the Phoenix essentials now.

Phoenix Tools

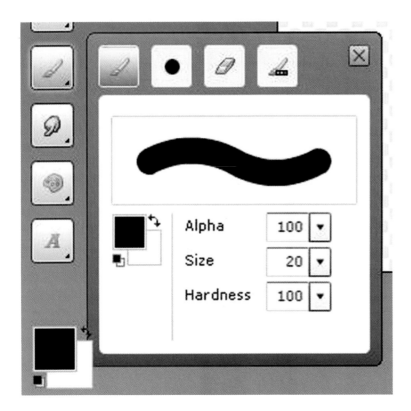

Phoenix comes equipped with many of the necessary tools needed for most all image manipulating. Before starting with any of the tutorials in this book, it's a good idea to familiarize yourself with the main tools.

All the tools are located on the left-hand side of the workspace. To select a tool for use, simply click on the icon for the tool you need.

Clicking on some of the tools opens a window or palette as shown here, where you can either select other tools in that toolset or choose settings for the tool you clicked.

So, let's get acquainted with some of these tools you'll be using, shall we?

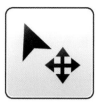

Transformation Tool—The Transformation Tool basically moves entire layers, or selected areas of your image, within the canvas at a time. With the Transformation Tool selected, you can drag the objects on your working canvas very easily. This tool also enables you to resize the selected object. Drag one of the "handles" on the bounding box around your selection to resize as needed. Then, simply double-click within your selection to confirm your transformation.

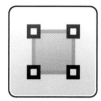

Distortion Tool—The next tool down is the Distortion Tool. Click the Distortion Tool icon, and handles appear on the corners of your image. Simply drag any of these boxes to skew the object, and then double-click in the selection to finish the change. The Distortion Tool makes it extremely easy to warp the perspective of your images.

Magic Wand—The Magic Wand Tool enables you to make selections based on color. After you click the Magic Wand Tool, clicking an area in your image selects all the surrounding pixels of similar color range. When you select the Magic Wand Tool, you'll see a window pop up beside the tool. Here, you can adjust the Tolerance setting of the tool. The higher the tolerance, the larger the range of colors selected becomes, down to a tolerance of 1, which will only select surrounding areas with the exact same color value of the pixel you clicked on. You also can choose to set Contiguous on or off. Unchecking this check box enables the Magic Wand to select colors within the entire image, whether joined to the point you initially clicked or not.

Lasso Selection—This tool enables you to make freehand selections in your image by dragging around the portion you want to select. To close your selection, simply release the mouse button. You can press Shift while dragging to add to the selection, or Alt while dragging to delete an area from the selection. When you click the Lasso Selection tool, you'll notice there's also an option to use the Polygonal Selection Tool. This tool is similar, except that you create selections with straight lines. The selection grows, adding corners with each click.

Rectangular Selection—Like the other selection tools, the Rectangular Selection Tool enables you to select and isolate regions of your image to alter. By dragging the tool on your image, you can make a rectangular selection. Holding Ctrl while you drag enables you to make a perfectly constrained square selection. You also have the option of using the Elliptical Selection Tool, which works the same as the Rectangular Selection Tool, except it enables you to create elliptical and circular selections.

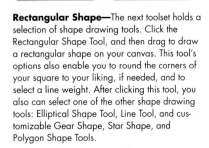

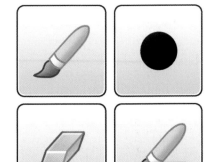

Rectangular Shape—The next toolset holds a selection of shape drawing tools. Click the Rectangular Shape Tool, and then drag to draw a rectangular shape on your canvas. This tool's options also enable you to round the corners of your square to your liking, if needed, and to select a line weight. After clicking this tool, you also can select one of the other shape drawing tools: Elliptical Shape Tool, Line Tool, and customizable Gear Shape, Star Shape, and Polygon Shape Tools.

Paint Bucket—The Paint Bucket Tool enables you to easily fill your image, or a selected area in your image, with the foreground color by simply clicking the tool on the canvas. By selecting the Gradient Tool from the same toolset, you can fill your image with a gradient color blend from the selected foreground color to the selected background color. You can set the foreground color by using the Eye Dropper Tool, which is also on this same toolset. Simply select this tool, and click on the portion of your image you want to sample your color from. This will select the color of the pixel you clicked on, and set it as your foreground color.

Paintbrush Tool—You could also paint specific areas of your image freehanded with the Paintbrush Tool. With this tool selected, drag anywhere on your canvas to paint with the current foreground color. The options also allow you to adjust the Alpha, Size, and Hardness of your brush to your liking by increasing or decreasing the amount in the tools options. There's also a Shape Brush Tool that enables you to paint with any of the included custom shapes. The Eraser Tool is also located among these tools. It works similarly to the Paintbrush, except it removes pixels from your image instead of adding them.

Smudge Tool—The Smudge Tool simulates dragging your finger through the image, smudging pixels in the direction you drag. This tool comes in handy when trying to distort elements to contour along warped paths. Also located in this toolset are the Blur and Sharpen Tools. What these tools basically do is apply a blurred or sharpened effect to the area in your image you click with the respective tool selected.

Liquify Tool—The Liquify Tool is similar to the Smudge Tool, in that the tool is used primarily by dragging from a starting point in your image to make the selected pixels conform to the path that you drag along. This tool especially comes in handy when trying to make subtle changes to elements in your image. For example, you could use the tool to enlarge or shrink facial features in a portrait. The Clone Stamp Tool enables you to duplicate a part of the existing image. Shift+click to establish an anchor point in the area to clone, and then drag to create the duplicate.

Text—The Text tool is just as it sounds. It allows you to insert text into your document. Select the tool and the desired settings (Font, Size, and so on), click the location where you want the text to appear, and type the text with your keyboard. You can select between any of the included fonts within the program itself, with the options of changing the text size, colors, bold, underline, and so on.

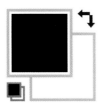

Selecting Colors—Below the tools in the bottom-left corner of your workspace, you'll notice two boxes, each filled with a color. These indicate the current foreground and background colors. The box on top is the foreground color, and the bottom or back box is the background color. Clicking the arrow icon to the top-right of this figure quickly inverts the color choices, making your background color your new foreground color. In order to change your foreground and background colors, simply click on the corresponding box. In the Select Color dialog box, select a color using the large color box and/or slider bar, or by inputting the Hex or RGB value of the color of your choice itself, provided you have the information of the color you seek.

Understanding Layers

Source Images: "Above the City" by Barsik, "Happy businessman" by Lise Gagne

Layers enable you to combine multiple images into one composite. You retain the ability to edit and alter images independently of each other to create the final piece. This tutorial will cover the basic use of layers and some of the various functions that can be applied to them.

To understand how layers work, imagine them as clear acetate sheets stacked on top of each other. In the example image at left, I started with the background image of the city skyline. Then I imported the figure of the man on top of it on a new clear plastic sheet. Let's go further in-depth to working with layers now.

1. First, I started by creating a new document. I selected Load Existing File on Phoenix's splash page, and then proceeded to upload my background image when prompted. This automatically inserted my background image onto a new layer.

2. Next, I imported the image of the man holding the umbrella. I selected File > Import. On the My Computer tab of the Resource Browser window, I clicked the browse button, selected the image of the man, and clicked OK to upload the image to my current document. When the file was uploaded to Phoenix, it automatically set it on a new layer above my background layer.

3. With the figure on a new layer, I was able to position him on the canvas without disturbing my original background layer. I lowered the umbrella man layer's alpha (opacity) to 50% by sliding the Alpha slider on the Layers sidebar halfway down. This enabled me to see the original background at the same time, helping me accurately position the figure to my liking. I then selected the Transformation Tool and dragged my figure where I wanted him. I double-clicked in the center of my selection to confirm the move. I then set the umbrella man layer's Alpha back to 100% on the Layers sidebar.

Note

For organizational purposes, it also helps to name your layers as you go. By double-clicking the layer in the Layers sidebar, typing a new name, and pressing Enter, you can change the layer name or label. In the case of this example, I decided to name my uploaded image as simply "Background."

4. I then needed to remove the sky portion of my umbrella man layer to make him appear to be placed on the background layer. I did this with a layer mask. With my umbrella man layer selected, I clicked drop-down list arrow for the options button in the Layers sidebar and selected the Mask Layer option. Initially, this option made my entire layer invisible. By selecting the Paintbrush Tool and painting on the Mask layer with white set as my foreground color, I was able to "draw" back in the parts I wanted to keep. I did this roughly at first, as I knew I would be fine-tuning it next.

5. To clean the edges, I selected the Eraser Tool, set the Hardness value to 90, and simply dragged around my figure to erase the rest of the unnecessary remnants on the layer's mask.

6. Working with layers also enables you to add certain adjustment edits and effects on layers independently of each other. In this image, I wanted to brighten the initial background layer. First, I selected the background layer in the Layers sidebar. I then selected Image > Brightness & Contrast and slid the Brightness slider in the Brightness and Contrast dialog box about 10 points to the right. I clicked OK to confirm the change.

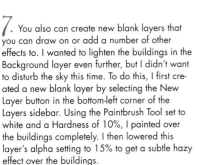

Note

By selecting File > Export Image, you can export a flattened version of your creation to your computer. In the pop-up menu, select the file type you want to save your image as, and click Save. It will prompt you to select a location to save the image to, and allow you to name the file at the same time. Then click Save, and your image will now be exported to your computer.

Note

Layers can be rearranged on the Layers sidebar at any time. To do so, select the layer you want to move on the Layers sidebar and simply drag it where you want. To delete a layer, select the layer you want to remove and click the Drop Layer icon on the bottom of the Layers sidebar.

7. You also can create new blank layers that you can draw on or add a number of other effects to. I wanted to lighten the buildings in the Background layer even further, but I didn't want to disturb the sky this time. To do this, I first created a new blank layer by selecting the New Layer button in the bottom-left corner of the Layers sidebar. Using the Paintbrush Tool set to white and a Hardness of 10%, I painted over the buildings completely. I then lowered this layer's alpha setting to 15% to get a subtle hazy effect over the buildings.

8. You can go on to add further effects and filters to layers. I wanted to slightly blur the background of this image to create a slight sense of depth. I selected my background layer once again, and clicked the Layer Filters icon at the bottom of the Layers sidebar. The Layer Filters dialog box appeared, offering a number of filters I could add to my layer. I clicked the Blur check box to check it. Then I was able to adjust exactly how much blur I wanted to apply by specifying horizontal (blur X) and vertical (blur Y) parameters. You can enter a value from 1-255 in each of those text boxes, with 255 being the strongest blur. In this case, I wanted to keep the effect minimal and entered 2 in both the blur X and blur Y text boxes. I then clicked OK to apply the effect.

Making Selections

Source Image: "Red Eye Frog" by Jan Pietruszka

Making selections is a necessary part of any selective image editing, such as when you're trying to apply effects to certain areas of an image. In this tutorial, I'll be showing you how, using a few different selection tools in Phoenix, I was able to add a neat out of bounds effect to a picture of a frog.

1. First, I wanted to start by isolating the frog from its background. I duplicated the original image layer, and then hid the original by clicking its eye icon, leaving the duplicate layer visible. I clicked the duplicate layer in the Layers sidebar. Then, I selected the Magic Wand Tool, set at a Tolerance level of 40, and simply clicked on an area of the background of the duplicate layer. The Magic Wand selected all adjoining pixels close in tonal proximity to the area clicked based on the amount of tolerance chosen in the Magic Wand's settings.

2. I noticed a lot of the background still remained deselected. I kept the Magic Wand Tool selected, but this time I held Shift as I clicked (Shift+click) on the remaining areas. Using Shift+click enabled me to add to my current selection and isolate the entire background. With the entire background selected, I chose Edit > Cut to delete the selection. Then I chose Select > Select None to make sure to remove my prior selection.

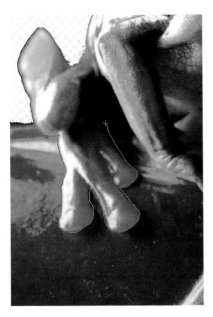

3. I still wanted to isolate the frog on its own layer. For areas that contain similar tones or for areas with complex backgrounds, I found it easier to use the Lasso Tool. With the Lasso Tool selected, I dragged around the frog to make a rough freehand selection.

4. I didn't need it to be perfect for now, as I would go in and fine-tune it later. With my frog selected, I chose Edit > Copy, then Edit > Paste. This pasted the selected frog onto a new layer, and I chose Select > Select None to remove my prior selection.

5. Next, I wanted to cut out a selection for the background. I went back to my original frog image layer, clicking the eye icon to redisplay it and then clicking the layer itself to make sure it was selected. I selected the Rectangular Selection Tool. I held down the Ctrl key as I dragged to make the selection. Doing so allowed me to select a perfectly constrained square.

6. With the portion of background selected, I pressed Edit > Copy, then Edit > Paste to paste my selection into a new layer. I clicked the eye icon for the original layer to hide it. I then moved the new layer with the cropped background area behind (below) the layer with the isolated frog.

7. I wanted to add a white border around the background selection to give the appearance of the background being a photograph. So, I selected the layer with the cropped background area. Using the Magic Wand Tool, I clicked the transparent area of the background square layer. I then chose Select > Invert Selection to create a selection around my background square. I added a new layer and made sure that it was selected, and then I used the Paint Bucket Tool to fill this selection in white after selecting white as the foreground color. This will be the basis for the frame, and this layer must appear in front of (above) the layer with the background selection.

8. Using the Rectangular Selection Tool, I then selected a section of the frame to remove on the layer with the white frame "base" I just created. I dragged a square marquee in the middle of the white frame base. Then I chose Edit > Cut to remove the middle, leaving me with a white border around the background.

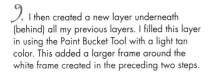

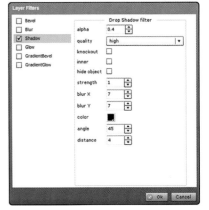

9. I then created a new layer underneath (behind) all my previous layers. I filled this layer in using the Paint Bucket Tool with a light tan color. This added a larger frame around the white frame created in the preceding two steps.

10. To fine-tune the rest of the image, I wanted to clean the edges of the exposed portion of the frog. Using the Eraser Tool set at 80% Hardness and 100% Alpha, I simply dragged around the frog on the layer where I copied it to soften the edges.

11. Finally, I wanted to set a shadow around the area of the image framed in white. I selected the layer with the background square in the layers list. I clicked the Layer Filters icon at the bottom of the layers palette. This opened the Layers Filter dialog box, which offers various effect options available to apply to a selected layer. I checked the box next to the Shadow option. This brought up the drop shadow options for the selected layer. I set the alpha setting to 0.4 to lessen the effect, then set the blur amount to 7 for both the X and Y variables. When I was satisfied with the shadow, I clicked OK. Then, I finished it off by doing the same for the frog layer.

2

Basic Tutorials

Casting Shadows

Source Image: "Jumpin' Jack Flash" by Don Bayley

One of the most important steps in compositing an image from multiple sources is creating believable shadows for your imported elements. Shadows make the elements appear to sit in their new environment more realistically and prevent the final image from looking like a simple "copy and paste" job. This tutorial will shed some light (pardon the pun) on the basics of creating simple cast shadows in an image.

1. The first, and most important, step is to determine where the light source is coming from in the image. You can do this by studying the existing light and shadows in the source image. In this case, I noticed a strong light hitting the guitar player from the front right, judging by the harsh light on the right side of his face. So I knew I wanted to cast a strong shadow going in the same direction, back and to the left away from our figure.

2. To create the shadow, I needed to duplicate the shape of the guitar player. A simple way to create this selection was to first extract the figure. I used the Lasso Tool and made a rough selection of the guitar player, chose Edit > Copy to copy the selection, and then chose Edit > Paste to paste the copied selection onto a new layer above the original image layer. I then pressed Ctrl+D to remove the selection marquee.

3. To finish this selection, I used the Eraser Tool set at 90% hardness, and simply erased the remaining background area from the layer with the copied figure.

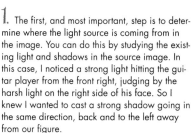

Tip

You can use the View menu to zoom in or out as you work, or press Ctrl+ + or Ctrl+ -. You also can press Ctrl+Tab to hide and display the sidebars to adjust your workspace.

Note

When extracting elements, I often create a new layer below the layer with the figure I want to extract, then fill this layer with a solid contrasting color. This enables me to easily see what portions of the image I'm removing and prevents me from accidentally erasing a portion I want to keep. In this case, I filled a new layer below the layer with the guitar player with red so I could easily see any remaining gray background areas.

4. With my figure extracted on a new layer, I then needed to create a selection around him. I did this by clicking the Magic Wand Tool on the transparent portion on this layer. This selected the entire outside area around him. To add additional areas to the selection, I pressed and held the Shift key while clicking. I did this in areas such as the space between the guitarist's right arm and body, or anywhere else that my initial Magic Wand selection failed to capture. Then, I chose Select > Invert Selection. This inverted the selection to create a marquee around the guitar player. With the figure still selected, I created a new layer above this layer, selected the Paint Bucket Tool and a black foreground color, and clicked within the selection marquee to fill it with black on the new layer. This will be the base for the shadow.

5. Next, I needed to skew the shadow to fit the ground's plane in the original image in the direction of our determined light source. Leaving the layer with the black shadow figure selected, I clicked the Distortion Tool. This automatically placed a bounding box with handles on the corners around the current layer—in this case, the base shadow. I dragged the top boxes down and to the left until the shadow was positioned along the path I determined. Then I dragged the base shadow layer on the Layers sidebar below the layer of the extracted guitar player. This placed the shadow behind the figure in the image. I also applied a slight blur to this layer by clicking the Layer Filters button on the Layers sidebar, clicking the Blur check box to check it, and leaving the Blur X and Blur Y settings at 4%. I clicked OK to apply the filter.

6. As shadows move farther away from the figure, they tend to grow lighter. One way you can achieve this effect in an image shadow is by using the Gradient Tool. I started by creating a selection around the shadow. Again, I did this by using the Magic Wand Tool and selecting the transparent area of the shadow layer, then inverting the selection. I then created a new layer below the extracted figure layer. To apply the gradient, I first set the foreground color to black, and the background color to white. I dragged the tool across the shadow selection on the new layer starting at the head of the shadow, and releasing at the base near the feet. I then set this layer's blend mode to "Overlay" on the layer palette and dropped the Alpha channel to 34%.

7. With the shadow still selected, I created another new layer below the extracted figure layer. As shadows are strongest directly where the figure meets the surface, I selected the Paintbrush Tool set at 0% hardness and 15% Alpha, and I painted in the area near the foot to make that area darkest in tone. Leaving the shadow selected ensured that the strokes would stay within the shadow area and not overpaint the background.

8. And finally, I added a shadow above the shoe itself to add dimension to the image. I created a new layer above the extracted guitar player on the Layers sidebar. I selected the extracted guitar player layer first and clicked Select > Selection from Layer. I then selected my new layer on the Layer sidebar and selected the Paintbrush Tool with the Hardness set to 0, Alpha set to 12, and black set as my foreground color. I painted over the shoe to darken it to make it appear as if it were in the shadow as well, completing the image.

Note

If you find you're getting jagged edges with this method, simply take the Eraser Tool set at a low hardness (0-10%), and drag along the edges of your selection to clean it up.

Matching Shadows

Source Images: "single car on autobahn" by Manfred Steinbach, "Cheeseburger" by Kelly Cline

One of the most important aspects of putting together photorealistic compositions from multiple source images is to match the lighting and shadows of the imported elements with their new environment. In this tutorial, I'll show how to add a cheeseburger image to a quiet street environment and apply a shadow that mimics an existing shadow in the original image.

1. First, I uploaded my image of a car on a street. I chose this background because there's a lot of space at the top for me to import a new image into, and the car itself has a very distinct shadow that will help illustrate the point of mimicking shadows even better.

2. Next, I chose File > Import, and imported the image of a cheeseburger. Doing so imported the burger onto a new layer above the original street layer. Using the Transformation Tool, I dragged the cheeseburger to center it in the open area in front of the car, double-clicking in the burger to finish the move.

3. I needed to get rid of the white background surrounding the cheeseburger on its layer. I clicked the Magic Wand Tool, set its Tolerance to 3, clicked the white background on the cheeseburger layer to select much of it, and then pressed Delete to delete it. I then selected the Eraser Tool, changed its Hardness option setting to 85%, and dragged along the edges of the burger to erase the rest of the background and isolate the burger.

4. To create the basis for the shadow, I needed to make a selection around the burger first. With the burger isolated on its own layer already, I took the Magic Wand Tool and clicked anywhere on the transparent area of the burger layer. This selected the blank area surrounding the burger. I then chose Select > Invert Selection to select the burger itself. I created a new layer by clicking the New Layer icon on the Layers sidebar, and filled the burger selection on that layer in black with the Paint Bucket Tool. I then chose Select > Select None to remove the selection marquee.

Note

Don't forget that you can click the close (X) button on the options box for the current tool to close the options while you work.

5. Here's where the mimicking fun comes into play! With the filled shadow layer still selected, I selected the Distortion Tool. By observing the visual cue provided by the car's shadow, I could see which direction the light comes from in the picture, and which way the burger shadow should flow. Copying the direction of the car's shadow, I dragged the handles around my shadow selection to line up parallel to the car's shadow. I dragged the upper two handles down and to the right to flip the shadow and establish the angle. I then dragged what used to be the bottom handles up and to the left to stretch the shadow all the way to the bottom of the burger. Happy with the shadow's placement, I double-clicked the shadow to finish the changes and dragged the shadow layer below the burger's layer in the Layers sidebar. In the Layers sidebar, I also changed the shadow layer's Alpha on setting to 47%. I used the Eraser Tool to clean off any jagged edges that may have appeared after I distorted the shadow.

6. Noticing that the car's shadow faded to a lighter tone farther from the car, I wanted to apply the same effect to the cheeseburger's shadow. Using the Magic Wand, I clicked on the cheeseburger's shadow on the shadow layer. I created a new layer by clicking the New Layer button on the Layers sidebar, and applied a gradient to it by first selecting the Gradient Fill Tool. I set black as my start color (leftmost slider arrow) and white as my end color (rightmost slider arrow), and then dragged the tool across the shadow selection starting from the base of the burger to the right end of the shadow. I changed this layer's blend mode setting to Overlay and lowered the Alpha to 25% on the Layers sidebar. I then chose Select > Select None.

7. The car's shadow also seemed to have a blue hue to it. In order to mimic this shadow as accurately as possible, I wanted to apply the same color saturation to the cheeseburger's shadow. I selected the original image layer, selected the Eye Dropper Tool, and clicked within the car's shadow. This sampled some of the blue tone for me and set it as my new foreground color.

8. I selected the burger's base shadow layer in the Layers sidebar. Using the Magic Wand Tool, I clicked inside the shadow again to select it. I created a new layer, moved it above the shadow and the gradient layers, and filled the selection with the blue color I sampled from the car's shadow in Step 7 using the Paint Bucket Tool. I changed this layer's blend mode setting to Overlay and dropped the Alpha to 54% on the Layers sidebar.

Note

Because there are a number of slight variations of blue within the car's shadow, the level of Alpha you set for your saturation layer may vary from my example. If you notice a lack of saturation in your attempt, you can simply open the Image > Hue & Saturation menu and raise the amount of blue in your shadow by sliding the Saturation slider to the right to your liking. It may take a bit of eyeball work, but just use the surrounding shadows as a cue on how much saturation to apply.

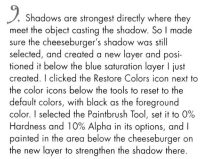

9. Shadows are strongest directly where they meet the object casting the shadow. So I made sure the cheeseburger's shadow was still selected, and created a new layer and positioned it below the blue saturation layer I just created. I clicked the Restore Colors icon next to the color icons below the tools to reset to the default colors, with black as the foreground color. I selected the Paintbrush Tool, set it to 0% Hardness and 10% Alpha in its options, and I painted in the area below the cheeseburger on the new layer to strengthen the shadow there.

10. I wanted to darken the backside of the cheeseburger, where the light wouldn't directly be hitting it. I clicked the burger layer in the Layers sidebar. I then selected the burger itself again by using the Magic Wand and selecting the transparent portion of the layer, and then choosing Select > Invert Selection to isolate the cheeseburger. I created a new layer above the cheeseburger layer and using the Paintbrush Tool set at 0% Hardness and 10% Alpha, I lightly painted the area of the burger that would be hiding in the shadows with black to create a slight shadowed effect.

11. And finally, noticing that the top of the car was illuminated by the sun, I created a new layer on top of the cheeseburger-shading layer. I changed the foreground color to white by double-clicking the foreground color box, and changing the R, G, and B values in the Color Picker dialog box to 255 and clicking OK. I then used the Paintbrush Tool and lightly painted the top of the bun to highlight it. I then set this layer's blend mode to Overlay.

Matching Lighting

Source Images: "Lounge room interior" by Auris, "Elephant sitting down with feet up" by Scott Hirko, "Sitting elephant" by Tristan de Haas

The core of creating believable compositions that involve the blending of two or more images is to match the tone and lighting of one image to the other. In this tutorial, I'm going to import a picture of an elephant into an image of a living room, which has its own distinct light. I'm going to attempt to match the room's lighting and apply it to the imported elephant.

1. I began with the background image of the living room. I chose File > Import and imported the image of the elephant onto its own layer. Using the Lasso Selection Tool, I roughly selected the elephant from its original background and pasted him onto a new layer using Edit > Copy and Edit > Paste. I chose Select > Select None to remove the selection marquee. In the Layers sidebar, I clicked the Eye icon for both the living room layer and the original elephant layer to hide them. Then, using the Eraser Tool set at 90% Hardness, I erased the remaining background area to finish extracting the elephant. Finally, I clicked the box for the Eye icon for the living room layer to redisplay it.

2. I lowered the Alpha setting in the Layers sidebar of the elephant's layer to 50% temporarily. Using the Transformation Tool, I dragged the elephant in position to sit on the sofa. Then, with the Eraser Tool, I erased the portions of the elephant overlapping the armrest and table, as I wanted those elements to appear to be overlapping the elephant in the image.

3. I then set the elephant layer's Alpha back to 100%. Noticing that the original background had an orange tint to it, I needed to match this tone with the elephant. With the elephant layer selected, I chose Select > Selection from Layer, and this created a selection around the isolated elephant. I clicked the New Layer icon on the Layers sidebar to create a new layer above the elephant layer. I clicked the Foreground Color Picker box, entered DBA12C in the HEX text box of the Color Picker dialog box, and then clicked OK. I then used the Paint Bucket Tool to fill the selection with the specified orange color. Note that you could also use the Eye Dropper Tool to sample an orange color from the living room image layer, but be sure to reselect the newest layer before filling the selection. I then chose Select > Select None.

4. I set the elephant fill layer's blend mode to Overlay in the Layers sidebar to give the elephant the orange tone I desired. This caused a more harsh tone than I wanted, so I lowered the Alpha setting for the layer to 80% to help lessen the effect until I was happy with the tone of the elephant against the original background.

5. Next I needed to add highlights and shadows to the elephant to match the lighting and the shadows in the original background. As the lights were coming down on the elephant from above, I wanted to add highlighting to the top of the elephant where the light would hit it. I selected the elephant layer and chose Select > Selection from Layer. I clicked the New Layer icon on the Layers sidebar to create a new layer above the elephant. I set the foreground color to white by clicking the Foreground Color Picker box, entering 255 for the R, G, and B values in the Color Picker dialog box, and clicking OK. Using the Paintbrush Tool set to 0% Hardness and 10% Alpha, I painted lightly on the areas on top of the elephant's head and trunk to create a highlighted effect, as if the lights above were hitting these exposed areas. I then set this layer's blend mode to Overlay in the Layers sidebar.

6. I continued this process over the rest of the surface of the elephant where there were existing highlights to strengthen these areas and lighten the general look of the elephant to suit the indoor lit surroundings.

7. Next, I wanted to deepen the elephant's shadows, as lightening the elephant tended to make the figure flat looking. I created a new layer for the surface shadows by clicking the New Layer icon on the Layers sidebar. I set the foreground color to black by clicking the Restore Colors button by the color selection boxes. With the selection around the elephant still active, I selected the Paintbrush Tool, set its Alpha setting to 8% in the tool options, and painted in the areas that needed shading, such as the areas under the elephant's neck and arms to deepen these areas. I then set this layer's blend mode to Multiply in the Layers sidebar.

8. With the lighting and shadows applied on the elephant, I still needed to situate him into the environment. To do so, I added shadows around the figure to sit him on the sofa better. I chose Select > Select None to deselect the elephant. I clicked the New Layer icon to create a new layer and dragged the new layer below the extracted elephant's layer. With the Eye Dropper Tool, I selected a dark reddish tone from an area of the shadows under the sofa on the original living room layer. Then I reselected the newest layer in the Layers sidebar. Using the Paintbrush Tool set to 10 Alpha, 20 Size, and 0 Hardness, I painted in shadows behind the elephant on the couch.

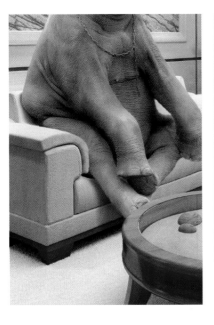

9. Then I did the same under the elephant's leg to create the effect of his leg casting a shadow over the couch in these areas as well.

10. I noticed there was a subtle reflection of the back of the sofa on the wall. To situate the elephant into this new environment accurately, I wanted to cast a slight reflection of the elephant onto the wall as well. I selected the layer with the extracted elephant. Using the Lasso Selection Tool, I made a rough selection around the back of the elephant and copied and pasted this selection onto a new layer (Edit > Copy and Edit > Paste). I then selected Edit > Transform > Flip Horizontal to mirror the segment for the reflection. Then I dragged this layer below the original elephant's layer.

11. I then set this layer's blend mode to Overlay in the Layers sidebar and used the Eraser Tool to erase the portions that were over-lapping the couch's reflection and the picture frame in the background.

12. Finally, I imported an elephant friend into the image and used the same steps as for the first elephant to blend him into his surroundings and complete the image!

Background Cloning

Source Image: "Stormy Weather" by Quavondo Nguyen

One of the most important techniques in image manipulation, whether it be for creative purposes or for photography retouching is effectively cloning out undesirable elements in an image. In this tutorial, I'll show how to remove this woman from the photograph and insert her back in as a ghostly apparition for effect.

1. To create our ghostly apparition, first I needed to remove the woman from the image. I started with the sky portion on the image. Using the Lasso Selection Tool, I selected a portion of the clouds in the sky, copied it (Edit > Copy), then pasted it (Edit > Paste) onto a new layer.

2. I selected the new layer in the Layers sidebar and chose Select > Select None to remove the selection marquee. Using the Transformation Tool, I moved the copied portion of the sky to cover the woman, resizing it as needed and pressing Enter to finish the transformation. Using the Eraser Tool with the Hardness set to 0, I softened the edges to blend it into the original sky. I continued this process until the woman and umbrella were completely covered in the sky portion of the image. Using darker areas of the sky to overlap darker areas of the original sky, and lighter areas of the sky for lighter areas of the original, will create a smoother blend when softening the edges.

3. I continued this same process for the grass and the mountains, copying a patch of each from the original layer and pasting it to its own layer. I made sure the horizon line of the pasted segments aligned properly with the horizon of the original background layer.

4. Cloning the dark foreground grass area took a little more work than the rest of the background, since there weren't any large, unobstructed segments I could cover a lot of space with at one time. Using the Lasso Selection Tool, I selected small sections of the exposed foreground grass on the original layer and pasted them just as I did earlier with the rest of the background.

5. I completed the same process for the street portion of the image until the woman was completely covered and my background was made clear. At this point, the background cloning process was complete.

6. To create the ghostly woman effect, first I hid all the pasted layers by clicking the Eye icon for each layer in the Layers sidebar so I could see the woman again. I then used the Lasso Selection Tool to make a selection around the woman on the original image layer, and pasted her onto a new layer and dragged the layer with the copy to the top of the Layers sidebar. Then I chose Select > Select None. Using the Eraser Tool, I extracted the woman from the selection until she was isolated on her own layer. I then redisplayed the hidden layers by clicking the Eye icon box for each layer.

> ## Note
>
> I then merged the grass layers in order to keep my Layers sidebar clean and organized. To do so, I selected all the grass layers on the Layers sidebar while holding down the Ctrl key. With the layers I wanted to merge selected, I selected Layer > Merge Layers.

7. To create the ghostly effect, I lowered the Alpha setting for the layer with the pasted extracted woman to 29% in the Layers sidebar. I then wanted to apply a subtle glow around her to enhance the effect, so I clicked the Layer Filters icon in the Layers sidebar. I clicked the Glow check box in the list of filters. I didn't want to overdo the effect, so I set the Glow's Alpha to 0.5 strength, set the quality to High, and entered a blur strength of 20 in both the Blur X and Blur Y text boxes, and set the Color to white. I clicked OK to apply the filter.

8. I then decided I still wanted the ghostly figure to cast a shadow. I copied the shadow from the original layer and pasted it onto a new layer and used the Eraser Tool to blend the shadow back in. I dragged the shadow layer below the layer with the extracted ghostly woman in the Layers sidebar.

Layer Masks

Source Images: "grass in woman's hands" by Dodz Larysa, "Sports – Golf" by Lugo Graphics

One of the handiest features in Phoenix is the ability to apply masks to layers. What this enables you to do is hide and reveal selected layer areas non-destructively. This is incredibly convenient because it means you can "draw" back in areas of layers you may have accidentally removed earlier, as erased portions of the image are never completely deleted. They are just hidden behind, well, the mask!

1. In this example, I opened an image of a woman holding a patch of grass in Phoenix. I used the File > Import command to add the image of a miniature golfer on a new layer. Because the image of the golfer was larger than my working canvas, I was prompted to resize the imported image. I selected Resize Image, which resized the golfer image to fit within my canvas. With the new layer with the golfer selected in the Layers sidebar, I lowered the layer's Alpha setting to 50 so I could have better visibility in positioning the golfer. I then used the Transformation Tool to resize and position the golfer on top of the patch of grass, pressing Enter when I was satisfied with the size and position. Finally, I returned the golfer layer's Alpha setting to 100 and chose Select > Select None.

2. Then, I applied a Layer Mask to the golfer layer. With the golfer layer still selected, I clicked the Options button drop-down list arrow in the Layers sidebar and clicked Mask Layer. This immediately hid the entire layer. But don't worry, the image wasn't gone! Using the Paintbrush Tool with the foreground color set to black (click the Restore Colors button and the color selection boxes if needed), I painted the golfer back in on the mask layer by simply roughly painting in the area where he was.

3. Then I used the Eraser Tool on the mask layer to remove the excess areas around the golfer, just as I would normally do when extracting a figure on a layer. The Mask came in handy immensely though; if you erased a portion of the golfer and decided you later wanted to add it back into the image, all you would have to do is take the Paintbrush and paint over the accidentally removed portion to reveal the section of the image hidden by the Mask.

4. I was happy with the placement of the golfer at this stage, but in order to sit him better onto his new surface, I needed to add a shadow. I selected the original layer with the woman and created a new layer above it by clicking the New Layer button in the Layers sidebar and dragged the layer below the layer with the golfer. And using the Paintbrush Tool set at 10% Hardness and 25% Alpha and the foreground color still set to black, I drew in the shadow across the surface for the golfer by hand.

5. Next, I wanted to make some of the grass overlap the golfer's feet and shadow to integrate him into the scene more convincingly. I used the Lasso Selection Tool and selected the area of grass from the original layer with the woman, selecting the area covering the golfer's feet and the shadows I just created. I then chose Edit > Copy and then Edit > Paste to create a new layer from within this selection. I dragged this layer to the top of the Layers sidebar. I also chose Select > Select None to remove the selection marquee.

6. Then I applied the Mask Layer choice from the Layers sidebar Options drop-down list to this grass layer. Just as with the golfer layer, this immediately made the pasted grass disappear. Then, using the Paintbrush Tool set at a very small size, I painted some of the grass around his feet and shadow to reveal blades of grass.

7. And finally, I added a bit of a blur to the woman's head in the background to make the golfer stand out more in the image. I selected the original layer with the woman in the Layers sidebar. I made a selection around the woman's head using the Lasso Selection Tool and copied and pasted it onto a new layer (Edit > Copy and Edit > Paste), leaving the new layer positioned just above the original layer in the Layers sidebar. Then I clicked the Layer Filters icon in the Layers sidebar. I clicked the Blur option to check it in the Layer Filters dialog box, entered 5 as both the Blur X and Blur Y settings, set the Quality to High, and clicked OK. Finally, I chose Select > Select None to remove the selection marquee.

Three Ways of Color Replacement

In this tutorial, I'm going to show three different ways to replace the color of an object. Changing colors enables you to not only enhance images, but also to inject unexpected punch into your Phoenix creations. In this case, you can make a luscious cluster of grapes look more like a sweet bunch of gumballs.

Source Image: "Grape 1" by Samuel Rosa

1. First, I started by simply adjusting an object's hue. I used the Lasso Selection tool to roughly select the element to adjust in the image. In this case, I wanted to replace the color of one of the grapes. I selected the Lasso Tool and dragged around the grape, finishing where I started to "close the loop."

2. Then, I copied the selection (Edit > Copy) and pasted it onto a new layer (Edit > Paste). Pasting the grape copy to its own layer enabled me to change its color there without altering the grape on the original image layer.

3. To change the color by adjusting the hue of the selection, I used the Hue & Saturation dialog box. After verifying that the new layer was selected in the Layers sidebar, I selected Image > Hue & Saturation. I moved the Hue slider by 84 points to the right, giving the selection a magenta tone, and clicked OK. I then chose Select > Select None to remove the selection marquee.

4. To clean the edges of the colored grape, I simply selected the Eraser Tool, changed the Size setting to 60 and the Hardness setting to 80, and erased the excess areas around the colored grape on the colored grape's layer, leaving the newly colored grape intact.

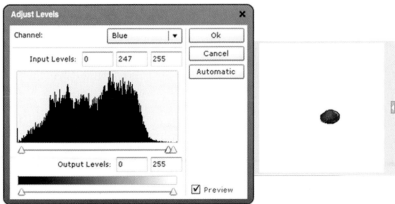

6. Then, with the new layer selected in the Layers sidebar, I selected Image > Levels. The Adjust Levels dialog box previews the selection at the right. I wanted to give the selected grape a green tone, so I selected Blue from the Channel drop-down list at the top of the dialog box. To drop some of the blue from the selection, thus making it appear greener, I dragged the midtone slider to the far right.

5. The second method to change a selection's color involves level adjustment. As I did previously, I isolated a grape by selecting it on the original image layer with the Lasso Selection Tool, and then copied (Edit > Copy) and pasted (Edit > Paste) it onto a new layer. I removed the selection marquee with Select > Select None and made sure the new layer was selected.

7. Next, I selected the Green channel from the Channel drop-down list. This time, I moved the midtone slider slightly to the left to raise the level of green in the selection. When I was happy with the new color, I clicked OK.

Note

Playing around with levels requires more trial and error than the previous method of changing the hue, as you'll never have the same result with two different images using the exact same technique. But with some experimenting, using levels will give you greater control over the tonal ranges in a selection more than simply adjusting the entire hue of an image.

Eye Dropper Tool

8. Then, I simply deleted the excess areas outside the green grape on its layer with the Eraser Tool, as in step 4.

9. Phoenix's handy, built-in Color Replacement Tool enables you to paint one color over another. I wanted to change the color of one of the grapes to an orange hue. I first selected the original layer in the Layers sidebar, and then selected the Color Replacement Tool. Then I needed to select the color I wanted to replace. I set the background color to the blue tone from the grapes by selecting the Eye Dropper Tool and clicking on the surface of one of the grapes. The background color determines the color that will be removed once I paint over it with the Color Replacement Tool.

10. Next, I changed the foreground color to orange. To do so, I clicked the Foreground Color box in the Color Replacement Tools options, selected the desired orange color in the Color Picker dialog box, and clicked OK.

11. Then, it was simply a matter of dragging on the grape to recolor on the original image layer. The Color Replacement Tool located the areas within the range of the blue background color I selected, and replaced the colors with the orange tone I selected for the foreground.

12. From there, I used my favorite method, creating layers as needed, to complete the rest of the grapes!

Precision Selection

Source Images: "Apples at the Cottage" by MentalArt, "Nerd Dinner" by Ryan J. Lane

We've already covered the Magic Wand Tool and its ability to select portions of images with similar colors. However, the tool can also be used to create simple selections around complex elements in your image. How? We trick the Magic Wand! Here's a neat little trick that allows you to create selections around your elements very quickly.

1. I started with an image of a bowl of apples I wanted to extract from its background. I needed to create a selection around this bowl. I started by clicking the New Layer icon on the Layers sidebar to create a new layer above my original layer. I then selected the Elliptical Shape Tool, set the foreground color to a bright green, and dragged to draw a circle roughly the same size of one of the apples.

2. Next, I reduced the Alpha setting for the layer with the green circle to 50% on the Layers sidebar so that I could see the apple's outline through the green circle. I clicked the Distortion Tool, dragged handles as needed to reshape the circle to match the apple's proportions, and then pressed Enter (you can also double-click within the selection box) to apply the changes. When I was happy with the size and shape of the green circle, I set the Alpha level on the layer back to 100%.

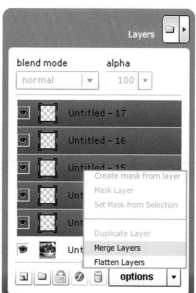

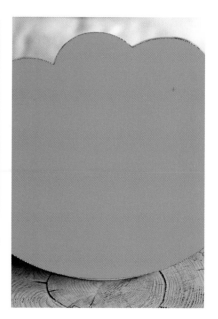

3. I repeated the process described in steps 2 and 3 for each element I wanted to extract from the original image. I created a new layer for each of the apples and the bowl, until every part that I wanted to keep was covered.

4. Next, I merged the layers with all the elliptical shapes. I pressed and held Ctrl on the keyboard as I clicked each layer with an elliptical shape on the Layers sidebar. Then, I pressed the Options drop-down list arrow at the bottom of the Layers sidebar and clicked Merge Layers. This combined the selected layers into a single layer.

5. With my elliptical shape layers all merged onto one layer, I selected this new layer in the Layers sidebar. Then, I selected the Magic Wand Tool and clicked anywhere within the green area to create a selection covering the apples and bowl.

6. I clicked the Eye icon beside the merged elliptical shape layer in the Layers sidebar to hide the layer. I then clicked the original apples layer in the Layers sidebar to select that layer. This placed the selection marquee around the bowl and apples.

7. I copied and pasted the selection onto a new layer (Edit > Copy and Edit > Paste), leaving the clean extracted bowl of apples. Using the Eraser Tool set at 85% Hardness, I refined any rough edges that remained. I imported a new background image (File > Import), dragged the layer with the imported image below the layer with the extracted bowl of apples in the Layers sidebar, and situated the bowl of apples on the table shown in the imported image using the Transformation Tool.

Lighting Effects

Source Image: "Graveyard Scenic" by tepic

In this tutorial, I'll show you how to add a bit of dramatic lighting punch to any of your photographs. With just the Gradient Tool and a few layer blend modes, you'll be able to add "artificial lighting" to any photograph in no time.

1. The first thing to do was to determine the light source of the image. In this case, the red candleholder held by the cherub was the obvious choice.

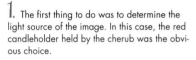

Note

You can use the slider above the image workspace to zoom an image to a comfortable working size.

2. I wanted to enhance the light first and cast some glow on the cherub. I accomplished this with the Gradient Tool. First, I created a new layer to hold the gradient by clicking the New Layer button in the Layers sidebar. I selected the Gradient Tool and then chose Radial from the Gradient Type drop-down list in the Gradient Tool options. This setting creates a gradient that radiates from a central point you specify. Changing the leftmost color on the Gradient Tool option slider sets the center color and will disperse from that color toward the rightmost color. I wanted to set the center color as a white, the highlight color. I double-clicked the leftmost slider arrow in the Gradient Tool option to open the Color Picker dialog box. I made sure that the R, G, and B values were all set to 255, and then clicked OK. Then, I double-clicked the rightmost slider arrow, entered #7F7F7F in the HEX text box to specify a mid-tone gray, and clicked OK.

3. With the gradient type and colors now selected, I dragged the Gradient Tool across the new layer, starting from the center of the red candleholder and dragging to the upper-left corner. This specified the diameter of the gradient on the new layer.

4. I then set the blend mode for the gradient layer by choosing Overlay from the Blend Mode drop-down list on the Layers sidebar. This created a highlighted effect using the white areas of the gradient. The midtone gray I selected does not show up with the Overlay Blend Mode selected, leaving a clean highlighted effect.

5. To create the effect of a shaded area behind the cherub, I used a similar process. This time, after creating a new layer with the New Layer button on the Layers sidebar and selecting the Gradient Tool, I set the Gradient Type to Linear in the Gradient Tool options. The Linear setting creates a straight gradient that disperses from the leftmost color selected to the rightmost. By double-clicking the left slider arrow in the options and using the Color Picker dialog box, I set the leftmost color to black (R 0, G 0, and B 0), and clicked OK. I left the rightmost color set to the previously specified midgray. I then dragged the Gradient Tool left to right across the new layer to create the linear gradient.

6. I set the linear gradient layer's Blend Mode to Overlay, as well, using the Blend Mode drop-down list and lowered the layer's Alpha level to 35% on the Layers sidebar. This enhanced the subtle shaded area around the back of the cherub, helping to create contrast against the brightness of the candle area.

7. Another important aspect of creating lighting and shadows is saturating them with the color of the source light and reflected light. In this case, the lit candleholder probably would cast a red reflection on the statue. I created a red glow effect the same way I created the previous lighting effects. I created a new layer and selected the Gradient Tool. This time, I selected a red tone for the leftmost color for the gradient by double-clicking the left arrow slider, choosing a red color in the Color Picker dialog box, and clicking OK. I left the rightmost color of the gradient set to the midtone gray. I selected Radial from the Gradient Type drop-down list, and then dragged from the candleholder toward the upper-left corner of the new layer to create a red gradient.

8. I set the red gradient layer's Blend Mode to Overlay, as well, using the Blend Mode drop-down list on the Layers sidebar. With the Overlay mode applied, the gray tones fail to show up and just the red cast light effect appears on the cherub figure.

9. And finally, I created another layer with the New Layer button on the Layers sidebar and added a smaller white to gray gradient on the layer right over the candleholder itself to create the illusion of a candle illuminating within. (I selected the Gradient Tool; changed the left gradient color to white by changing the R, G, and B values in the Color Picker dialog box all to 255; and dragged on the new layer.) I set this layer's Blend Mode setting to Hardlight and lowered the Alpha to 90% using the Layers sidebar. From here, you can continue to add or remove Overlay highlight and shadow layers depending on your own personal preference.

Surface Reflections

Creating reflections may seem like an easy image-editing task upon first glance. Simply copy your image, then flip it vertically, right? That idea may work on images with elements sitting on a flat plane, but what happens when the image has any sort of depth and perspective or doesn't sit on a single plane? As you'll see in this tutorial, the seemingly simple task of creating a mirrored effect can be quite a challenge.

Source Image: "Indian Water Dragon" by Global Photographers

1. First, I needed to create open space on the bottom half of the source image to make room for the reflection. I selected the Transformation Tool, dragged the lizard to the top half of the existing canvas, and pressed Enter. This left most of the bottom half of the image empty and available to hold the reflection. Select white as the foreground color, select the Paint Bucket Tool, and click the transparent area below the lizard image to fill it with white, making the background complete.

Note

If you need to add more space at the bottom of an image in a case like this, you can increase the canvas size by selecting Image > Canvas Resize and enter the desired canvas Height and Width. Uncheck the Constrain Proportion check box to resize just one dimension. Click Apply to finish resizing the canvas.

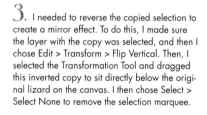

2. Because the lizard isn't resting flat on the surface, there are several different points of depth on this image, so simply copying and flipping the figure to create the reflection would not work. In order to accomplish a convincing reflection, I needed to assemble the reflection in sections. I started with the head and body of the figure. Using the Lasso Tool, I created a rough selection around the head and body of the lizard, copied it (Edit > Copy), and then pasted it (Edit > Paste) onto a new layer.

3. I needed to reverse the copied selection to create a mirror effect. To do this, I made sure the layer with the copy was selected, and then I chose Edit > Transform > Flip Vertical. Then, I selected the Transformation Tool and dragged this inverted copy to sit directly below the original lizard on the canvas. I then chose Select > Select None to remove the selection marquee.

4. The reflection should appear underneath the original lizard in the image. There are a couple of ways to accomplish this. I did it the easy way by selecting the Eraser Tool set to 100% Alpha and simply erasing the parts of the reflection that were overlapping the original lizard, creating the illusion that the lizard sits on top of the reflection.

5. Next, I needed to align the reflection of the arms to appear directly under the original lizard's front feet. Because of the multiple planes of depth in this image, I needed to create the arm reflections on a separate new layer. With the Lasso Tool I made a rough selection around both of the figure's arms on the original lizard layer. I selected one arm with the Lasso Tool, then while holding down the Shift key, I made a selection around the other arm to add the second selection to the first. I copied (Edit > Copy) and pasted (Edit > Paste) this onto a new layer, and then dragged the layer above the one with the reflection of the body.

6. Just as I did with the reflection of the lizard's head and torso, I flipped the layer with the copied arms vertically using Edit > Transform > Flip Vertical. I chose Select > Select None to remove the selection marquee. Then with the Transformation Tool, I aligned the inverted arms to sit directly below the figure's front feet on the canvas. I then erased the areas overlapping the original figure with the Eraser Tool set at 100% Alpha. Then, I reduced the Eraser Tool's Hardness to 10% and made a soft erase around the edge where the arms' reflections met the body's reflection to create a soft blend.

7. I noticed there were some remnants of the lizard's original reflection on parts of the white surface in the original image, in an area where I wanted to add in the lizard's back leg reflections. To remove these, I selected the original layer and clicked the New Layer icon on the Layers sidebar to create a new layer directly above the original layer. I selected the Paintbrush Tool with white set as the foreground color and painted over the areas where the original reflections were.

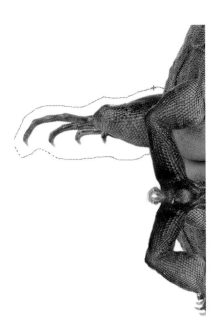

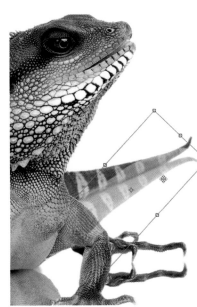

8. Once the white surface was clear, I continued the reflection process. Using the same method as before, I continued on with the lizard's back legs. I selected the back legs on the original layer using the Lasso Tool, copied and pasted them onto a new layer, flipped them vertically, and then used the Eraser Tool to clean the edges.

9. For the lizard's tail, I noticed a simple vertical flip was not going to do the trick since it was on an angle and would not align properly that way. As with the other segments, I selected the tail on the original layer and copied it onto a new layer. With the tail reflection layer as my active layer, I selected the Transformation Tool, which enables you to move a selection and rotate the selection around a center point. I then hovered the mouse slightly outside one of the corner points until the curved arrow mouse pointer appeared. I dragged to rotate the tail in the appropriate direction to align along the same angle as the lizard's original tail. I pressed the Enter key to confirm the changes. Then, I used the Eraser Tool to clean the edges.

10. Once I had my reflection layers positioned correctly, I held down the Ctrl key while clicking each reflection layer in the Layers sidebar. This selected all the layers. I clicked the Options drop-down list arrow on the Layers sidebar, and clicked Merge Layers. Because this wasn't supposed to be a direct mirror surface but rather a reflection on a shiny surface, I wanted to lower the opacity of the reflection. On the Layers sidebar, I changed the Alpha setting of the merged reflection layer to 48%. With the reflection layer still selected, I clicked the Layer Filters icon at the bottom of the Layers sidebar. I clicked the Blur check box to check it, entered 2 on both the Blur X and Blur Y text boxes, and clicked OK to apply the blur.

11. Reflections often tend to grow lighter and more diffuse farther away from the subject casting them. In order to achieve this effect for our reflection, I first needed to select the entire reflection. I selected the merged selection layer in the Layers sidebar. I selected the Magic Wand Tool, and on my merged reflection layer I clicked the transparent portion. Then I chose Select > Invert Selection to select the reflection rather than the transparency. I created a new layer above the reflection layer by clicking the New Layer icon on the Layers sidebar and selected the new layer. I selected the Gradient Fill Tool, left the default white (left slider arrow) and black (right slider arrow) gradient colors selected, and filled the selection on the new layer with a gradient. I dragged from the lower-right toward the upper-left to place the white tones in the gradient on the end of the reflection that is farthest from the figure. I set this layer's Blend Mode to Add and reduced its Alpha to 16 in the Layers palette, creating a gradual transition from darker to light on the reflection.

12. Finally, I wanted to fade the ends of the reflections farthest from the figure even further. I created a new layer (New Layer icon in the Layers sidebar) above the gradient layer. I selected the Paintbrush Tool set at 0% Hardness and 10% Alpha, and set the foreground color to white (click the Switch Between Foreground and Background Colors bent double arrow near the color boxes to reverse the default colors and make white the foreground color). I then painted over the ends of the reflections to fade them into the white background even further.

Motion Blur

Source Images: "Dangerous Jump" by barsik, "Snowboarder – Winter Sports" by Eric Limon

Motion blur is an effect often applied to sports images to evoke a sense of speed. In this tutorial, I'll take two images of snowboarders soaring in different directions and show how to apply a motion blur effect to them to enhance the appearance of motion.

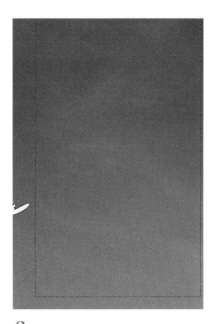

1. I started with an image of a snowboarder accelerating horizontally. I loved the original photograph but I wanted to apply a motion blur effect to the image to further enhance the action in this shot.

2. Because I would be blurring just the background, I first needed to extract the figure from the image. I used the Lasso Tool to make a rough selection around the snowboarder, and then I copied and pasted this selection onto a new layer with Edit > Copy and Edit > Paste. I then chose Select > Select None to remove the selection marquee. Using the Eraser Tool set at 100% Alpha, I cleaned off the edges so only my snowboarder remained.

3. Next, with the snowboarder extracted on his own layer, I wanted to remove him from the background layer. I hid the layer with the extracted snowboarder, and then I made a copy of my background layer, as I'll need the preserved original background later on. I did this by first selecting the background layer. I then clicked the Options button drop-down list arrow on the Layers sidebar and clicked Duplicate Layer. I then made the original background layer invisible for the time being. I reselected the duplicated background layer, and then used the Rectangular Selection Tool to select a clear portion of the sky and copied and pasted it onto a new layer with Edit > Copy and Edit > Paste. I would later use this selection to cover up the snowboarder.

Note

It might help to disable the background layer when extracting elements in your images. To do so, click the Eye icon next to the layer you want to make invisible on the Layers sidebar. This will hide the layer in your workspace. To make this layer visible again, simply click the box on the left of the layer you want to make visible to bring the Eye icon back up, and your layer back to the workspace.

4. Using the Transformation Tool, I moved the copied sky layer over to cover the snowboarder, dragging the handles as needed to resize the copied sky area to cover any remaining parts of the snowboarder. Then, using the Eraser Tool set at 0% Hardness, I erased and softened the edges of this sky portion to blend into the original sky better, making sure not to expose the snowboarder. This doesn't need to be done perfectly, as minor imperfections in blending will all but disappear once we apply the blur effect to the background.

5. Next, I merged the layer(s) with the sky portions used to cover the snowboarder with the copy of the original background. I held down Ctrl and clicked the background and sky portion layers on the Layers sidebar. (Holding down Ctrl while clicking layers enables you to select multiple layers simultaneously.) With these layers selected, I clicked the Options drop-down list arrow on the Layers sidebar and clicked Merge Layers. Then I could apply the motion blur to this layer, which I left selected. I clicked the Layer Filters icon on the Layers sidebar and clicked the Blur check box in the Layer Filters dialog box. I set the Blur X strength to 10, the amount of horizontal blur I wanted. Then I set the Blur Y strength to 0, since I didn't need any vertical blur for the motion effect. I set the Quality to High, then clicked OK to apply the blur.

6. I wanted to re-add some of the unblurred snow around the snowboarder. First, I hid the blurred layer. I redisplayed the original background layer and selected the layer. Using the Lasso Tool, I made a rough selection around the snow below the snowboarder and pasted it onto a new layer with Edit > Copy and Edit > Paste. I dragged the newly pasted layer to the top of the list in the Layers sidebar and hid the original background layer again.

7. I redisplayed the layers with the blur and the isolated snowboarder. I then selected the layer with the snow selection copied in step 6. To blend the snow into the rest of the image, I selected the Eraser Tool set at 0% Hardness and erased the edges to soften them.

8. You can use the same process outlined in steps 1 through 7 to apply a vertical motion blur effect. So, after saving I opened another photo of a snowboarder who appeared to be jumping upward in the image.

9. I used the same steps as for the previous image. The exception was that I reversed the strength for the two axes when specifying the Blur options, setting the Blur X strength to 0, and setting the Blur Y strength to 10. This created a vertical blur effect to my background instead, giving the appearance of the motion blur running in an upward direction.

Perspective Sign

Source Images: "Bus stop billboard" by Zoom Studio, "Aviary - Phoenix" by Meowza Katz

The Distortion Tool is an important feature of Phoenix that enables you to scale and skew an object to fit the perspective of a new background you want to incorporate the object into. For example, in this tutorial, I'll show you how to take a one-dimensional poster and easily integrate it into the natural setting of a bus stop.

1. I started with a specific image to use as the poster, so I needed to locate a source background image with an area to hold the poster that was roughly the same proportions as the source poster image. Choosing a background with different proportions would create the risk of skewing the poster image undesirably. I opened the source background image in Phoenix.

2. To import the source poster image, I selected File > Import and this prompted me to upload a new picture. I selected my Aviary poster image file and clicked OK. When the upload was complete, the poster image was automatically placed on a new layer above the background image.

3. To distort the poster so it fit the perspective of the white bus stop sign area, I selected the poster layer in the Layers sidebar and then selected the Distortion Tool. Four handles or control points appeared around the poster image, one on each corner. I dragged these corners to their respective counterparts on the original bus stop sign, so that the top-left handle on the Aviary image lined up with the top-left corner of the bus stop, and so on. I pressed the Enter key to finish the selection.

4. I was happy with the general placement of the poster, but I wanted to situate it into its environment even better, so I pretended this poster was protected by a sheet of glass. To create a reflection of the bus stop roof on the glass over the poster, I selected the original bus stop layer in the Layers sidebar and then used the Lasso Tool to create a rough selection around the overhang end of the roof. I chose Edit > Copy, then Edit > Paste. This copied the selection onto a new layer, which I dragged above the other layers in the Layers sidebar. I then chose Select > Select None.

5. To reverse the glass to make it more suitable for a reflection, I made sure that the new layer was selected in the Layers sidebar, then I chose Edit > Transform > Flip Vertical. Then, with the Transformation Tool, I dragged this selection down to position it over the poster. I opened the Blend Mode drop-down list on the Layers sidebar and clicked Screen. Finally, I used the Eraser Tool to remove the parts of the layer outside the poster area, which wouldn't be reflected on the glass in a real setting.

6. To further integrate this poster into the bus stop sign area, I wanted to add a little bit of shadow along the edges of the poster. I clicked the poster layer again in the Layers sidebar. I then clicked the Magic Wand Tool on the transparent area surroundings of the poster. Then, I chose Select > Invert Selection to select only the poster on the layer. I clicked the New Layer button on the Layers sidebar to create a new layer above the poster's and made sure that the layer was selected. I selected the Line Tool and changed its Line Weight to 7 pixels and the foreground color to black in the tool options, and then I dragged along the right and bottom edges of the poster. This created a shadowy effect giving the appearance of sinking the poster deeper into the bus stop sign. I lowered the Alpha of this layer to 50% in the Layers sidebar so it wasn't overly dark and chose Select > Select None to remove the selection marquee.

7. And finally, I wanted to add a subtle reflection of the sidewalk onto the poster. Again, I used the Lasso tool to select a nearby area of sidewalk on the original bus stop layer, copied the selection to its own layer, and dragged the layer above the poster layer. I flipped the selection vertically, then used the Distortion Tool to change the perspective of the selection to a vertical reflection of the rest of the sidewalk. In the Layers sidebar, I changed the layer Blend Mode to Lighten and lowered the Alpha to 50% to make the reflection more subtle. I then erased the portions of this selection that weren't on the poster.

Changing Skin Color

Source Images: "Pretty Lady with Madonna Lily" by neoblues

Whether altering a person's skin color to situate him in a new environment better, or to completely change the person's racial appearance, recoloring skin tones is a fun and challenging step in photo manipulation. In this tutorial, I'll go the dramatic route of altering a woman's race completely for effect.

1. First, I wanted to extract the areas of the image I wanted to recolor. In this case, that meant selecting all the exposed skin in the source image. Using the Lasso Tool, I roughly selected the figure from the image and copied (Edit > Copy) and pasted it (Edit > Paste) onto a new layer. I chose Select > Select None to remove the selection marquee, and I hid the original layer by clicking its Eye icon in the Layers sidebar. Then, I selected the new layer and used the Eraser Tool to clean off the remaining white edges, leaving just the skin portion.

2. I wanted to change her skin color to a darker tone, so I needed to first remove some of the pinkish hue from her skin and drop the saturation level slightly. With the layer holding the extracted figure selected, I chose Image > Hue & Saturation to open the Hue & Saturation dialog box. I moved the Hue slider to the right to change the setting to 15, and dropped the Saturation to a setting of -30 by moving the slider to the left. I then clicked OK to close the dialog box, and redisplayed the original layer by clicking its Eye icon in the Layers sidebar.

3. To darken her skin and give it some new color, I created a new layer above the layer with the extracted figure by selecting that top layer in the Layers sidebar and clicking the New Layer button at the bottom of the sidebar. I selected a darker skintone as the foreground color using the foreground color box below the tools. I then used the Paintbrush Tool set at 100% Alpha and 100% Hardness to paint over her skin in a darker tone.

4. I set the Blend Mode drop-down list setting for the layer with the painted skin tone to Multiply and lowered the Alpha of this layer to 70% on the Layers sidebar. Then, using the Eraser Tool set at 100% Alpha and 85% Hardness, I removed all the excess areas not directly on my figure's skin.

5. This darkened the figure's skin tone, but left a flat appearance to her. In order to fix this problem, I needed to blow out the highlights some more. I did this by selecting my original image layer again. I then clicked the Options button drop-down list arrow on the Layers sidebar and chose Duplicate Layer. I dragged the duplicated layer to the top of the list of layers in the Layers sidebar. With the duplicated (top) layer selected, I chose Image > Levels. In the Levels dialog box, I slid the Midtone slider (the middle slider under the Input Levels diagram) to the right to about the 185 mark to deepen the dark areas of the image, then slid the Highlight slider (slider on the furthest right) to the left to around the 225 mark to blow out the highlights in the image. (This also readjusted the Midtone setting slightly.) I then clicked OK to apply the changes. I then dropped the Contrast on the layer by about 15 points (Image > Brightness & Contrast) and dropped the Saturation by 60 (Image > Hue & Saturation), and applied the Hardlight Blend Mode to this layer with an Alpha setting of 55% using the Layers sidebar.

6. To further accentuate the highlights, I added another new layer using the New Layer button on the Layers sidebar. I then set the fore-ground color to white and used the Paintbrush Tool with the Hardness set to 0 and Alpha set to 10% to paint over the existing highlights in areas such as around the figure's cheek and neck, over her lip, lightly on her cheeks, and on the tip of her nose. I set this layer's Blend Mode to Overlay on the Layers sidebar.

7. I wanted to bring back some of the pink tone from her original lip color back into the image as well. I selected my original image layer again, made a rough selection around her mouth with the Lasso Tool, and then copied (Edit > Copy) and pasted (Edit > Paste) this selection onto a new layer. I removed the selection marquee (Select > Select None), and then I dragged this lip layer to the top of the list in the Layers sidebar. Using the Eraser Tool set at 50% Hardness on the lip layer, I refined the edges of her lips by erasing any areas of skin around them. I then set this layer's Alpha to 30% in the Layers sidebar, and this gave my figure's lips a pink hue. I then applied the same process to her eyelids.

8. At this point, I could've called the image complete. But for an added element, I clicked the Options button drop-down list arrow on the Layers sidebar and selected the Flatten Layers option. This merged my entire image into a single layer. I removed the white background from this merged layer with the Eraser Tool. I selected File > Import and imported another source file to serve as the new background. I dragged the layer holding the imported image below my merged layer in the Layers sidebar. I then clicked the Layer Filters button on the Layers sidebar, clicked Blur to check it, applied a slight blur of 5 points to both the Blur X and Blur Y axes to add a sense of depth, and clicked OK.

Note

When importing an image into an existing document of smaller size, you'll be prompted to resize the image to continue. Selecting Resize Image will resize the imported image to fit in your current working canvas. Selecting Resize Canvas will increase the canvas size to the size of the larger imported image. And selecting Crop Image won't change the size of either the imported image or the canvas. It will, however, crop the imported image to fit the current canvas size.

Note

If you want to flatten the layers in your image but are afraid to lose your layered working file, flatten your image, press Select > Select All, and then Edit > Copy. This copies the flattened layer onto your clipboard. Then, click the Undo button or choose Edit > Undo to return to the full layered image. You can then use Edit > Paste to paste the copied flattened image onto a new layer over the rest of the document. This inserts the flattened layer to work on, while maintaining all the layers underneath.

Creating Lightning

Source Image: "Shining Moon, Church, City Lights" by Don Bayley

How lightning forms in nature is still a matter of debate in the scientific community. Personally, I think it all begins with the Paintbrush Tool. In this tutorial, I'll show how to easily turn a photo of an ordinary night sky into an electrifying lightning storm.

1. First, I created a new layer by clicking the New Layer button on the Layers sidebar so I could draw in some lightning bolts by hand. I selected the Paintbrush Tool and set the brush Size to 3 in the tool options. I wanted the edges slightly softened, so I adjusted the brush Hardness setting to 90%. I set the foreground color to white by clicking the foreground color box in the tool options and using the Color Picker dialog box to choose white (R, G, and B values all set to 255). I made sure that the new layer was selected, and painted in a few lightning bolts.

2. Looking at photos of actual lightning, I noticed lightning is never universally one thickness throughout the bolt. So I drew in additional lightning bolts of varying sizes around the initial strokes on the same layer, alternating between a size 1 and 2 Paintbrush.

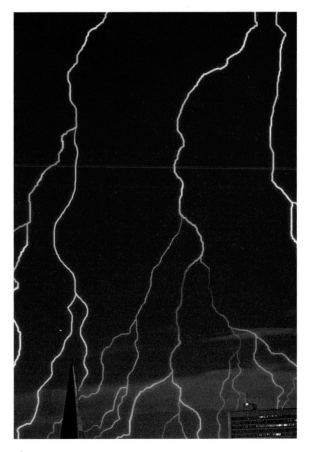

3. I wanted to fade the lightning in some of the areas, giving the appearance that portions of the lightning were partially hidden behind clouds. I selected the Eraser Tool and set 0% Hardness and 20% Alpha in the tool options. Working on the layer with the drawn lightning, I clicked the tool sporadically on random areas of the lightning to give it a diffused look in those areas, as shown by the yellow orb, the Eraser Tool, in the figure above.

4. I then wanted to create a slight glow effect around the lightning. To do this, I clicked the Layer Filters icon on the bottom of the Layers palette with my lightning layer selected. This opened the Layer Filters dialog box. I clicked the Glow check box to check it, enabling a number of customizable options for the Glow filter. I set the Alpha to 0.7, changed the Quality drop-down list setting to High, gave the glow the Strength of 2, and blurred it by entering 12 points in both the Blur X and Blur Y text boxes. I then changed the color to a blue tone using the Color drop-down palette to help the glow blend into the night sky. I clicked OK, applying a nice subtle glow around the lightning.

5. Next, I added highlights around the clouds where the lightning was originating from. I created a new layer by clicking the New Layer button on the Layers sidebar, and then I dragged the new layer below the lightning layer in the sidebar. I then made sure white was still set as the foreground color. I selected the Paintbrush Tool, specified at 0% Hardness and 5% Alpha in the tool options, and painted on the new layer around the sky near the top of the lightning bolts. Then, I opened the Blend Mode drop-down list on the Layers sidebar and clicked Overlay. To strengthen the highlight directly where the lightning touches the sky, I created another new layer below the lightning bolt layer and painted with the Paintbrush tool around the tops of the lightning bolts, with the foreground color still set to white.

6. To enhance the effect further, I added a layer with gradient lighting effect to the sky. I clicked the New Layer button in the Layers sidebar, and then dragged the new layer to the top of the list. I selected the Gradient Fill Tool, left the slider arrows set to white on the left and black on the right of the Gradient scale (double-click a slider arrow to open the Color Picker dialog box to change a gradient color), and selected Radial from the Gradient Type drop-down list in the tool options. Starting from a point in the upper-right area of the new layer, I dragged the tool diagonally toward the upper-left corner to create the gradient. Then, I applied the Overlay Blend Mode to this layer and set its Alpha to 30% using the Layers sidebar.

Foggy Day

Source Images: "Cemetery path, Unitarian Church" by Brian Nolan, "Smoke" by Hermann Danzmayr

*f*og is often a desired effect in cinema. It has the ability to add a spooky element to a setting. Fog effects also can be applied to photography to change a photo's mood. In this tutorial, I'll show you how to create a fog effect on a cemetery scene, adding an eerie mood to the image.

1. There are a few points to keep in mind when creating a foggy image. First, fog usually makes the elements it covers more desaturated. So the first thing I wanted to do with this image was drop some of the color. I chose Image > Hue & Saturation. In the Hue and Saturation dialog box, I dragged the Saturation slider to the left to -40, and then clicked OK.

2. In real photos of heavy fog, background elements become increasingly less and less visible the farther they are from the camera. An easy way to pull off this effect convincingly is to apply a gradient to the image. I clicked the New Layer button in the Layers sidebar to create a new layer above the original layer. I selected the Gradient Fill Tool, left the default white to black gradient specified (double-click a slider arrow to open the Color Picker dialog box and change the color), and made sure that Linear was selected as the Gradient Type setting in the tool options. I then dragged from upper-left to lower-right. Next I opened the Blend Mode drop-down list on the Layers sidebar and clicked Screen so that only the light tones of the gradient would be visible. I also changed the layer's Alpha setting in the Layers sidebar to 80%.

3. I wanted the foreground elements unfogged to enhance the depth of the image. I did this by simply erasing the areas of the gradient layer covering the foreground tombstones. Using the Eraser Tool set at 40% Hardness, I dragged on the tombstones right on the gradient layer to delete those portions of the gradient layer.

4. Next, I wanted the top portion of the image completely covered in fog. I first set the foreground color to white. (You can click the Switch Between Foreground and Background Colors bent arrow to flip the default colors.) Using the Paintbrush Tool set at 0% Hardness, I simply painted in the sky area of the gradient layer in white. If you notice visible edges on the areas you painted in, simply add a bit of blur to the layer to smooth it out. For this image, I clicked the Layer Filters icon on the Layers sidebar and clicked Blur in the Layer Filters dialog box. I then entered 15 blur in both the Blur X and Blur Y text boxes, chose High from the Quality dropdown list, and clicked OK.

5. Fog that's closer to the camera is more defined than the fog that's farther away. One way to achieve this effect is to simply paint in the foreground fog by hand. An even easier way is to use a source image of smoke. So I chose File > Import and uploaded an image of smoke to the document using the Resource Browser. The imported image appeared on a new layer.

6. I then desaturated the smoke image layer by choosing Image > Desaturate with the layer still selected. Then I clicked the Transformation Tool, dragged the right handles to stretch the image horizontally, and double-clicked the image to finish the transformation. I also used the Transformation Tool to move the smoke image to the bottom of the image area. This gave the appearance of the smoke dispersing across the ground level in the image foreground. When I was happy with its placement, I pressed the Enter key to confirm the transformation. I applied a bit of blur to this layer (as in step 4), with a strength of 7 for both the Blur X and Blur Y settings. Then I applied the Screen Blend Mode to this layer and dropped the layer's Alpha to 40% in the Layers sidebar.

7. Still wanting to keep my foreground relatively uncovered by the fog, I selected the Eraser Tool set at 0% Hardness and simply erased the portions of the smoke layer covering the foreground tombstones.

8. And finally, it was time to add a few final touches to the image. I clicked New Layer in the Layers sidebar to create a new layer above the others. I changed the foreground color to white (double-click the foreground color box below the tools; specify 255 for the R, G, and B values in the Color Picker dialog box; then click OK), and then filled the entire new layer white with the Paint Bucket Tool. Then I dropped this layer's Alpha setting in the Layers sidebar to 20%. This gave the entire image more of a hazy effect I desired.

9. I also wanted the entire image to possess more of a monotone feel to it. So I created another new layer (New Layer button on the Layers sidebar) and filled this layer in with a navy blue tone. To choose the color, I clicked the foreground color box below the tools, entered 0020a2 in the HEX text box, and clicked OK. I then used the Paint Bucket Tool to fill the new layer with the blue color. I opened the Blend Mode drop-down list and clicked Overlay and then adjusted the layer's Alpha to 10%, both in the Layers sidebar. This gave the image a subtle blue hue to it throughout.

Snowy Day

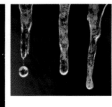

Another neat effect you can apply to photos rather simply is the appearance of snow. As with anything, there are several ways of accomplishing the same end result. In this tutorial, I'm going to show you a quick way to make any scene look as if it's amidst a snowstorm in just a few easy steps.

Source Images: "Barbary macaque, Gibraltar" by Stephan Hoerold, "Icicle" by Griszka Niewiadomski

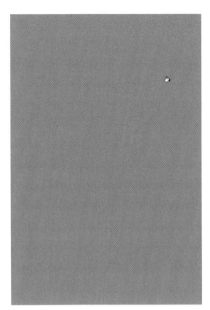

1. As snow tends to lighten the environment it surrounds, I wanted to brighten the overall look of the image and drop some of the saturation. After opening the original image, I chose Image > Brightness & Contrast. In the Brightness and Contrast dialog box, I raised the Brightness setting to 50 and lowered the Contrast setting to -15, and then clicked OK. Then I chose Image > Hue & Saturation. In the Hue and Saturation dialog box, I dragged the Saturation slider left to set its level to -70, and then clicked OK. This brightened and dulled the scene a bit, which gave me a good point to start from.

2. I still wanted to create a hazy look to the entire image. So I created a new layer by clicking the New Layer icon in the Layers sidebar, making sure the layer was above the original image layer. I selected white as the foreground color (click the Restore Colors and then Switch Between Foreground and Background Colors buttons by the Color selection boxes) and filled the new layer with white using the Paint Bucket Tool. Then I lowered the Alpha setting for this layer to 15% in the Layers sidebar.

3. Often times, snowy images tend to have a blue tint to them. I wanted to apply that same look to my image. I created another new layer by clicking the New Layer icon on the Layers sidebar. I clicked the Restore Colors button, clicked the Foreground Color selection box, entered 4BA3DD in the HEX text box to choose a blue foreground color, and clicked OK. I used the Paint Bucket Tool to fill the new layer with the specified light blue. I then applied the Overlay Blend Mode and changed the Alpha setting of this layer to 65% in the Layers sidebar.

4. With the mood of the image set, it was time to bring in the actual snow. This could be done in any number of ways. I could simply draw in the flakes by hand using the Paintbrush Tool, but there are easier ways. I found a picture of random white splatters across a black surface and imported this image using the File > Import command. Because the imported image was larger than the canvas, I was prompted to resize the image. I clicked Resize Image to shrink the imported image to fit my canvas. I selected the Transformation Tool, dragged the bottom center handle straight down to have the snow layer fill the whole canvas, and pressed Enter. I set the snow layer's Blend Mode to Screen, so only the whites of the layer were visible, giving a great base for snow.

5. I wanted to give the snow a bit of a motion blur to create the appearance that the flakes were actually falling and not just suspended in mid air. With the snow layer still selected, I clicked the Layer Filters button in the Layers sidebar and clicked Blur to check it in the Layer Filters dialog box. I set the Quality of the blur to High, and entered 10 in the Blur X and Blur Y text boxes. I clicked OK to apply the blur effect to the snow layer.

6. I then merged the snow layer with a blank new layer to rasterize it (See Note) when I was happy with the blur. Then, using the Transformation Tool, I rotated the layer and then dragged the top and side handles to make sure the snow filled the whole image, finally pressing Enter to create the appearance that the snow was blowing at an angle.

Note

If you want to commit to a particular layer filter and make it a permanent fixture to your layer, there's a simple way to do so. First, create a blank new layer. Then Ctrl+click the layer with the filter on it and the new blank layer in the Layers sidebar. Then, click the Options button drop-down list arrow and click Merge Layers. This procedure rasterizes the filter on the newly merged layer, making it editable like any normal layer. This technique can be used in conjunction with any of the layer filters.

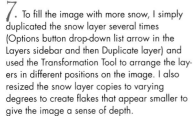

7. To fill the image with more snow, I simply duplicated the snow layer several times (Options button drop-down list arrow in the Layers sidebar and then Duplicate layer) and used the Transformation Tool to arrange the layers in different positions on the image. I also resized the snow layer copies to varying degrees to create flakes that appear smaller to give the image a sense of depth.

8. I clicked the New Layer icon in the Layers sidebar to create a new layer above the original layer and set the foreground color to white using the Foreground Color selection box. Working on the new layer, I selected the Shape Brush Tool, and chose the brush with the splattered look (Brush 4). With white as my foreground color, I clicked the tool on various parts of the top of the monkey's head and back to make it look as if snow had fallen and stuck to the figure.

9. And as a final optional touch, I added icicles to the bottom of the monkey's chin for even further effect. I imported an image of icicles (File > Import), and erased out as much of the surrounding background as I could from this layer, leaving my icicles intact. Using the Transformation Tool, I resized the icicles to fit proportionately under the monkey's face. In the Layers sidebar, I changed the layer's Blend Mode setting to Screen and lowered the Alpha to 81%, achieving the look I desired.

Rainy Day

I personally love the rain. I love the sense of freshness as the showers wash away the city grime to start anew. But any photographer knows that a sure way to ruin his camera is to leave it sitting in the rain. So how do we get that beautiful picture of the rain-covered street without endangering our camera? Easy! We wait for the rains to die down, then take our photograph, and then add in the rain later in Phoenix!

Source Image: "Off to kindergarten" by Ingvald Kaldhussæter

1. First, I wanted to set a darker mood in the original photograph. After opening the image in Phoenix, I chose Image > Hue & Saturation, and lowered the Saturation to -35, lowered the Brightness to -15, and clicked OK. This created a gloomier tone, which was more suitable for a rain-covered scene.

2. To set the scene, I wanted to create the appearance that the ground was covered in rain. To do so, I needed to create reflections. I used the Lasso Selection Tool, and roughly selected the girl from the original image and copied and pasted her onto a new layer with Edit > Copy and Edit > Paste. I chose Select > Select None to remove the selection marquee. Using the Eraser Tool, I removed the remaining background to extract the figure on its own layer. (I temporarily hid the original layer by clicking its Eye icon to create this screen shot.)

3. With the layer with the extracted girl still selected, I then chose Edit > Transform > Flip Vertical to flip the layer. Then, using the Transformation Tool, I dragged the selection under the girl down to create the illusion of the reflection below her image on the original layer, pressing Enter to finish the move. I then lowered the Alpha setting for this reflection layer to 50% in the Layers sidebar.

4. Next, I flattened the image by selecting Layer > Flatten Layers. I wanted to add some blur to the ground around the girl's feet. I selected the Blur Tool and dragged the ground to soften the appearance.

5. To add to the effect, I created ripples around the base of the girl's feet on the ground. Using the Liquify Tool set with the Pressure of 2 and a Size of 20, I dragged the tool in semi-circles around the girl's feet starting with the outer left side and dragging around the girl's foot to the right side to create the appearance of ripples. Using the Liquify Tool set at a larger size, I also displaced the rest of the reflections slightly to create a light wave effect on the water.

6. I repeated the overall process to create reflections of the trees in the background, creating subtle reflections of the distant trees on the surface of the ground. I copied and extracted them to their own layer, and flipped them. Then, I clicked the Layer Filters icon on the Layers sidebar and applied a Blur to the trees. I set the Blur X value to 15, the Blur Y value to 4, and pressed OK to apply the blur to the layer.

7. To create the rain, I first created a new layer by clicking the New Layer icon on the Layers sidebar and dragging the layer to the top of the list in the Layers sidebar. I set white as the foreground color by clicking the Restore Colors button and then clicking the Switch Between Foreground and Background Colors button. I then selected the Shape Brush Tool, selected the splattered brush (Brush 4) in the tool's options, and chose a brush size over 100. I created a series of splatters across the top of the canvas on the new layer.

8. I then selected the Transformation Tool and dragged the bottom center handle down to the bottom of the canvas to stretch the splattered drawing layer; then I pressed Enter to confirm the transformation.

9. I wanted the rain to fall at an angle, so I selected the Transformation Tool again, moved the mouse pointer just below and to the right of the lower-left handle, and dragged to the left to skew the selection. I then dragged the upper-left and lower-right handles diagonally to resize the selection so the rain would fill the image. I pressed Enter to confirm this transformation. I then lowered the Alpha setting for this layer to 15% on the Layers sidebar.

10. Next, I wanted to add a slight blue tint to the image. To do this, I created a new layer by clicking the New Layer icon on the Layers sidebar. I selected a blue foreground color and filled the layer using the Paint Bucket Tool. I set this layer's Blend Mode to Overlay and lowered the Alpha to 10%.

11. And finally, I selected the Liquify Tool again and dragged across the surface of the original image some more to add a few more ripples to the ground to make it appear as if rain were falling and plopping on the ground.

Flood

Source Image: "Victorian English Shop" by Stephen Geer

Creating realistic water reflections is a difficult challenge. Not only do you need to copy the content to create the reflections, but you also must set the color, tone, and displacement to truly give it the liquid appearance. In this tutorial, I'll show you a few of the key techniques for creating realistic water reflections using this image of a storefront I'm gonna set amidst a flood.

1. Because of the multiple planes of perspective (the sides of the buildings) in the image, I needed to assemble the water reflection one wall at a time. I started with the front wall of the foreground building. Using the Polygonal Selection Tool, I made a selection around the front wall (including a small portion of the woman in the lower-left corner), copied this selection (Edit > Copy), then pasted it onto a new layer (Edit > Paste). I chose Select > Select None to remove the selection marquee.

2. With the new layer selected in the Layers sidebar, I chose Edit > Transform > Flip Vertical. I realized right away that a simple vertical flip wasn't going to give a convincing reflection. I selected the Transformation Tool, dragged the building copy down in front of the original building, then dragged just below the upper-right selection handle to align the bricks on the front face of the wall to fit parallel to the bricks on the original wall, pressing Enter to finish the transformation when I was satisfied with the alignment.

3. I noticed that the short wall on the side of the protruding windows still didn't align properly. Still working on the reflection layer, I used the Polygonal Selection Tool to select the short wall. Then I used the Transformation Tool to change the angle of the reflection (again dragging an area between handles) and line the wall up parallel to the short wall in the original image, pressing Enter to finish the transformation.

4. Then I needed to trim the reflection down to the water line. I first hid the reflection layer by clicking its Eye icon in the Layers sidebar, but I left the layer selected. Using the Polygonal Selection Tool, I made a selection around the base of the original house. I clicked the box for the Eye icon to redisplay the selection layer and then chose Edit > Delete to delete the area directly covering the base of the house from the reflection layer.

5. I then repeated the overall process outlined in steps 1 through 4, creating a reflection layer for each face of each building, making sure to place the buildings further back in the image lower on the Layers sidebar but above the original building layer. (Also make sure to reselect the original layer so that you don't copy and paste blank areas from another layer.) I didn't worry about overlapping the woman in the foreground at this point, as I planned to add her back in later on. I made sure to choose Select > Select None to remove any remaining selection marquee.

6. After I assembled the rest of the reflection layers, it was safe to merge those layers into one. Holding down the Ctrl key, I clicked each of the reflection layers on the Layers sidebar, and then clicked the Options drop-down list arrow and selected Merge Layers.

> ## Note
> Make sure that the reflections are positioned so that they fill all of the foreground; you don't want to have to go back and fill missing spaces in later steps.

7. I wanted to darken and dull the reflection a little more in comparison to the original image. I selected the merged reflection layer and chose Image > Brightness & Contrast. In the Brightness and Contrast dialog box, I dragged the Brightness slider left to set it to -27, and dragged the Contrast slider left to set it to -47. I then clicked OK to apply the changes.

8. I also wanted to add a slight blue tone to the reflection to make it look more like water. With my reflection layer still selected in the Layers sidebar, I chose Select > Selection from Layer to make a selection around the entire reflection. I created a new layer above the reflection layer by clicking the New Layer icon on the Layers sidebar and filled this selection with blue after setting the foreground color to blue and selecting the Paint Bucket Tool. In the Layers sidebar, I set this layer's Blend Mode to Overlay and set the Alpha to 16%. I chose Select > Select None to be sure to remove the selection marquee.

9. Now it was time to bring the woman back into the image. Hiding the other layers and selecting the original image layer, I made a rough selection around the woman using the Lasso Selection Tool and pasted her onto a new layer with Edit > Copy and Edit > Paste. I chose Select > Select None to remove the selection marquee. Using the Eraser Tool, I finished extracting her from the background on the new layer.

10. I dragged the layer with the copied woman to the top of the list in the Layers sidebar. Using the Eraser Tool, I erased the lower portions of her legs to make them look like they were under water.

11. Realizing the woman needs a reflection herself, I simply duplicated the layer with the woman on it by clicking the Options drop-down list arrow on the Layers sidebar and clicking Duplicate Layer. I dragged the copied layer below the blue overlay layer to give the same saturation to the woman's reflection. I then chose Edit > Transform > Flip Vertical to flip the layer vertically, used the Transformation Tool to move the reflection in position and adjust the shape so the ends of the legs matched up, and then used the Eraser Tool to clean the area around the base of the legs.

12. Then I wanted to add a few ripples and imperfections to the water surface. I merged the main reflection layer with the woman's reflection layer using the process described in step 6. Then, using the Liquify Tool set at a low Pressure of 1 and a Size of 23, I simply dragged on the reflection layer to create my ripples in the water.

Note

In my working file, I left unmerged copies of my reflection layers available to examine the process involved in that further. These layers are not necessary for the final image.

Day to Night

Source Image: "Model Home III" by jhorrocks

There are several ways to turn a daytime photo of a house into a nighttime scene. The least technically challenging method would be to sit outside the same house in the same position with a camera for 12 hours and snap a photograph in both day and night settings. But for those without the spare 12 hours a day, there's a quicker way to achieve this same effect right in the comfort of the indoors using Phoenix.

1. First, I extracted the foreground. I copied the original image layer in the Layers sidebar first, as we'll need the original later. To copy the layer, I selected the layer in the sidebar, clicked the Options drop-down list arrow, and clicked Duplicate Layer. With the copied layer selected, I used the Polygonal Selection Tool to select the angular outlines of the house and foreground. With the house and rest of the foreground selected, I copied (Edit > Copy) and pasted (Edit > Paste) this selection onto a new layer. After selecting the new layer in the Layers sidebar, I chose Select > Select None and then used the Eraser Tool to clean off any of the remaining edges that needed extracting.

2. Next, I wanted to create a darker night sky. I clicked the New Layer icon on the Layers sidebar, then dragged the new layer below my extracted house layer in the Layers sidebar. I next selected the new layer and filled it with a gradient. I selected the Gradient Fill Tool and chose Radial from the Gradient Type drop-down list in the tool's options. Then, by double-clicking the arrow sliders to open the Color Picker dialog box, I set the leftmost color to a dark shade of blue (Hex value #0D3499) and the right color to an even darker shade (#000050), clicking OK to finish each color selection. I dragged the tool from a point just above the peak of the roof towards the edge of the image until I was left with a night sky gradient I was happy with.

3. I then needed to darken the extracted house foreground layer to match the night sky. I selected the extracted house layer in the Layers sidebar. I chose Image > Brightness & Contrast to open the Brightness and Contrast dialog box. I lowered the Brightness to -100 and lowered the Contrast to -70 using the sliders, and clicked OK. I then chose Image > Hue & Saturation menu and used the sliders in the Hue and Saturation dialog box to drop the Saturation level to -70 and dropped the Brightness on this menu to -40, clicking OK to finish.

Tip

Holding Shift while making a selection will add to the current selection if one was present initially. This makes it easier because you can make selections in segments instead of trying to get it all in one shot. This works with any of the selection tools, so feel free to use what works best for you.

4. I wanted to add a blue tone to the house. With the extracted house layer selected, I chose Select > Selection from Layer. This automatically selected all the content on the extracted house layer. I created a new layer above the extracted house layer by clicking the New Layer icon on the Layers sidebar. With the new layer selected, I then filled the selection with a dark blue using the Paint Bucket Tool. In the Layers sidebar, I changed this layer's Blend Mode setting to Overlay and dropped the Alpha to 70%. Finally, I chose Select > Select None to remove the selection marquee.

5. The house looked lonely in this state, so I decided to add a suggestion of the presence of people by lighting up the windows. Using the Polygonal Selection Tool, I made a selection around the glass panes of one of the windows, pressing and holding the Shift key as I selected each subsequent pane of glass. The Rectangular Selection Tool can also be used in this case, if you find it easier. I then clicked the New Layer icon on the Layers sidebar to create a new layer, dragged it above the blue blend layer on the Layers sidebar, and filled the selection with a yellow tone on the new layer using the Paint Bucket Tool. I then chose Select > Select None to remove the selection marquee. I repeated this process to light several of the other windows of the house.

6. I then selected each yellow window layer and added a slight blur. First I clicked the Layer Filter icon on the Layers sidebar. In the Layer Filters dialog box, I clicked the Blur check box to check it, entered a strength of 2 in both the Blur X and Blur Y axes text boxes, and selected High from the Quality drop-down list. I also wanted to apply a glowing effect around the window panes. With the Layer Filters dialog box still open, I clicked the Glow check box to check it. I set the Glow's Strength to 2, entered 12 in the Blur X text box, and entered 17 in the Blur Y text box. I changed the color to a yellow-ish orange tone. Finally, I clicked OK to apply the blur and glow. I repeated the process to apply a blur and glow to each of the other yellow window layers.

> ### Note
> It might help to hide the gradient and blue blend layers during this step in order to more clearly see the windows while you work.

7. I wanted to create the effect of the light from the windows casting a glow on the lawn below. I copied each of the window glow layers onto new layers by using the Duplicate Layer choice from the Options drop-down in the Layers sidebar. I then dragged the copied layers below the original layers in the sidebar. I selected the Transformation Tool, dragged each copied window glow to the general position where I wanted it to appear (the porch roof or front lawn), and pressed Enter to finish the change. Then, using the Distortion Tool, I added the proper perspective effect to each copy by dragging the bottom two handles further out to the proper angle to make it appear as if the light was emanating from the windows, and then I pressed Enter to finish.

8. I clicked Select > Selection from Layer on this layer. With this area still as my current selection, I selected the original image from the Layers palette. I copied this area and pasted it onto a new layer and dragged it to the top of the palette. This created the effect of the window casting light on the ground. I set this layer's Alpha to 50%, and using the Eraser Tool set to 0% Hardness, I lightly dispersed the light to fade further from the original window. I chose Select > Select None to remove the selection marquee.

9. In order to light up the streetlight, I created a new layer by clicking the New Layer icon on the Layers sidebar, set white as the foreground color using the color boxes below the tools (click a box, specify the color in the Color Picker dialog box, and then click OK), and painted over the lamp with the Paintbrush Tool. With the new layer still selected, I then clicked the Layer Filters icon on the Layers sidebar. In the Layer Filters dialog box, I clicked the Glow check box to check it. I changed the Alpha level to 0.95, entered a Strength of 2, and set the Blur X and Blur Y values to 30. I then changed the Glow's color to a yellowish orange color, and clicked OK.

10. I then created a new layer (New Layer icon) and, using the Elliptical Shape Tool, I drew a circle. (White should still be selected as the foreground color.) I selected the Transformation Tool and dragged the circle over the streetlight, pressing Enter to the finish the change. I clicked the Layer Filters icon on the Layers sidebar, and clicked the Blur check box in the Layer Filters dialog box to check it. I changed the Blur X and Blur Y values to 88 and clicked OK. Finally, I lowered the Alpha setting for the layer to 72% using the setting on the Layers sidebar.

11. And just as I did for the glow on the ground from the windows, I selected the original image layer, used the Elliptical Selection Tool to select the area directly surrounding the streetlight, and copied and pasted the selection to a new layer with the Copy and Paste commands on the Edit menu. I dragged this layer into position under the layer where I created the light glow, softened the selection's edges using the Eraser Tool, and set the layer's Alpha to 50% in the Layers sidebar. I then chose Select > Select None to remove the selection marquee.

12. And to finish the effect, I wanted to add stars and a moon to the night sky. I created a new layer for the moon using the New Layer icon on the Layers sidebar. Using the Paintbrush Tool with the foreground color still set to white, I drew a circle for the moon. Using the Eraser Tool set to a large diameter, I clicked on a portion of the circle to create a crescent shape. I applied a slight glow around the moon, starting by clicking the Layer Filters icon and then clicking Blur to check it. I changed both the Blur X and Blur Y settings to 22, set the color to a light blue tone, and clicked OK.

13. And for the stars, I just created another layer and painted them in with the Paintbrush Tool of varying sizes, finally setting this layer's Alpha to 40% to complete the night sky effect.

In the Clouds

Source Images: "Sky" by Airyelf, "Eternal Dream" by Portugal2004

Most of us can remember spending afternoons as children looking up at the clouds and seeing all sorts of things, from people, to trains, to dragons, with our visions limited only by how far our imagination could take us. In this tutorial, we're gonna go back to our childhood and put our dreams and imagination back in the clouds where they belong.

1. In this example, I'm going to attempt to place this statue of a woman into the clouds. For the sake of brevity, I'll explain how I assembled her arm and hand, as the same method can be applied to the rest of the image to complete the piece. I started by loading up the image of the sky, then I imported the image of the statue onto its own layer using the File > Import command. Using the Transformation Tool, I dragged the statue layer roughly where I wanted it in the composition and pressed Enter to apply the change.

2. I then set this layer's Blend Mode to Screen in the Layers sidebar. This gave me the base for my clouds I'll work around. Using the Transformation Tool, I then resized the figure to a size I felt fit the composition well, and pressed Enter to confirm the decision.

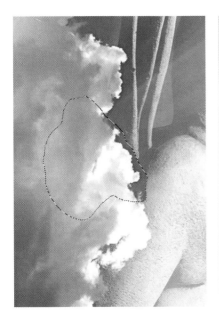 

3. Now came the hard part. To assemble the actual figure from portions of the clouds, I worked in many segments. For example, I started with the shoulder area of the figure. Looking at the contour of the figure's shoulder, I tried to find an area of the clouds that closely resembled the shape of the shoulder. Working on the original clouds layer, I selected the area I wanted with the Lasso Selection Tool. I then copied (Edit > Copy) and pasted (Edit > Paste) this portion of the clouds onto a new layer, but kept my statue's Screen layer on the top layer.

4. Using the statue as a guide but working with the newly pasted layer selected, I used the Transformation Tool to resize and rotate my copied cloud segment to fit the direction and shape of my original figure's shoulder, pressing Enter to finish the change. Then, using the Eraser Tool set at 0 Hardness, I softened the edges of the pasted selection to help them blend better into the scene.

5. I continued copying, pasting, and transforming selections from the original cloud layer onto new layers until the main part of the figure's arm was complete. Then I merged the cloud segments for the arm together by pressing and holding the Ctrl key while clicking the cloud layers I wanted to merge in the Layers sidebar. I clicked the Options drop-down list arrow and clicked Merge Layers. Because I wanted the clouds to overlay only the highlighted areas of the figure, I erased portions of the clouds to expose the sky in the figure's shadowed sections.

6. Next, I assembled the figure's hand. Because I wanted to keep the details of the hand, I kept all the fingers isolated. To do this, I needed to find an area in the original clouds that most closely resembled the shape of the fingers. I selected this area with the Lasso Selection Tool and copied it onto a new layer.

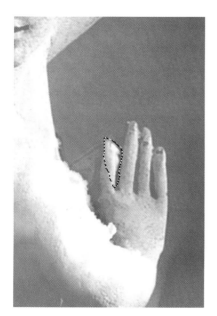

7. Then I continued the same process as I did for the arm, using the Transformation Tool to situate each segment onto the desired finger area, making sure I left the sliver of sky between the fingers visible to keep each finger isolated. I then merged the finger layers together as before.

8. After the arm and hand were complete, I needed to soften some of the graininess still apparent from the statue's stone texture. Using the Liquify Tool set at 2 for Pressure and a Size of 20, I dragged the tool in circles directly on the statue layer to soften the edges of the statue to blend it better with the clouds, and blur the visible grain.

9. On the left is what my figure looked like after I had completed this same process for the rest of the statue. I could leave it at this, but I wanted to add a little more pop to the image.

10. I wanted to slightly darken the shaded areas of the figure a little more. So I selected the Paintbrush Tool with black set as the foreground color (clicking the Restore Colors button near the color boxes below the tools quickly resets the foreground color to black). In the tool's options, I set the Alpha to 12% and the Hardness to 0. I then painted the desired areas to darken them on a new layer (New Layer icon) above the statue's Screen layer. Then I set this layer's Blend Mode to Overlay and dropped this layer's Alpha to 33% in the Layers sidebar.

11. Then, I selected white for my foreground color (if you reset the colors as noted in the previous step, you can simply click the Switch Between Foreground and Background Colors button). On a new layer (New Layer icon), and with the Paintbrush Tool still selected, I painted in the edges of the clouds to enhance the brightness of these areas to create a stronger highlighted effect.

12. I noticed that my figure was now covering most of the sunrays that were peeking out from behind the clouds in the original image. For a final effect, I wanted to bring these rays back into the image to create the appearance they were emerging from behind my newly created cloud figure. Using the Lasso Selection Tool, I created a rough selection of the rays from the original clouds layer, and pasted it onto a new layer behind my cloud layers (just above the original cloud layer in the Layers sidebar). Using the Transformation Tool, I dragged this selection to the right so the rays appear to be emerging from behind the cloud figure. Then using the Eraser Tool set at 0 Hardness, I softened the edges to blend into the original sky.

Behind Glass

Source Images: "Snow Globe" by Jim Larkin, "Arts & Crafts Snowman" by Jim Jurica

How did that ship get inside the bottle? It's a fascinating question that has delighted curious kids for generations. Lucky for us, placing the subject of a photo behind glass is much easier than building a ship in a bottle, as you'll see in this tutorial.

$1.$ I started with the image of the snow globe for the background. Then, I imported the image of the snowman figure I wanted to encapsulate in the globe using the File > Import command. The snowman appeared on a new layer. After selecting the Transformation Tool, I dragged the snowman over the snow globe and roughly positioned him where I liked. Then I pressed Enter on the keyboard to confirm the new position.

$2.$ Next, I extracted the snowman from his original background. I clicked the Eye icon beside the snow globe layer in the Layers sidebar to hide the snow globe for the time being. I then clicked the snowman layer to reselect it. Using the Eraser Tool set at 90% Hardness and 100% Alpha, I dragged on the sky around the snowman to remove it. I also dragged on the snow in the lower corners to round them off so they would fit inside the globe.

$3.$ After the figure was extracted, it was time to set it behind the glass. I redisplayed the snow globe layer by clicking the box for its Eye icon in the Layers sidebar and made sure that the layer was selected. Using the Lasso Selection Tool, I selected the glass portion of the snow globe on the original snow globe layer. I copied and pasted (Edit > Copy and Edit > Paste) this selection onto a new layer and then removed the selection marquee (Select > Select None). Then, I pasted the copied layer twice more so I had three copies, and dragged all three copies above the layer with the extracted snowman. I then hid the lower two of the duplicates temporarily by clicking the Eye icon beside each. On my visible glass copy layer, I set the Alpha to 26%. This provided the basis for the glass effect over our figure by creating a hazy look over it.

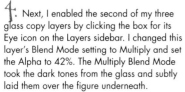

4. Next, I enabled the second of my three glass copy layers by clicking the box for its Eye icon on the Layers sidebar. I changed this layer's Blend Mode setting to Multiply and set the Alpha to 42%. The Multiply Blend Mode took the dark tones from the glass and subtly laid them over the figure underneath.

5. I redisplayed the third of the glass copy layers by clicking the box for its Eye icon on the Layers sidebar. I set the layer's Blend Mode to Overlay and changed the Alpha setting to 61%. This had the opposite effect of the Multiply Blend Mode applied in the previous step, pulling out the shine from the glass image and laying it over the snowman.

6. I wanted to add more glare to the glass. I did this manually with the Gradient Tool. First, I created a new layer by clicking the New Layer button in the Layers sidebar and then I dragged the new layer above the glass copy layers. With the new layer selected, I made a circular selection slightly smaller than the size of the snow globe using the Elliptical Selection Tool. I selected the Gradient Fill Tool with white set as the left slider arrow color and black set as the right slider arrow color (the defaults). I dragged from the top down over the circular selection to fill it with white at the top gradating to black at the bottom. I then set this layer's Blend Mode to Screen in the Layers sidebar. This only left the white portions visible, creating a smooth glare effect. I then set the layer's Alpha to 65%.

7. I wanted to add a bit of saturation to the glare. With the elliptical selection still selected, I created a new layer above my glare layer by clicking the New Layer icon. Using the Eye Dropper Tool, I selected the light brown tone from the glass area (not the wood area) in the original snow globe layer, selecting the layer before clicking a brown area to set the color as the foreground color. Then, I reselected the newest layer by clicking it, selected the Paint Bucket Tool, and then clicked in the selection on the new layer to fill it. I set this layer's Blend Mode to Overlay and set the Alpha to 55%. I then chose Select > Select None to remove the selection marquee.

8. Finally, I wanted to surround the snowman with flakes of falling snow. I added a new layer, selected the Paintbrush Tool, and set its size to 3 and the foreground color to white. (You can switch the foreground and background colors to quickly set the foreground color to white.) I then simply drew in some snow dots over the figure. I duplicated this layer by clicking the Options button drop-down list arrow in the Layers sidebar and then clicking Duplicate Layer. I then reselected the layer where I drew the snowflakes (it should be second in the Layers sidebar list), and chose Image > Invert Colors to make the snowflakes black. Then I selected the Transformation Tool and dragged the layer with the inverted snowflakes down slightly so the black flakes appear as shadows below the white flakes, adding a sense of depth. Finally, I set the Alpha for the layer with the snowflake shadows to 15%.

Tattoo Art

Source Images: "Back in Shape" by PeskyMonkey, "Egyptian pharaoh miniature" by Mmedia Multimedia, "Egyptian papyrus detail" by Jose I. Soto

Tattoo Art can be some of the most beautiful art you'll find anywhere. With the entire human body as a walking canvas, some call it the truest form of art imaginable. But tattoos can be costly, not to mention permanent. In this tutorial, I'm going to show how to apply a tattoo to your skin using Phoenix before you go and shell out all that cash (and flesh) for a real one.

1. For this image, I decided to go with an Egyptian themed set of tattoos for the figure, the original image of a fighter that I opened in Phoenix. First, I found a nice straightforward perspective image of the Sphinx and imported it using the File > Import command. Because the photo of the fighter was taken with the same symmetrical perspective, I thought the Sphinx would be a good fit to tattoo on the figure's back.

2. I first placed the image of the Sphinx roughly where I would eventually want it. To do so, I first lowered the Sphinx layer's Alpha to 50% in the Layers sidebar so I could also see the original image underneath and align the Sphinx properly in the center. Using the Transformation Tool, I then was able to drag the Sphinx to an area I was happy with and to resize the Sphinx to my liking. I pressed Enter to apply the changes. I then reset the Sphinx layer's Alpha setting to 100 in the Layers sidebar.

3. I wanted to remove the background from the Sphinx tattoo image, as I wanted the Sphinx to be isolated. The background didn't need to be removed perfectly, as I would be applying a layer Blend Mode to this image in the next step, which would hide the rest. So I selected the Magic Wand Tool set at 32 Tolerance, and clicked in the white area surrounding the Sphinx. I chose Edit > Cut to remove the selected white background and then Select > Select None to remove the selection marquee.

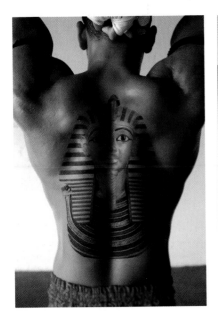

4. With the Sphinx layer still selected, I opened the Blend Mode drop-down list on the Layers sidebar and clicked Multiply. This blended the image of the Sphinx onto the figure, while retaining the shadows and texture of the fighter's original skin. I noticed that this caused the Sphinx to look a little too dark and oversaturated. I chose the Image > Hue & Saturation menu, dragged the Saturation slider left to -42 in the Hue and Saturation dialog box, and then clicked OK. I then chose Image > Brightness & Contrast, dragged the Brightness slider right to a setting of 32, dragged the Contrast slider right to a setting of 11, and clicked OK. I then was happy with the look of the tattoo.

5. Next, I wanted to add some hieroglyphic art to the fighter's arms. I used File > Import to import a Papyrus image. Using the Lasso Selection Tool, I made a rough selection around one of the figures in this glyph on its original layer, and used Edit > Copy and Edit > Paste to paste it onto a new layer. I then clicked the Eye icon beside the original Papyrus layer in the Layers sidebar to hide that until later. I then clicked the extracted glyph layer in the Layers sidebar to reselect that layer.

6. Using the Transformation Tool, I rotated the figure from the glyph and aligned it to fit the direction of the fighter's left arm. When I was happy with the general placement, I pressed Enter to confirm the transformation.

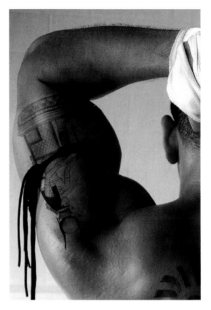

7. I applied the Multiply Blend Mode to this layer as well and lowered the Alpha to 90% in the Layers sidebar. Also finding this portion looking too dark on the figure, I chose Image > Brightness & Contrast. I specified 48 for Brightness and 16 for Contrast and clicked OK. I then chose Image > Hue & Saturation, lowered the Saturation to -35, and clicked OK. I wanted to displace the tattoo to fit the contour of the figure's arm a little better, as it still appeared a little flat. I selected the Liquify Tool, set its Pressure to 1 and the Size to 139 in the tool options, and lightly dragged down the edges of the figure to create the illusion the tattoo was wrapping around the figure's arm.

8. Using the same methods as I did with the tattoo on the figure's left arm, I redisplayed the original Papyrus layer by clicking its Eye icon box in the Layers sidebar. I then selected the other glyph figure, and copied and pasted it to its own layer with Edit > Copy and Edit > Paste. I then clicked the Eye icon for the Papyrus layer to hide it again. Working on the new glyph layer, I rotated and changed settings for the layer to apply the tattoo to the figure's right arm, as shown in steps 6 and 7.

9. And finally, I felt like I lost a little of the shine from the figure's original skin once it was covered by the tattoos. I created a new layer by clicking the New Layer icon in the Layers sidebar, and dragged the new layer to the top of the list. I set the foreground color to white. I then selected the Paintbrush Tool, set it to 0% Hardness and 8% Alpha in the tool options, and lightly painted in highlights over the tattoos in the areas that were no longer visible with the tattoos covering them. This helped give the image a little more depth and rounded out the arms.

Graffiti

Source Images: "Grunge Kitchen 4" Shaun L., "Berlin Street Art" by Richard Kershaw, "Graffiti" by xbauerx, "Monster King" by Berkeley Robinson, "Graffiti 4" by Alejandro González G., "Graffiti" by Bianca de Blok, "Urban Tex Churs" by Jason Antony, "Soul Taggin 1" by Jason Cross, "Stop Bomb" by Bonifacio Pontonio

Under the cover of dark, the entire world becomes a blank canvas for graffiti artists the world over. From bridges to alleyways, no space is off limits to these artists. In this tutorial, I'm going to show how, using Phoenix, you could do the unexpected and cover the interior of a kitchen with spray paint. And you won't even need to get your hands dirty.

1. The first thing I needed to do was find an unlikely scene to cover in graffiti, so I decided to tag a kitchen. I chose an image of a rundown kitchen to create the illusion that this kitchen was abandoned and overtaken by vandals.

2. The next step was to locate source images of graffiti. I wanted to find sources of various sizes that would fit into the different surface sizes I would cover with graffiti. I used the File > Import command to import the first graffiti source image into a new layer in the document.

3. Noticing that this graffiti source image was similar in proportion to the closest cabinet door, I decided to apply the source image to that area. I needed to skew it to fit the perspective of the cabinet. First, I lowered the Alpha setting for this graffiti source layer to 50% in the Layers sidebar so I could see the cabinet to which I needed to align the graffiti source image. After clicking the Distortion Tool, I aligned the corner handles with the four corners of the cabinet to fit the perspective of the original photo.

4. I wanted the original cabinet's texture to show through, so I applied the Multiply Blend Mode to this graffiti layer and increased the Alpha to 75%.

5. Next, I imported my second graffiti source image with File > Import. I noticed this piece was tall rather than wide. So I located a section of my image would fit best in. To do so, I lowered the Alpha setting for the second graffiti source layer to 50% in the Layers sidebar so I could see through the image.

6. Noticing that the furthest cabinet was relatively similar in proportion to the second graffiti source image, I decided to apply the source to that area. Again, with the Distortion Tool selected, I aligned the corners of the second graffiti image on its layer with the corners of the cabinet. I set this layer's Alpha to Multiply and reset the Alpha to 93%.

7. I also wanted to cover the walls in the background with graffiti as well. So I imported my third graffiti source image into the document and aligned it against the back wall as I did with the other pieces, using the techniques presented in the earlier steps.

8. The graffiti in the third source image was covering some items I wanted exposed—for example, the mirror, sink, and the cabinet. Using the Polygonal Selection Tool, I made a selection around the elements I wanted exposed on the third image's layer and chose Edit > Cut to remove each area. I chose Select > Select None after cutting the last selection. Using the Eraser Tool set to 95% Hardness, I fine-tuned and erased any portions I may have missed and any round corners the Polygonal Selection Tool couldn't select until I was left with the graffiti sitting comfortably on just the exposed wallpaper area. I then set this layer's Blend Mode to Hard Light and set the Alpha to 77% in the Layers sidebar.

9. I imported my fourth graffiti image into the document and aligned it to the nearest set of drawers using the Distortion Tool as before.

10. Applying the Multiply Blend Mode pulls out the dark colors of the layer and hides the lighter tones. Because I wanted the lighter toned figure of the fourth graffiti source image to remain prominent, I decided to apply the Overlay Blend Mode to this layer instead of the Multiply as I did in the upper cabinets. This way, the cartoon figure remained visible, yet the wood texture from the original image still showed through giving me the effect I desired. I changed the Alpha of this layer to 74%.

11. Using these same techniques, I finished the rest of the image by importing in appropriately proportioned graffiti sources and applying them to the remaining areas I wanted to cover.

Face Swap

Source Images: "Beauty in Petals" by Aldra, "Confident standing portrait of a handsome student" by Yuri Arcurs

One of the first things a lot of people do when starting to learn image manipulation is a simple face swap. How would your head look on Angelina Jolie's body? How would you look as one of the 12 disciples in Leonardo Da Vinci's "The Last Supper"? In this tutorial, I'll show you the basic steps in the simple face swap. And in no time, you'll be putting yourself in any image you like, whether you're welcome or not!

1. I started with these two images. Selecting appropriate source images is probably the most important part of the process. Choosing two images where the perspectives match and have generally the same lighting will make the process a whole lot easier.

2. I wanted to blend the young man's face onto the woman's body. I started by opening the image of the woman in Phoenix. I then chose File > Import and uploaded the image of the man into the same document. I selected the man layer and used the Lasso Selection Tool to make a rough selection around the man's face. I copied this selection (Edit > Copy) and pasted it (Edit > Paste) onto a new layer. I chose Select > Select None to remove the selection marquee. I then clicked the Eye icon next to the original layer with the man on it on the Layers sidebar to make the layer invisible, since I wouldn't be needing it anymore.

3. Next, it was time to align the man's face to the woman's body. First, I clicked the man face layer in the Layers sidebar and lowered the layer's Alpha setting to 50%. This enabled me to see the woman's face in the background as a guide for positioning the man's face on top. Using the Transformation Tool, I resized and rotated the man's face to align with the woman's face using her facial features as a guideline. I lined it up so that the man's eyes were directly over the woman's, the man's nose aligned with the woman's, and so on. When I was happy with the placement, I pressed Enter and confirmed the transformation. I then set the man face layer's Alpha back to 100%.

4. Blending the man's face into the woman's head on the original layer was the next step. Making sure the man's face layer was still selected, I selected the Eraser Tool and in the tool's options adjusted the Hardness to 0, set the size to 130, and the Alpha to 25%. I then lightly clicked around the edges of the face to get a soft blend between the two images, making sure to preserve the man's main facial features: his eyes, nose, and mouth.

5. Next, it came time to adjust the tone of the image. I noticed the man's face was lit more brightly than the woman's, so I needed to darken it slightly. With the man's face layer still selected, I chose the Image > Brightness & Contrast command. In the Brightness and Contrast dialog box, I dragged the Brightness slider left to a setting of -30, and dragged the Contrast slider right to 11. I clicked OK to apply the change. The face still didn't look right, as the man's complexion was more of an orange color, whereas the woman's skin tone leaned more toward pink. I fixed this by choosing Image > Hue & Saturation and moving the Hue slider to the left by -10 to give the man's face a more pink appearance as well. The pink tone was still a little too deeply saturated in comparison to the woman's, so with the Hue and Saturation dialog box still open, I slid the Saturation slider left to -10, as well, and clicked OK.

6. Then I needed to match the sharpness of both images. With the image of the man showing softer features, I needed to apply a slight sharpening to him. I did this by copying the man's face layer by clicking the Options drop-down arrow in the Layers sidebar and then clicking Duplicate Layer. With the new layer selected, I chose Filters > Sharpen. I lowered this layer's Alpha to 50% in the Layers sidebar to alleviate some of the sharpening effect the filter caused.

7. And finally, I wanted to darken some of the shadows around the man's face in areas that were darker on the original woman's face. I created a new layer by clicking the New Layer icon on the Layers sidebar. I selected the Paintbrush Tool and set the Hardness to 0% and set the Alpha to 15%. With black as my foreground color (click the Restore Colors button by the color boxes below the tools to reset black as the foreground color if needed), I simply painted in the areas around the man's nose and around his lips to darken these areas. I set this layer's Blend Mode to Overlay in the Layers sidebar to give a nice saturated darker shadow around these areas.

Liquify—Melting

Personally, I'm not a big fan of the summer. I swear, I could melt just standing still outside in the sun. No, I'd rather sit here in my air-conditioned studio and make the rest of the world around me melt. In this tutorial, I'm going to show how to do just that, and melt this poor, unsuspecting frog.

Source Image: "Frog" by an Jan Pietruszka

1. To create the appearance that the frog was melting, I wanted to create a series of drips flowing from the frog. I first made a duplicate of my original layer (Layer > Duplicate Layer), in case I made a mistake and wanted to go back to the original layer and start over. Using the Liquify Tool set at 5 Pressure, I dragged the tool to roughly create a drip flowing from the tip of one of the frog's fingers. I dragged this portion to flow down the leaf.

2. To add some more realism to this effect, I wanted to add a blob to the end of the drip. With the Liquify Tool still selected, I dragged the tool in a circular shape toward the end of the drip to expand this area, creating the look of a blob.

3. Then I continued the same process for the rest of the frog's fingers, making sure to take gravity into account and dragging the drips to flow down the contours of the leaves. For the drips further back in the image, I lowered the Pressure of the Liquify Tool to 4 to lower the amount of drip distance.

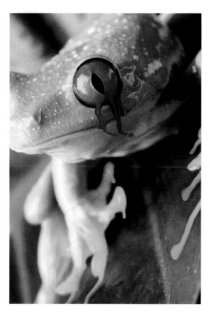

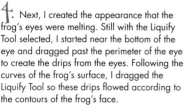

4. Next, I created the appearance that the frog's eyes were melting. Still with the Liquify Tool selected, I started near the bottom of the eye and dragged past the perimeter of the eye to create the drips from the eyes. Following the curves of the frog's surface, I dragged the Liquify Tool so these drips flowed according to the contours of the frog's face.

5. And again for the drips on the frog's back, I dragged the Liquify Tool, this time with the Pressure setting lowered to 3. I dragged subtle drips along the surface of the frog's skin. I started with a lighter area of the skin and dragged down along the curve of the frog. I continued this process until I was satisfied with the number of drips around the frog.

6. I then wanted to add some depth to the drips, as they still had a flat appearance to them. I did this by creating a new layer (New Layer icon on the Layers sidebar) to add shadows and highlights to the drips. I selected the Paintbrush Tool and chose 10% Hardness and 15% Alpha in the tool options. I also set black as the foreground color (click the Restore Colors button by the color selection boxes, if needed). With the new layer selected in the Layers sidebar, I painted around the edges of the drips. This created the appearance of shadows and made the drips appear more prominent. I set this layer's Blend Mode to Overlay and lowered the Alpha to 75% in the Layers sidebar to keep the shadows saturated with the frog's original color.

7. To create the highlights, I created a new layer (New Layer icon) and selected white as my foreground color (Switch Between Foreground and Background Colors button near the color selection boxes). With the Paintbrush Tool still selected, I roughly painted in the highlights on the drips on the opposite edge of the shadows.

8. I then selected the Eraser Tool and set it to 50% Hardness. I erased the excess of the painted highlights and this formed the highlights to fit the shape of the path of the drips.

Liquify—Displacement

Aviary

There are plenty of uses for the Liquify Tool. In this tutorial, I'll show how you can use a subtle approach to displace objects in order to situate them over the curves and contours of the wrinkles in a person's clothing.

Source Image: "Plain white T shirt" by Sue Colvil

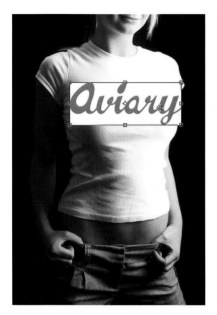

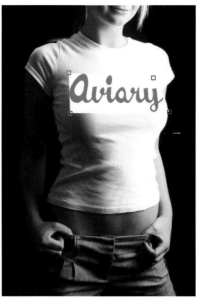

1. In this first example, I wanted to simply place the Aviary logo on the woman's shirt. After opening the original image, I used the File > Import command to import the logo onto a new layer. Working on the new layer, I selected the Transformation Tool, resized the logo, and dragged it into roughly the position I wanted, pressing Enter to finish my change.

2. I realized the woman was not directly facing forward to the camera, so the logo didn't sit properly. I selected the Distortion Tool and skewed the logo to an angle by dragging the corner handle boxes until the logo was at the shape and angle I desired. I pressed Enter to apply the change.

3. With the logo layer still selected, I then opened the Blend Mode drop-down list in the Layers sidebar and clicked Multiply. This made the texture of the shirt visible through the logo layer. I noticed the logo was still too clean look-ing, as it sat over the wrinkles of the shirt uncon-vincingly. This is where the Liquify Tool came into play. I selected the Liquify Tool and changed its Pressure setting to 2 and set the Size to 21 in the tool options. I lightly dragged the tool on the wrinkles on my logo layer. Dragging along the contours of the wrinkle lines gave a much more realistic look to the distor-tion. This created a wavy effect, as if the logo were rolling directly over the wrinkles. I then used the Eraser Tool to smooth out any edges that may have gone blurry during the liquifying process.

4. Next, I needed to apply lighting effects to the logo. I made a selection around the logo by selecting the Magic Wand Tool, setting the Tolerance to 60, and clicking within the Aviary letters on the logo layer. I pressed and held Shift, and then clicked again in the dot of the eye to add it to the selection. I then clicked the New Layer icon on the Layers sidebar to create a new layer. I used the Gradient Fill Tool to apply a gradient across the selection on the new layer, leaving the default colors selected (white for left slider, black for right slider) and dragging from right to left on the layer. In the Layers sidebar, I selected Screen from the Blend Mode drop-down list and lowered the Alpha to 50% so that only the light portions of the gradient appear, giving the lighting effect over the letters I wanted.

5. I created a new layer and painted over the sleeve and collar areas on new separate layers in the same blue as my original logo (I selected the Eye Dropper tool and clicked in the letters on the logo layer to select the right color), then I applied the Multiply Blend Mode to this layer in the Layers sidebar. This added matching trim to the shirt, making it look more interesting than the original plain white T-shirt.

6. And finally, I added a lighting effect over the entire image. I copied the original layer, and dragged the layer copy to the top of the list in the Layers sidebar. I opened the Blend Mode drop-down list in the Layers sidebar and clicked Hard Light, and lowered the Alpha to 25%. The image was complete.

7. This technique can also be applied to full-scale images over an undulating surface area. In this case, I used the File > Import command to import an image of the Phoenix and Hummingbird on a new layer.

8. Again, using the Distortion Tool, I roughly skewed the painting to the perspective of the original image, pressing Enter to apply my change.

9. I applied the Multiply Blend Mode to this layer in the Layers sidebar. Then, using the Liquify Tool, I dragged the areas around the wrinkles again to make the imported image appear as if it were curving to the contours of the shirt.

10. Using the Eraser Tool, I erased the parts of the painting that were exposed past the shirt in the layer with the imported image. Then, I did as I did in step 6: I copied the original image layer, moved it to the top of the list over top of the painting layer, and applied the Hard Light Blend Mode to give it the extra boost of lighting effect.

Liquify—Texturizing

Source Image: "Ladybird" by Serdar Yagci, "Architectural Mix 3" by Benjamin Earwicker

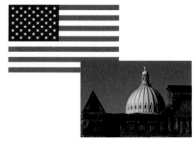

Ah, the many uses of the Liquify Tool. We've already seen how it can be applied to reshape and form anything from subtle effects to extreme cases. You also can use it to texturize and add interesting patterns to nearly any figure, as I'll show in this tutorial, applying the flag of the United States of America onto the back of a Ladybird (Johnson?).

1. First, I needed to get rid of the original spots on the ladybug in the original image by painting the orange color of the ladybug's shell right over the spots. Using the Eye Dropper Tool, I sampled the orange colors from directly around the spot I was to paint over on the original layer. Then I clicked the New Layer icon in the Layers sidebar to create a new layer. Using the Paintbrush Tool, I simply painted over the spots with the brush's Hardness set to 0 to create a soft blend into the original image. I had to work back and forth between the layers and tools, selecting various shades of orange on the original layer with the Eye Dropper Tool and painting them on the new layer with the Paintbrush Tool.

2. When the spots were covered, I flattened the image by clicking the Options button drop-down list arrow in the Layers sidebar and clicking Flatten Layers. Next, I wanted to desaturate the shell so that I could apply the colors of the flag onto it. Using the Lasso Selection Tool, I roughly selected the shell and copied and pasted it onto a new layer (Edit > Copy and Edit > Paste). Then I chose Image > Desaturate, followed by Select > Select None. Using the Eraser Tool, I erased around the shell to leave only the actual shell desaturated.

3. Next, I imported the image of the American flag onto a new layer using the File > Import command. I set the layer's Alpha to 50% so that I could see the ladybug. Using the Transformation Tool, I rotated the flag and positioned it in the area I wanted it over my ladybug, pressing Enter to finish the transformation.

4. Using the Liquify Tool, I dragged the stripes to fit the contours of the ladybug's shell. By using the tool set to 200 Size, I dragged near the center of the stripe and dragged up and to the right along the ladybug's back to create the round contour.

5. Using the Eraser Tool, I then removed the edges of the flag, leaving only the portion directly over the ladybug's shell. I then chose Image > Hue & Saturation, and in the Hue and Saturation dialog box dragged the Saturation slider left to -14 and dragged the Brightness slider right to 15. I clicked OK to apply the change.

6. I wanted to bring in some of the original highlights and shadows from the ladybug that are less prominent in the image since covering them with the flag. So I duplicated the desaturated shell layer by clicking the Options button drop-down list arrow in the Layers sidebar and clicking Duplicate layer. I dragged the new layer to the top of the list in the Layers sidebar, above the flag layer. I set this layer's Blend Mode to Overlay and this exposed the original highlights on top of the shell.

7. I wanted to change the background to a blue tint, as I would be importing a new background image. So I made a rough selection around the exposed background areas original image, and used Edit > Copy and Edit > Paste to paste the selection onto a new layer. With the new layer selected, I chose Image > Hue & Saturation, dragged the Hue slider to the right to 154, dragged Saturation setting to the right to 14, and clicked OK. Then I applied the Hard Light Blend Mode to this layer in the Layers sidebar.

8. Next I chose File > Import and imported an image of the Capitol building onto a new layer. I positioned the Capitol building image on its layer with the Transformation Tool, pressing Enter to finish the transformation.

9. I brightened the Capitol building layer to match my ladybug's sky by opening the Brightness & Contrast menu from the Image tab and setting the Brightness to 65 and the Contrast to -12. I then pressed OK to confirm the adjustment. Then, using the Eraser Tool set at 0 Hardness, I erased the hard edges to create a smooth blend. Then I clicked the Layer Filters icon on the Layers sidebar. I clicked Blur in the Layer Filters dialog box to check it, entered 10 for both the Blur X and Blur Y settings, and clicked OK.

10. And finally, I selected the areas of the stem that the ladybug was crawling on and copied them onto a new layer with Edit > Copy and Edit > Paste. Then I clicked the Layer Filters icon on the Layers sidebar. I clicked Blur in the Layer Filters dialog box to check it, entered 5 for both the Blur X and Blur Y settings, and clicked OK. This created a less harsh blend from the stem to the sky.

Clowning Around

I'm sure we all have one: that undeniable uncle who's generally regarded as the family "clown." In this tutorial, I'm going to give this special man in our life the make-up he was born to wear. That's right, we're going to make him an actual clown. The techniques presented here are not exclusive to crazy uncles, as they can be applied to a photo of nearly anyone.

Source Image: "old man making a face" by Bela Tibor Kozma

1. First I wanted to lay a white foundation covering most of the man's face. I made a rough selection around his face with the Lasso Selection Tool, and then copied and pasted this selection onto a new layer with Edit > Copy and Edit > Paste. I chose Select > Select None to remove the selection marquee.

2. To make this section white, I needed to drop most of the original skin color. With the new layer still selected, I chose Image > Hue & Saturation. In the Hue and Saturation dialog box, I dragged the Saturation slider left to lower the Saturation level to -85 and then clicked OK. This left just a hint of color in his face to maintain some realism, as no white make-up will make a person completely white.

3. I was happy with the saturation level, but I wanted the selection noticeably lighter. So I chose the Image > Brightness & Contrast menu. In the Brightness and Contrast dialog box, I dragged the Brightness slider right to a setting of 50, and dragged the Contrast slider left to -11 until I was happy with the look of the white paint. I then clicked OK to apply the change.

4. I didn't want the make-up to cover the man's eyes and mouth area, so I used the Eraser Tool to erase these areas on the copied layer, exposing the man's eyes and tongue from the original layer beneath. I then dragged the Eraser around the figure's head as well to remove any excess areas that weren't directly part of his face.

5. I wanted to add blue patches around the figure's eyes next. I clicked the original layer in the Layers sidebar, and then I roughly selected the areas around his eyes with the Lasso Selection Tool. To make the second selection, I pressed and held the Shift key while dragging on the image. With both areas selected, I then copied and pasted (Edit > Copy and Edit > Paste) the selection onto a new layer. I then dragged the new layer above the original and white paint layers in the Layers sidebar. I chose Select > Select None to remove the selection marquee.

6. To change the color of the areas around the eyes on the newest layer, I made sure the layer was still selected in the Layers sidebar. I then chose Image > Hue & Saturation. In the Hue and Saturation dialog box, I dragged the Hue slider to the right until I was happy with the tone for this segment of paint, about 170. I then lowered the Saturation by dragging its slider left to -11 to lessen the color a tad. I clicked OK to apply the changes.

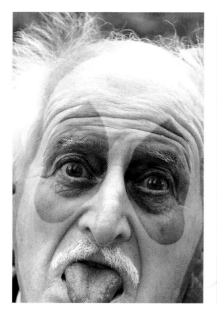

7. As I did earlier on the white paint layer, I removed the areas within the figure's eyes on this layer with the Eraser Tool. Using the Eraser Tool set at 90% Hardness, I also shaped the patches around his eyes by erasing around the edges until I was satisfied with the shape of the segments.

8. I then wanted to create the appearance of a black outline around the make-up. With the blue eye make-up layer still selected, I chose Select > Selection from Layer to do just that—create a selection around my active layer. I clicked the New Layer icon in the Layers sidebar to create a new layer, and then dragged the new layer below the eye make-up layer. Then I chose Select > Modify > Expand, entered 2 in the Selection Expand text box, and clicked OK to expand the selection by 2 pixels. I clicked OK to finish applying the modification.

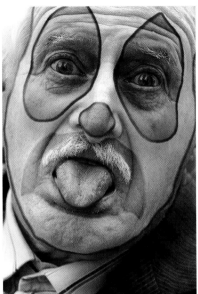

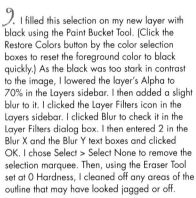

9. I filled this selection on my new layer with black using the Paint Bucket Tool. (Click the Restore Colors button by the color selection boxes to reset the foreground color to black quickly.) As the black was too stark in contrast to the image, I lowered the layer's Alpha to 70% in the Layers sidebar. I then added a slight blur to it. I clicked the Layer Filters icon in the Layers sidebar. I clicked Blur to check it in the Layer Filters dialog box. I then entered 2 in the Blur X and the Blur Y text boxes and clicked OK. I chose Select > Select None to remove the selection marquee. Then, using the Eraser Tool set at 0 Hardness, I cleaned off any areas of the outline that may have looked jagged or off.

10. Next, I wanted to add a spot of red make-up to the man's nose. Using the same method I used to create the eye make-up, I selected the original layer in the Layers sidebar, selected the area I wanted with the Lasso Selection Tool, copied and pasted it onto a new layer, and then dragged the new layer to the top of the list in the Layers sidebar. Because the skin already had a pink complexion to it, I didn't need to alter the color too much. Instead, I chose Image > Brightness & Contrast, used the sliders to lower the Brightness by -23 and raise the Contrast by 11, and clicked OK. This gave the nose a red color. Then I applied an outline to this area just as I did with the blue area around the eyes, using the techniques covered in steps 8 and 9. I used Select > Select None when finished to remove the selection marquee.

11. Then, starting from the original layer, I used the same methods to color the area around the figure's mouth. This time, after selecting Image > Hue & Saturation, I dragged the Hue slider to the right to 63 to give the segment a green color, and then clicked OK. I applied an outline to this section as well. And finally, I erased the tongue area on this layer using the Eraser Tool and then chose Select > Select None.

12. And finally, I added a single tear down the clown's cheek using the same methods used in the rest of the image. Just for dramatic effect!

Coloring Line Art

Source Image: "Just Follow My Hues" by Meowza Katz

Not only is Phoenix useful in creating photorealistic images, but you also can use it to have fun colorizing line drawings. In this tutorial, I'll show you a simple way to use the tools and features in Phoenix to color a line drawing of his feathered friend, the toucan.

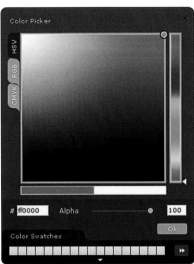

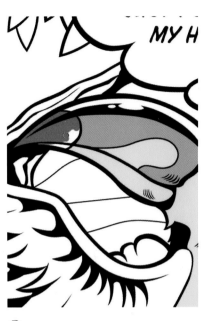

1. The first thing I did was set the line art layer's Blend Mode setting in the Layers sidebar to Multiply. This preserves the black outlines so that color layers are added below the original layer; the outlines will always remain on top and the white areas will appear invisible. I selected the blank layer below the outline layer. (You could click the New Layer button to add a new layer and then drag it below the original layer, if needed.) I then selected white as the foreground color and used the Paint Bucket Tool to fill the transparent layer with white.

2. Next, I selected the Paintbrush Tool. In the tool's options, I clicked the upper Color selection box to open the Color Picker dialog box. I slid the top slider (H) to select the hue I wanted, and then used the other controls in the dialog box to fine tune the color. Once I had the color I wanted, I clicked OK.

3. To start laying down a coloring for a portion of the image, I created a new layer directly below the original outlines layer by clicking the New Layer icon in the Layers sidebar and then dragging the new layer into position. With the new layer selected, I used the Paintbrush Tool to paint each of the sections that I wanted to fill with the current foreground color. I then changed foreground colors as needed to paint the various sections. By painting segments on new layers instead of directly on the line art layer, I'm able to go back and make edits and adjustments to these sections without destroying the original line art.

Note

Phoenix is set to JPEG as its default File Type. Because the line art was a GIF image, I had to specify this when uploading my image by changing the Files of Type option to "gif (*.gif)" in the file uploading prompt.

4. At this point, you could call the image complete with the base colors down. But I like adding a few effects to line art colorizations to make them more interesting. First, I wanted to add a light source to this image, in this case, the sun. Using the Magic Wand Tool, I selected the sky portion between the trees on my base color layer. With this selection isolated, I created a new layer. I then selected the Gradient Fill Tool, specified a yellow hue for the left arrow slider and orange for the right arrow slider, and changed the Gradient Type to Radial. I then dragged on the selection, starting from the point where I wanted the sun to appear. This added the appearance of light from the sun. I then chose Select > Select None to remove the selection marquee.

5. To add the sun itself, I created a new layer and positioned it above the layer where I just added the glow. I set the foreground color to white. I selected the Paintbrush Tool, set it to 0% Hardness and 60 pixels for Size, and then simply painted in the sun by clicking once in the middle of the gradient glow created in the previous step.

6. Next, I added some highlights to the surrounding elements. Again, using the Magic Wand Tool, I selected segments of my image that I wanted to edit on the base color layer. For example, I selected the tree. I then created a new layer for the highlights. I used the Eye Dropper Tool to select the yellow color from the sun gradient on its layer, making that color the foreground color. I then reselected the new layer in the Layers sidebar, and using the Paintbrush Tool set at 0% Hardness, I painted highlights on the branches of the trees on the areas adjacent to the gradient. The selection marquee prevented the highlights from painting over unwanted areas. When I was finished adding highlights to an area, I chose Select > Select None.

7. Another way to increase the lighting effect of the sun was by playing with layer Blend Modes. I created another new layer and left the yellow foreground color selected. I then selected the Elliptical Shape Tool and drew a circle, holding down Shift as I dragged to draw a perfectly constrained circle over the sky and sun. I clicked the Layer Filters icon in the Layers sidebar, clicked the Blur check box to check it, entered 50 in both the Blur X and Blur Y text boxes, and clicked OK. I then chose the Overlay Blend Mode and set the Alpha to 70% for the layer in the Layers sidebar. This furthered the glow effect over the surrounding elements of the sun.

JUST FOLLOW
MY HUES...

8. I added gradients to other areas in the image to make it appear more dimensional. I created a new layer above the base colors layer to hold the gradients. I then returned to the base color layer, and used the Magic Wand Tool to select the colored area to which I wanted to apply the gradient. I reselected the gradients layer and selected the Gradient Fill Tool. In the tool's options, I specified a color as close as possible to the color I selected on the base colors layer for the left color arrow slider and chose a slightly darker version of the same color for the right color arrow slider. I then dragged over the selection to apply the gradient. I continued this process until the rest of the colored areas in the image (except for the sky) had a gradient effect.

9. I also added a gradient effect to the sky using layer Blend Modes. I selected the segments that made up the sky in my base color layer. Then on a new layer added just above the base colors layer, I created a white to black gradient from top to bottom with the Gradient Tool. I set this layer's Blend Mode to Overlay and it gave the background sky a nice subtle gradient effect.

10. To add further shading, I created a new layer above the layer containing the color gradients created in step 8, and painted in some darker areas with the Paintbrush Tool on the bottom portion of the toucan's body, beak, and below its eye.

11. I clicked the Layer Filters icon in the Layers sidebar, clicked the Blur check box to check it, entered 15 in both the Blur X and Blur Y text boxes, and clicked OK. I then set the Alpha to 20% for the layer in the Layers sidebar. This gave a nice shading effect to add some final depth to the figure.

3

Sprucing Up
Photography

Enhancing Saturation

Source Image: "Bite Me!" by spxChrome

Enhancing saturation is one sure fire way to get people to notice your photographs. Selectively increasing the saturation around focal elements in your images can give these areas the needed punch to really leave a vibrant mark on the viewer. In this quick tutorial, I'll be taking a seductive photo of a cherry and bumping up the vibrancy in the image with just a few easy steps.

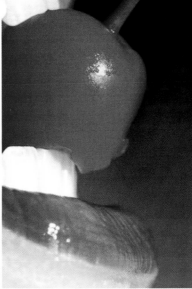

1. First, I wanted to raise the overall contrast in the image. I chose Image > Brightness & Contrast. In the Brightness and Contrast dialog box, I lowered the Brightness setting to -12 and raised the Contrast to 9. I clicked OK to confirm the changes, which gave the image a slight boost in contrast.

2. To brighten the teeth, I made a rough selection around the teeth with the Lasso Selection Tool (using Shift+drag to select the second set of teeth) and copied (Edit > Copy) and pasted (Edit > Paste) this selection onto a new layer, then chose Select > Select None to remove the selection marquee. With the copied teeth layer selected, I chose Image > Hue & Saturation. In the dialog box, I lowered the Saturation setting to -40, raised the Brightness slightly to 4, and clicked OK.

3. Using the Eraser Tool set with 100 Size, 48 Hardness, and 70 Alpha, I erased any area of the lips and cherry on the copied layer that happened to get desaturated in the process, leaving just the teeth exposed.

4. And to increase the vibrancy in the cherry, I selected the original image layer in the Layers sidebar. Using the Lasso Selection Tool, I selected the cherry and pasted it onto a new layer with Edit > Copy and Edit > Paste. I chose Image > Hue & Saturation. This time, I lowered the Hue to -6, raised the Saturation to 12, and lowered the Brightness to -12, clicking OK to apply the changes. This gave the cherry a very bright red color that I desired.

5. And finally, I bumped up the Saturation in the original background layer some more. I selected the green background area directly behind the cherry using the Lasso Selection Tool and pasted it onto a new layer (Edit > Copy and Edit > Paste). I chose Select > Select None to remove the selection marquee. I then chose Image > Hue & Saturation, changed the Saturation setting to 21, and clicked OK. This applied a more saturated green hue to the area, giving great contrast to the red in the cherry so it popped even further. I was finished. By selectively increasing and decreasing the saturation levels in certain parts of your photographs, you can quickly make the important elements in your pictures stand out.

Borders

Y ou can choose to add a border to a photograph for a number of reasons, and the possibilities for the types of borders you can add are endless. The right border can add a certain class or element to an image, making important aspects of an image stand out or adding more mood to a picture. In this tutorial, I'll show you how to create several different styles of borders and touch on why to apply certain borders to images.

Source Images: "bw-toddler1" by canadian,"bride and groom share a kiss" by Alex Ustin, "Call Center Stress" by Photoganda Inc., "Vintage Paper" by Cornelius

1. **Simple Border:** The easiest border to create is a thin, single-colored border. To do this, I chose Select > Select All to create a selection around the entire photograph in Phoenix. Then I chose Select > Modify > Border, which opened the Selection Border dialog box, where I could enter a width. I entered 2 and clicked OK to confirm the size. The selection around the entire image was transformed into a 2-pixel wide selection border surrounding my image. (Zoom in to 140% or so to see the selection border better.) I clicked the Restore Colors button near the color selection boxes to reset the foreground color to black, and then used the Paint Bucket Fill Tool to fill the 2-pixel selection around my image to create the simple 2-pixel border. I then chose Select > Select None to remove the selection marquee. This type of simple border is effective to use on images with a lot of surrounding white to help delineate the image without obstructing the focal point of the photo.

2. **Simple Thick Border:** To create a thicker, single-colored border, simply input a higher number (up to 20) after choosing Select > Modify > Border and click OK. Then proceed with filling the border as in Step 1. A thicker border more prominently delineates the photograph from its surroundings, especially if the photograph is to be placed on a wall or a website with a white background.

3. **2-Color Border:** To create a duotone border, I first created a 20-pixel black border around the image just as I did for the Thick Border, but I created a new layer above the photo before filling the selection to create the border on its own layer. I then chose Select > Select None. To create the thin white border inside, I selected the Magic Wand Tool and clicked in the transparent portion inside the black border on its layer. Then, I chose Select > Modify > Border, entered 4 for the thickness of the inside border, and clicked OK. I selected white as the foreground color, used the Paint Bucket Tool to fill the smaller border with white, and then chose Select > Select None to remove the selection marquee. This created a two-color border. This technique is particularly effective because not only does the black outline delineate the light portions of the image, but the thin white border also isolates the dark elements within the image as well.

  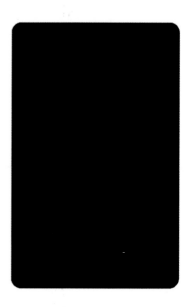

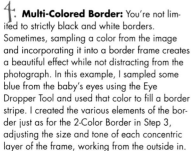

4. Multi-Colored Border: You're not limited to strictly black and white borders. Sometimes, sampling a color from the image and incorporating it into a border frame creates a beautiful effect while not distracting from the photograph. In this example, I sampled some blue from the baby's eyes using the Eye Dropper Tool and used that color to fill a border stripe. I created the various elements of the border just as for the 2-Color Border in Step 3, adjusting the size and tone of each concentric layer of the frame, working from the outside in.

5. Next, I'll show a couple of stylized borders you could apply to a photo like this wedding photograph. Wedding photographs usually require a certain sense of elegance. Keep the nature of the original photo in mind when selecting borders for the image.

6. Feathered Border: First, I wanted to apply a feathered border to the image. This type of stylized border helps to create a soft, dream-like quality to images, which would be a perfect effect for the wedding photograph. I first clicked the New Layer icon on the Layers palette to create a new layer above the photo. I filled the new layer with white using the Paint Bucket Tool. I created another new layer, and selected black as the foreground color. I selected the Rectangular Shape Tool and set Corner Rounding to 80 in the tool's options. I dragged on the newest layer to create a rounded rectangle, leaving a white border around the image.

7. With the rounded black rectangle layer selected, I chose Select > Selection from Layer. I then clicked the white fill layer in the Layers sidebar and selected Edit > Cut to cut the rounded rectangle shape out of the white fill. I then deleted my black rectangle layer by clicking it and clicking the Drop Layers icon in the Layers sidebar, and chose Select > Select None to remove the selection marquee. I selected the white border layer in the Layers sidebar, and then clicked the Layer Filters icon. I clicked the Blur check box to check it, entered 20 in both the Blur X and Blur Y text boxes, and clicked OK. I duplicated this layer, reopened the Layer Filters dialog box, clicked Blur, set the duplicate layer's Blur strength to 40 for both Blur X and Blur Y, and clicked OK. I then duplicated both the 20 strength and 40 strength blurred layers to enhance the white fill around the image. You can duplicate these layers as much as you want and increase/decrease the amount of blur to apply the exact amount of feathered effect around your image that you wish.

8. **Floating Border:** Another effect we can apply to an image is a floating effect. This really makes an image stand out, as it gives the appearance the photograph is elevated off the screen or page. To do this, I first flattened the wedding photograph with the feathered border. I then selected the Rectangular Selection Tool and created a selection around the photograph, and copied and pasted this onto a new layer.

9. With the copied layer selected from the Layers sidebar, I clicked the Layer Filters icon in the Layers sidebar. I clicked the Shadow check box to check it in the Layer Filters dialog box. I lowered the Alpha setting to 0.5 to subdue the shadow so it wouldn't be overpowering. I then entered 10 in both the Blur X and Blur Y text boxes, changed the Distance to 5, and clicked OK.

10. Finally, I'm going to show how to lend a darker mood to an image via the border you create. Using this image of a screaming woman, I'm gonna apply borders to complement her frustrated mood.

11. **Vignette border:** First, I'm going to show how to create a dark vignette border around the figure. I used the same technique as for the feathered effect on the wedding photograph, but I started by creating a new layer and filling it with black instead of white. I then created another new layer, set the foreground color to white, and used the Rectangle Tool to draw a rounded rectangle. I chose Select > Selection From Layer, clicked the black fill layer in the Layers sidebar, and used Edit > Cut to remove the rectangle. Finally, I deleted the white rectangle layer and chose Select > Select None to remove the selection marquee.

12. Applying the same Blur as in Step 7, I was able to create a nice vignette effect around the photograph. What this does is isolate the woman in the image even further, emphasizing her feeling of being trapped, which I felt from the original image.

13. **Grunge border:** And finally, I'll show how to apply a grunge border around the image. Grunge borders are most effective when applied to images that you want to have an aged or a rough look. I used the same image from the previous border tutorial for this one, as the figure in the image showed a sense of anger, which would lend perfectly to the raw style of the grunge border. So first I imported an image of old weathered paper using the File > Import command.

14. I inverted this layer (Image > Invert Colors) and desaturated it (Image > Desaturate). I then chose Image > Brightness & Contrast, lowered the Brightness to -45 and raised the Contrast by 45, and clicked OK.

15. I then applied the Screen layer Blend Mode to this layer in the Layers sidebar. This gave me a grungy border around the image, giving it the raw, gritty feel I felt complements the original photo very well. And that was it. A number of ways to enhance your images with appropriate borders!

Dodge & Burn

Source Image: "Senior" by Jordan Chesbrough

"Dodging" and "burning" an image sounds like a dangerous practice just in name alone. But these techniques enable you to enhance an image rather than destroy it. Dodging enables you to lighten overly dark areas in the image, while burning enables you to darken tones where needed. In this tutorial, I'll show how to apply these effects to a portrait for dramatic effect. This method can be applied to any number of images to make them pop.

1. The first thing I did was to darken and add overall contrast to the image to create a more dynamic appearance to start with. I chose Image > Brightness & Contrast, and in the Brightness and Contrast dialog box, I dragged the Brightness slider left to -18 and the Contrast slider right to 12. I clicked OK to finish the change.

2. I opted not to use the Dodge/Burn Tool in Phoenix and rather went the manual route. First, I wanted to burn (darken) the original shadows on the figure. I did this by creating a new layer (New Layer icon on the Layers sidebar) above the original layer and filling it with a midtone gray (HEX #7F7F7F in the Select Color dialog box opened by double-clicking the Foreground color selection box) using the Paint Bucket Tool. I set this layer's Blend Mode to Overlay in the Layers sidebar, making the gray no longer visible.

3. I clicked the Restore Colors button by the color selection boxes to reset the foreground color to black. Then, I selected the Paintbrush Tool and set its Hardness to 0 and Alpha to 10% in the tool options. I then painted on the gray overlay layer. I painted over the areas that were already shaded in the original image. This increased the depth of the original shadows by burning these areas rather than painting in any new shadows. What this essentially does is enhance the dark or shadowed areas in the image.

4. When I set this layer's Blend Mode back to Normal in the Layers sidebar, I could see exactly where I painted on the figure to enhance the shadows, as shown in the image accompanying this step. After I finished examining my painting, I reset the layer's Blend Mode to Overlay.

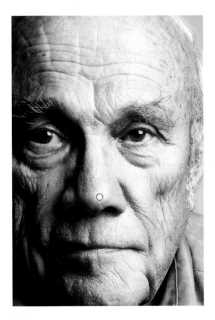

5. To dodge (lighten) areas in the image, I again created a new layer by clicking the New Layer icon on the Layers sidebar. I filled the new layer with the same midtone gray (HEX #7F7F7F in the Select Color dialog box opened by double-clicking the Foreground color selection box) using the Paint Bucket Tool, then set the layer's Blend Mode to Overlay in the Layers sidebar. This time I selected white as the foreground color (click the Restore Colors button and then the Switch Between Foreground and Background Colors button) and painted over the existing light areas in the figure, such as the tip of his nose and cheekbone with the Paintbrush Tool set to 10% Alpha and 0 Hardness.

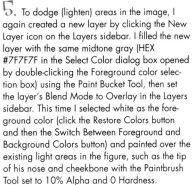

6. When I set this layer's Blend Mode to Normal in the Layers sidebar, I could see exactly where I painted the figure to enhance the highlights, as shown above. After I finished examining my painting, I reset the layer's Blend Mode to Overlay.

7. When I was content with the amount of dodge and burn applied, I flattened the image into a single working layer by clicking the Options button drop-down list arrow in the Layers sidebar and clicking Flatten Layers. As this technique frequently bumps up the saturation level, I wanted to lower it back down. With the image flattened, I chose Image > Hue & Saturation. In the Hue and Saturation dialog box, I dragged the Hue slider to the right to 11 and moved the Saturation slider left to -17 to alleviate some of the image's pink tint, and clicked OK.

8. To enhance the mood of the image even further, I wanted to apply a subtle gradient lighting effect to the image. I created a new layer (New Layer icon in the Layers sidebar) and selected the Gradient Fill Tool. In the tool's options, I chose Radial as the Gradient Type and left the default white (left) and black (right) colors selected. I dragged from the center of the image diagonally to a corner to create the gradient on the layer.

9. I selected the Overlay Blend Mode for this layer in the Layers sidebar. I noticed it created more of a harsh effect than I wanted. So, with the gradient layer still selected in the Layers sidebar, I chose Image > Brightness & Contrast, raised the Brightness to 52 and dropped the Contrast to -67, and clicked OK.

10. And finally, I added a bit more of a yellow tone to the whole image. I created a new layer and filled it with a dark yellow brown color (double-click the Foreground color selection box, set the HEX to #807900, and click OK) using the Paint Bucket Tool. I then chose the Overlay Blend Mode for this layer and lowered the Alpha for the layer to 18% in the Layers sidebar, and the image was complete. This is a very quick method to add pop to any of your portraits!

Compositional Cropping

Cropping is a fairly simple process. You simply select a section of your image and isolate it. But trying to figure out when and where and how much to crop your image can be a daunting task, and is often left to the tastes of each individual creator. In this section, I'll go over a few different ways to crop images and give my own reasons why I decided to crop them the way I did.

Source Images: "Blonde in Blue Dress" by Fidelio Photography, "I can't believe it!" by Andrés Peiró Palmer, "Red Rose" by Rob Hunt, "Ladybug in a twig 01" by arlindo71

1. The most obvious reason to crop a photograph is to remove distracting elements within the image. For this first image, I wanted to isolate the woman for a nice clean portrait photograph.

2. Using the Rectangular Selection Tool, I made a selection around my figure in the image. When I was happy with the selection, I selected Image > Crop Selection, and I was left with just my cropped figure. By doing this, I eliminated the excess background and all focus in the picture is directed on the woman now.

3. Sometimes, you might have a photograph with emotions you really want to emphasize. As for the case of my next image, I wanted to enhance the dramatic effect of the screaming woman.

4. Again, I used the Rectangular Selection Tool and drew a rectangle framing the woman's face and cropped to the selection using Image > Crop Selection. You can see that this instantly brings a stronger sense that the danger, which has the woman terrified, is drawing near. This is an old cinematic trick that can be applied to photographs to emphasize the emotion within them.

5. Sometimes you'll have a great photograph, but something about it looks really bland and you can't quite put your finger on why. For example, I found this gorgeous image of a red rose, but the composition was lacking. Often, simply moving the image so it's not sitting directly in the center of your composition, often referred to as the "Rule of thirds" in photography, can add that needed kick. So in this example, I'm going to enlarge the canvas and sit the rose low on the image to create a somber mood.

6. The original image was 849 × 565 pixels. With this image open in Phoenix, I selected Image > Canvas Resize. I unchecked the Constrain Proportion check box, as I didn't want my new composition to retain the proportions of the original image. I entered 1200 in the Width text box and 1600 in Height text box in the Resize Canvas dialog box, and clicked Apply.

7. With the rose layer still selected in the Layers sidebar, I selected the Transformation Tool and dragged the image to the lower-left area of the composition, pressing Enter to finish the move. I then set the foreground color to white, selected the Paint Bucket Tool, and filled the transparent area on the layer with white. I added a border to the image and I was done. This was a nice way to add a whole new mood to the image, by simply moving the subject matter away from the center.

8. There'll be times when you have an image that's cropped to your liking, and the subject sits just as you want in the image, but you still think that you can improve the composition. It may be you've been looking at your image for too long and need a fresh new look at it for your own personal sake.

9. In the case of this image, I decided to rotate the image clockwise by 90 degrees. To do so, I chose Edit > Transform > Rotate 90 CW. Doing this gave a whole new look to the image. The ladybug was no longer walking casually across the branch, but rather now appeared to be struggling up the branch on her way to loftier goals. With my image rotated, I selected the Rectangular Selection Tool, made a selection, and cropped the image down a tad more using Image > Crop Selection.

10. I added a subtle dark green border to complement the image and I was done. Sometimes when you want a whole new perspective on an image, you do just that. Change the perspective! And there you have it, a number of ways to crop all sorts of images to enhance their mood or emphasize certain portions of your photographs.

Cross Processing

Source Images: "Cowgirl in the Heat" by Alexander Hafemann, "Instant Film Border" by sx70

In traditional film photography, *cross processing* involves intentionally processing color film in chemicals intended for a different kind of film. This basically creates wild, unnatural colors and images generally high in contrast. This photographic style was highly popular in the 1980s. Digital photo manipulation allows today's digital photographers to recreate similar effects, and I'll show you how to mimic this developing style right in Phoenix.

1. Finding the right image that will work with this effect is the first step. Fashion portraits tend to work the best, in my opinion, for subject matter. So I chose this picture of a girl dressed up in western garb and large sunglasses, as it was reminiscent of a dated style that will lend to the nostalgic feeling typically associated with cross-processed images.

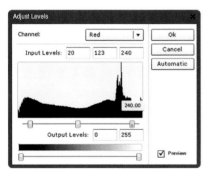

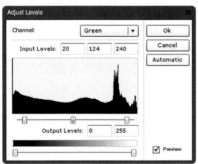

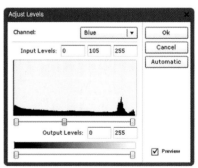

2. I needed to adjust the Levels in the image, so I chose Image > Levels to open the Adjust Levels dialog box. I opened the Channel drop-down list and clicked Red so I could adjust the levels for the red channel first. I wanted to blow out the red in the highlights some more. Under Input Levels I dragged the black (left) slider to the right to the 20 mark, slid the white (far right) slider to the left to the 240 mark, and slid the midtone (middle) slider to the 123 mark.

3. I then selected Green from the Channel drop-down list and applied the same Input Levels settings (20 black/left, 124 midtone/middle, 240 white/right) to increase the green within the highlights as well.

4. I selected Blue from the Channel drop-down list. Under Input Levels, I left the black (left) and white (right) sliders as they were, and just slid the midtone slider to the left to the 105 mark. This increased the amount of blue overall in the image, especially in the shadows. As cross-processed images tend to have a lot of blues in their shadows, this effect would work particularly well here.

5. I clicked OK to apply the Levels settings, and the image appearance changed as shown in the picture for this step. I chose Image > Hue & Saturation. In the Hue and Saturation dialog box, I dragged both the Hue and Saturation sliders to the left to -12. I clicked OK to apply the changes. I chose Image > Brightness & Contrast, lowered the Brightness setting to -15 and raised the Contrast to 8, and then clicked OK. This gave the entire image a really blue look, a good starting point.

6. I wanted to bring back more yellow into this image, so I created a new layer (New Layer icon on the Layers sidebar). With the new layer selected, I clicked the Foreground color selection box, entered BDBD00 in the HEX text box of the Select Color dialog box, and clicked OK to specify a mustard yellow foreground color. Then I selected the Paint Bucket Tool and filled the new layer with the color. In the Layers sidebar, I set the layer's Blend Mode to Overlay and lowered the Alpha to 25%. Choose Image > Hue & Saturation and play around with the Hue and Saturation levels to fine tune the layer's color level if you're not happy with the look of your image at this point.

7. Next, I wanted to increase the amount of green in the image just a tad more as well. So I created another new layer (New Layer icon on the Layers sidebar) and filled it with a green tone (HEX 639026 in the Select Color dialog box) using the Paint Bucket Tool; I set this layer's Blend Mode to Overlay and lowered the Alpha to 30%.

8. And just to bring back some of the blue in the shadows I lost, I created another new layer (New Layer icon on the Layers sidebar) and filled it with blue (HEX 00A0D4 in the Select Color dialog box) using the Paint Bucket Tool; I set this layer's Blend Mode to Overlay, as well. I lowered the Alpha for this layer to 43%.

9. Then, I wanted to apply a vignette effect to the image. I created a new layer by clicking the New Layer icon on the Layers sidebar. I selected the Gradient Fill Tool, chose Radial from the Gradient Type drop-down list in the tool options, and left the default white (left) and black (right) gradient colors selected. Working on the newest layer, I dragged diagonally from the middle towards a corner to create the radial gradient. I set this layer's Blend Mode to Overlay and low-ered the Alpha halfway to 50% in the Layers sidebar.

10. When I was happy with the look, I flat-tened the entire image by clicking the Options button drop-down list arrow and clicking Flatten Layers. Noticing the image was still a tad on the blue side, I chose Image > Hue & Saturation, slid the Hue slider to the left to -10, and clicked OK. Remember, cross processing tends to create wild unexpected colors, so specific colors are not required. Achieving the look you want is all personal preference.

11. And finally, for an added effect, I added an old film border around the image. I found a pic-ture of an old film border and imported it into its own layer using the File > Import command.

12. I set the frame layer's Blend Mode to Multiply in the Layers sidebar so that the photo-graph showed through the white portion of the frame. I noticed this left a lot of the photo out-side of the frame exposed as well. I simply took the Rectangular Selection Tool and selected the portion of the photograph visible within the frame and selected Select > Select Inverse, then cut this portion out (Edit > Cut) to remove the unwanted area, and my image was done!

Selective Desaturation

Source Images: "Healthy Elegance" by Ink Studios, "Young artist" by Two Humans

Selective desaturation, you'll learn, is one of the easiest techniques to grasp in photo manipulation. Removing the color from some parts of the image while leaving other areas fully colored can produce some of the most stunning effects in photographs. In this tutorial, I'll show two ways selective desaturation can be used to produce two very different looking images.

1. The first reason to use selective desaturation is to make certain elements in a photograph pop. For example, in this example image, I wanted to make the apple that the woman is carrying the focal point of the image. By desaturating everything but the apple, the viewer's eyes will automatically be drawn to the vibrancy of the apple.

2. To achieve this effect, I simply made a rough selection around the apple using the Lasso Selection Tool and pasted it onto a new layer (Edit > Copy and Edit > Paste). I then chose Select > Select None to remove the selection marquee.

3. I then selected the original image layer in the Layers sidebar and chose Image > Desaturate. This transformed the original image to grayscale while leaving the copied apple layer above it in full color. I then increased the contrast of the original image layer by choosing Image > Brightness & Contrast, lowering the Brightness to -6 and raising the Contrast to 15, and clicking OK.

4. I then selected the copied apple layer in the Layers sidebar and used the Eraser Tool to erase the colored areas around the apple on the apple layer, leaving a clean green apple. I was pleased with the general image composition, but I wanted to make the image pop even further. So I decided to make the apple red, a more vibrant color to the eyes. I selected the Color Replacement Tool. I used the color selection boxes in the tool's options to select red as the foreground color and green as the background color. (I used the Pick Color button in the Select Color dialog box to sample the green from the original apple.) I then used the Color Replacement Tool set to 220 Tolerance to paint over the apple directly on the apple layer, easily converting the apple to the red tone. The image was complete!

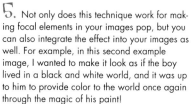

5. Not only does this technique work for making focal elements in your images pop, but you can also integrate the effect into your images as well. For example, in this second example image, I wanted to make it look as if the boy lived in a black and white world, and it was up to him to provide color to the world once again through the magic of his paint!

6. Just as I did with the previous image, I selected the sun that the boy was painting and pasted it onto a new layer. I then desaturated the original layer with Image > Desaturate.

7. Using the Eraser Tool, I selected the painted sun layer and proceeded to erase around the brush and erased the majority of the upper portion of the sun to make it appear as if those areas were yet to be painted so that this photo looked like it was taken right in the middle of the painting process.

8. I then erased the rest of the surrounding elements around the sun to leave a partially painted sun until I was left with what you see above.

9. And finally, I selected the yellow paint area within the cup that the boy is holding from the original image layer and pasted it onto a new layer with Edit > Copy and Edit > Paste. This gave the appearance that the boy was actually dipping from his cup of yellow paint and applying it to his image. With just a few simple steps, you can see how selective desaturation can also aid as a story-telling tool when used properly.

Selective Inversion

Source Images: "Red wine" by Plainview, "beez attack" by Roel Dillen

$\mathcal{S}$elective inversion is the process of inverting the colors in select portions of an image for effect or to enhance the mood of an image. In this tutorial, I'll be showing two ways to use the process of selective inversion for two different effects.

1. You can use selective inversion to add an extra interesting element to a photograph. In this example, I've applied the effect to an image of a wine glass to enhance the symmetry of the picture. First, I wanted to create a black border around the image as an added element to the image. I created a new layer by clicking the New Layer icon on the Layers sidebar. I chose Select > Select All to make a selection around the entire image. Then I chose Select > Modify > Border, entered 20 in the Selection Border text box, and clicked OK. I made sure that black was selected as the foreground color (click the Restore Colors button), selected the Paint Bucket tool, and clicked in the selection. I then chose Select > Select None to remove the selection marquee. This created a 20-pixel black border around the image.

2. I created a new layer by clicking the New Layer icon in the Layers sidebar. I then used the Rectangular Selection Tool to make a selection around the entire left half of the image. Using the Paint Bucket Tool, I filled this entire selection in black. (The foreground color should still be set to black.)

3. When I set this layer's Blend Mode to Invert, this inverted the color of everything directly below the rectangular fill, creating the simple selective inversion effect I desired.

4. Finally, I selected the original layer again and raised its contrast. I chose Image > Brightness & Contrast, lowered the Brightness to -15 and raised the Contrast to 15, and clicked OK. The first example of selective inversion was done.

5. The technique also could be used to enhance certain portions of an image. I wanted to emphasize the subjects, the bee and the flower, in this picture.

6. On a new layer (New Layer icon in the Layers sidebar), I first created a black square over the bee by selecting the Rectangular Shape Tool with the foreground color set to black (Restore Colors button) and dragging a square covering the bee.

7. Then, I chose Select > Selection from Layer to create a selection around the square fill. I chose Select > Modify > Border, entered 20 in the Selection Border text box, and clicked OK to create a 20-pixel selection around the square fill.

8. I then filled this border in with white. With the 20-pixel border area still selected, I created a new layer by clicking the New Layer icon. I selected the Paint Bucket Tool and set my foreground color to white (click Restore Colors, and then click Switch Between Foreground and Background Colors). I clicked inside the border selection to fill this area, and then chose Select > Select None.

9. I needed to create a black border around the square now. I made a selection from the layer with the white square border using Select > Selection From Layer. I then chose Select > Modify > Border, entered 10 in the Selection Border text box, and then clicked OK to create a 10-pixel border selection this time. I clicked the New Layer icon in the Layers sidebar to create another new layer. I then clicked the Restore Colors button to reset the foreground color to black, and used the Paint Bucket Tool to fill the 10-pixel border selection with black this time. Finally, I chose Select > Select None to remove the selection marquee.

10. I then selected the white border layer again. I chose Select > Selection from Layer to select the white contents. I then chose Edit > Cut to remove this selected area from the square so that the image content below could show through. I then deleted the white border layer. I then merged the square and the black border layers. I did so by Ctrl+clicking each layer in the Layers palette. Then, I clicked the Option button drop-down list arrow in the Layers sidebar and clicked Merge Layers. I then repeated this procedure to create a frame around the front of the flower as well.

11. I wanted to invert the colors in the background and leave the area of the bee and flower intact. With the layer with my black squares selected, I clicked Select > Selection from Layer to make a selection around the bee and flower frames. I then selected my original image layer in the Layers sidebar and copied and pasted (Edit > Copy and Edit > Paste) this selection onto a new layer. I then deleted the black borders layer. I selected the original image layer again and chose Image > Invert Colors. I then chose Image > Brightness & Contrast, raised the Contrast to 33, and clicked OK.

12. And finally, I wanted to add a subtle shadow behind my bee and flower layer. So I selected the layer with my bee and flower and selected the Layer Filters icon on the bottom of the Layers sidebar. I clicked the Shadow check box to check it in the Layer Filters dialog box. I lowered the Alpha setting for the shadow to 0.75, raised the quality setting for the Shadow to High, raised the amount of blur to 6 in both the Blur X and Blur Y text boxes, and clicked OK. This showed another way to use selective inversion to not only take a normal image and add unexpected interest to it, but also to enhance the existing action in the image.

Aging a Photo

Source Images: "Cocker" by Joan Vicent Cantó, "Very Old Paper" by Daniel Mogford

Here's a neat effect to make any of your personal photographs look aged and damaged. In this tutorial, I'll be taking a portrait of a dog on a fence and make it appear as if it's been sitting up in my leaky attic for the last thirty years.

1. The first thing I wanted to do was lower the saturation level of the original image that I opened, as older images tend to lose a lot of their color as they age. I chose Image > Brightness & Contrast, dragged the Brightness slider right to 37, dragged the Contrast slider left to -16, and clicked OK. I then chose Image > Hue & Saturation menu, dragged the Saturation left to -70, and clicked OK.

2. I then wanted to apply a yellowish tint to the entire image. I created a new layer by clicking the New Layer icon on the Layers sidebar. I then clicked the Foreground color selection box, entered D89B13 (mustard yellow) in the HEX text box, and clicked OK. I used the Paint Bucket Tool to fill the new layer with the mustard yellow color. I set the mustard layer's Blend Mode to Overlay and lowered the Alpha to 48% in the Layers sidebar. This gave the image a sepia look that older photos tend to have.

3. Next, I wanted to give the image some texture. So I took a scanned image of old paper and imported it into the document using the File > Import command.

4. I duplicated this layer by clicking the Options button drop-down list arrow in the Layers sidebar and clicking Duplicate Layer. I set the duplicate layer's Blend Mode to Overlay and the original layer's Blend Mode to Multiply in the Layers sidebar. This made the image appear a little too dark, so with the Multiply layer still selected, I chose Image > Brightness & Contrast, changed the Brightness to 19, the Contrast to 21, and clicked OK.

5. Then, it was time to add some damaging effects to the photograph. I imported a photo of a damaged wall using File > Import.

6. First, I desaturated the wall image on its new layer (Image > Desaturate). I then set the layer's Blend Mode to Screen in the Layers sidebar. As the Screen Blend Mode only makes the lighter portions of a layer visible, I needed to lower the brightness of this layer. I chose Image > Brightness & Contrast, lowered the Brightness to -91 and raised the Contrast to 53 by dragging the sliders, and clicked OK. This added a nice weathered look to the image.

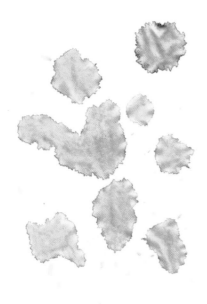

7. And one more damaging effect I wanted to apply to this image was the appearance of having been damaged by water over time. So I took an image of coffee stains on a piece of paper and imported it onto a layer using File > Import.

8. I set this stain layer's Blend Mode to Multiply in the Layers sidebar. I then chose Image > Brightness & Contrast, changed the Brightness to 10, and clicked OK. I wanted to offset the stains slightly to make it appear as if only the left side of the image has been affected by the water damage. Making the damage less uniform in the image will create a more realistic appearance. So I selected the Transformation Tool and rotated the stain and dragged it so that the left side of the image was most affected by the damage, and pressed Enter to finish the change.

9. Finally, I wanted to set the whole image on top of a weathered piece of paper. I flattened the entire image first. I then found an image of a damaged piece of cardstock and imported it using File > Import.

10. I then dragged the merged dog layer above the cardstock layer in the Layers sidebar. I temporarily hid the merged dog layer by clicking its Eye icon in the Layers sidebar. Using the Magic Wand Tool, I selected the outer white background on the cardstock layer. With this area selected, I redisplayed the merged dog layer by clicking the box for its Eye icon, and selected the layer. I then chose Edit > Cut to remove this area from my image, making the photo the shape of the cardstock. I then chose Select > Select None to remove the selection marquee.

11. I then duplicated the cardstock layer twice to get two more working copies of this layer, and desaturated them (Image > Desaturate). To make each duplication, I selected the cardstock layer, clicked the Options button drop-down list arrow in the Layers sidebar, and clicked Duplicate Layer. I moved both of the new layers above the merged dog layer in the Layers sidebar. I set the top cardstock copy layer's Blend Mode to Overlay and Alpha to 45 in the Layers sidebar. With the layer still selected, I chose Image > Brightness & Constrast, dragged the Brightness slider right to 30, and clicked OK. I then selected the second cardstock copy layer in the Layers sidebar and set its Blend Mode to Multiply. This added the cardstock's original texture to the dog portrait to situate it onto the paper better.

12. And lastly, I selected the Eraser Tool and set its Hardness to 0 and Alpha to 25% in the tool options. I dragged the Eraser Tool around the edges of the merged dog layer to create a smoother blend onto the card.

Photo Retouching

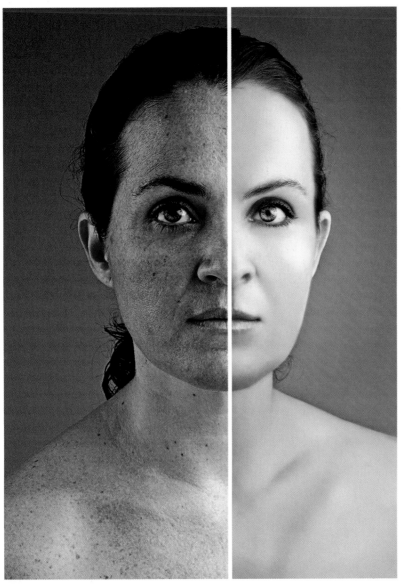

Photo retouching is the fine and sometimes controversial art of refining images; retouching is often associated with media publications glorifying celebrities. That doesn't mean you can't use similar techniques to touch up your own photos! After all, we're all stars in someone's eyes. In this tutorial, I'll be showing you general tips for removing wrinkles and blemishes from your photographs to make them ready for your first magazine spread!

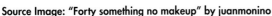

Source Image: "Forty something no makeup" by juanmonino

1. First I wanted to generally smooth out the skin of the figure to remove most of the surface blemishes. I clicked the New Layer icon on the Layers sidebar to create a new layer above the original image layer. Then, I selected the Paintbrush Tool and set the Hardness to 0 and set the Alpha to 10% in the tool's options. I clicked the foreground color selection box in the Paintbrush Tool options to open the Color Picker dialog box. I clicked the Pick Color (Eye Dropper) button in the dialog box, and then I sampled a color from the original image layer by clicking on the figure's cheek area, which I'll be smoothing first. I clicked OK to confirm the color selection, and I proceeded to paint on the new layer to build up color around her cheek area, smoothing out the skin in the process.

2. Because removing wrinkles is a huge part of the retouching process, I wanted to remove the wrinkles under the woman's eyes particularly in this step. So I proceeded to continue painting around this area to cover the wrinkles there. Not sticking to just my first selected color, I occasionally used the Foreground color selection box and the Pick Color button to select varying shades of skin color from the area I would be painting on for a more natural, realistic look.

3. I continued this same process over the figure's forehead to smooth out the blemishes around the area. Make sure to retain the image's original highlights and shaded areas by sampling the colors within the highlights and shadows, respectively, and painting in these areas with these tones. To keep the skin looking natural, it's a good idea not to go too far with the painting. Leaving traces of some of the pores and other natural elements visible on the skin creates a more natural look.

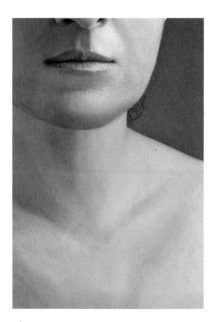

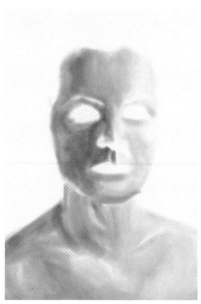

4. I did the same around the figure's body area to remove her aging spots. It's good practice to frequently disable and enable your painted layer to make sure you're coloring consistent to the colors and contours of the original image.

5. When I was finished with this process, I was left with a painted layer that looked like this. Notice I never painted solidly with a single color, as I wanted the original woman's skin texture to show through to some extent still. What this does is give the woman's skin an overall smoother look, which I was after.

6. Next, I flattened the painted layer with my original image layer by clicking the drop-down list arrow on the Options button in the Layers sidebar and clicking Flatten Layers. I then duplicated this layer by clicking the Options button drop-down list arrow and clicking Duplicate Layer. With the duplicated layer selected, I clicked the Layer Filters icon in the Layers sidebar. I clicked the Blur check box to check it, entered 3 for both the Blur X and Blur Y settings, and clicked OK. Using the Eraser Tool, I then erased the eyes, nose, hair, mouth, and image background to expose these features from my unblurred layer directly beneath. The blurred layer smoothed out the remaining blemishes on the skin even further, giving the figure an even more smoothed out appearance overall.

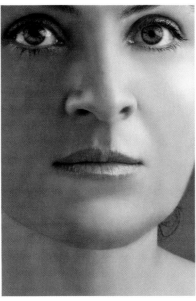

7. I wanted to add more life to the woman now. So I subtly added some make-up effects to her. I created a new layer and used the Paintbrush Tool set at 0 Hardness and 20% Alpha and painted in a pinkish hue over her eyes to simulate eye shadow. I then set this layer's Blend Mode to Overlay and this added the pinkish tone to her skin that made her look more vibrant around the eyes.

8. Then, I did the same around her lips, giving the impression she had just applied a fresh coat of lipstick.

9. I wanted to lighten and add more color to her hair, as well. Similar to the technique we used for the eyes and lips, I created a new layer by clicking the New Layer icon in the Layers sidebar, selected an orange foreground color using the Foreground color selection box, and roughly painted over her hair with the Paintbrush Tool. I changed this layer's Blend Mode to Overlay in the Layers sidebar, giving the figure's hair the color and tone I wanted. You could always go on to adjust the hair color to your liking by opening the Hue and Saturation dialog box and playing around with the Hue slider to see the variations of hair color you could apply, and adjusting the brightness slider to increase the amount you want applied.

10. I selected white as the foreground color (click the Restore Colors button and then the Switch Between Foreground and Background Colors button). I created a new layer by clicking the New Layer icon in the Layers sidebar. I then selected the Paintbrush Tool and painted over her eyes on the new layer. I set the layer's Blend Mode to Overlay, as well, in the Layers sidebar. Then I added a shine to the eyes by creating another new layer and painting over the existing highlights of the woman's eyes with the Paintbrush Tool and set this layer's Blend Mode to Overlay as well, and lowered the layer's Alpha to 56%.

11. To make the eyes even stronger, I decided to apply some mascara to the figure's eyelashes. Now obviously there is no Mascara Tool in Phoenix! But by creating another new layer (New Layer icon), setting the foreground color to black (Restore Colors button), painting over her lashes with the Paintbrush Tool, and setting the layer's Blend Mode to Overlay in the Layers sidebar, I was able to darken the lashes around her eyes, making her irises pop even more.

12. I wanted to add a rosy glow to the woman's cheekbones to further accentuate the youthful look we're striving for in this image. So I created a new layer (New Layer icon) for the cheeks, selected a rose foreground color, and used the Paintbrush Tool to paint her cheekbone areas lightly. I then applied the, you guessed it, Overlay Blend Mode to this layer in the Layers sidebar to give the cheeks the subtle pink hue I desired.

13. And to enhance the overall appeal of the photo even further, I wanted to brighten the background. So I selected the merged layer and made a selection around the entire background area (Select > Select All) and copied and pasted it onto a new layer. I then chose Image > Hue & Saturation, changed the Saturation setting to 53 and the Brightness to 15, and clicked OK to create a lighter more colorful background for the figure. I then used the Eraser Tool to erase the woman from the copied background layer so the figure would show through.

14. Finally, I added a Radial Gradient on a new layer to create a slight vignette effect to focus the composition on the woman's face. I created the new layer, selected the Gradient Fill Tool, and selected Radial from the Gradient type drop-down list in the tool's options. I also left the default white and black gradient colors selected. I dragged diagonally from the middle to a corner of the new layer to create the gradient. I lowered this layer's Alpha to 30% and set the layer's Blend Mode to Overlay in the Layers sidebar. And that was it! A retouched photo ready for the cover of a glamour magazine. (Although I personally think she was just as beautiful before.)

Coloring Hair

Getting your hair colored could be a time-consuming process. Booking an appointment with your hairdresser, coordinating your schedule with theirs, not to mention the cost associated with it these days. So before you spend all that time and money, why not give your hair a test run first? In this tutorial, I'll show a quick and simple way to color your hair in Phoenix, and you don't even need an appointment.

Source Image: "Manifesto" by Katja De Bruijn

1. I decided to color the woman's hair in a funky blue/purple and gold streaked color. Of course, you could easily use the same technique to color her hair any myriad of more natural hair colors, but I went with a blue/purple for the sake of dramatic effect. First, I created a new layer. Then, I set the foreground color to a deep blue and selected the Paintbrush Tool. I dragged the Paintbrush to paint over the woman's hair. Don't worry if you paint too far outside the confines of her hair for now. Just make sure to leave the roots of her hair, where it joins her forehead, exposed.

2. I then switched to the Shape Brush Tool and selected the splatter-shaped brush (Brush 4). With this brush selected, I zoomed into the image 150% and drew in the roots of her hair, still working on the layer where I painted blue earlier. Using this brush creates a more natural blend as the appearance of the splatter begins to look like hairs as I drag it across the canvas.

3. Then, I set this layer's Blend Mode to Overlay. If you were unhappy with the color of the figure's hair at this point, you could choose Image > Hue & Saturation and slide the Hue slider around to see a variation of alternate colors you could apply instead.

4. Noticing that the color blended into the head a little roughly around the edges still, I decided to clean it up a bit. I selected the Eraser Tool set to 0 Hardness, and carefully softened the edges to blend them better.

5. To add the gold streaks, I simply selected my original image layer again. Using the Lasso Selection Tool, I selected portions of her hair roughly where the streaks will go. I copied the selection and pasted it onto a new layer (Edit > Copy and Edit > Paste) and dragged this layer to the top of the Layers sidebar.

6. Then, using the Eraser Tool set to 150 Size, 0 Hardness, and 23% Alpha, I erased portions of the hair to leave several dispersed gold streaks. Make sure to follow the contours of the hair during this stage, as it'll create a much more natural appearance.

7. With the hair colored now, I wanted to adjust the color of the woman's make-up to match her new 'do better. In the original image layer, I made a rough selection around the woman's cheeks using the Lasso Selection Tool (press Shift while dragging to make the second selection), then copied and pasted this onto a new layer. I selected Select > Select None to remove the selection marquee. I decided to give her cheeks a purple tint to match the purple in her hair. So with my copied cheek layer selected, I chose Image > Hue & Saturation, slid the Hue slider left to -46, and clicked OK to apply the color I desired. I then took a soft Eraser Tool and cleaned the edges of my selection to blend her new cheeks into her face cleaner.

> ## Note
>
> Alternately, you can use the Feather feature to blend the cheeks back onto the face. With the woman's cheeks selected, choose Select > Modify > Feather, input a Value of 25, and press OK. Then, copy (Edit > Copy) and paste (Edit > Paste) the feathered selection onto a new layer and delete your first cheeks layer, for a quicker alternate technique.

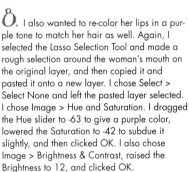

8. I also wanted to re-color her lips in a purple tone to match her hair as well. Again, I selected the Lasso Selection Tool and made a rough selection around the woman's mouth on the original layer, and then copied it and pasted it onto a new layer. I chose Select > Select None and left the pasted layer selected. I chose Image > Hue and Saturation. I dragged the Hue slider to -63 to give a purple color, lowered the Saturation to -42 to subdue it slightly, and then clicked OK. I also chose Image > Brightness & Contrast, raised the Brightness to 12, and clicked OK.

9. Then I selected the Eraser Tool and simply erased out the area around her lips and inside her mouth leaving only her purple lips intact.

10. And finally, I wanted to color her eyes brown to go together with the gold in her hair. So I created a new layer and selected a dark brown as the foreground color. On the new layer, I painted over her irises using the Paintbrush Tool. I set this layer's Blend Mode to Overlay, and her eyes were colored brown as simple as that. And then I was done! A quick and easy makeover, and you don't even need to leave a tip.

Enhancing Eyes

Eyes are the most striking thing we notice about a person when we see them, whether it be in person or in photographs. Although enhancing your eyes could be a costly and dangerous process in real life, it's actually a simple and painless procedure digitally! Using a couple blend modes, I'll show how to make your eyes POP in photographs!

Source Image: "Chocaholic" by Nuno Silva

1. First I selected the Lasso Selection Tool and made a selection around the figure's eyes in the photo I opened. (I pressed and held Shift while selecting the second eye to add it to the selection.) I then copied this selection and pasted it onto a new layer with Edit > Copy and Edit > Paste. I then chose Select > Select None. Initially, I just wanted to raise the overall brightness of the eyes. So, with the copied eye layer selected, I chose Image > Brightness & Contrast. In the Brightness and Contrast dialog box, I raised the Brightness to 11 and the Contrast to 36, and clicked OK.

2. Then, I selected the Eraser Tool and working on the eye copy layer, erased the areas I didn't need brightened, leaving just the white, iris, and pupil area on the copied layer. At this point, I decided to raise the Saturation of the iris, as well. So I chose Image > Hue & Saturation, raised the Saturation setting to 12, and clicked OK.

3. To make the iris stand out even more, I decided to draw a dark outline around the edges. I created a new layer (New Layer icon on the Layers sidebar) and clicked the Restore Colors button by the color selection boxes to reset the foreground color to black. I then selected the Paintbrush Tool, set the Size to 7 and Hardness to 50, and roughly painted a dark outline around the iris of each eye. It appeared overdone at first, but I simply set the layer's Blend Mode to Overlay and lowered the Alpha to 40% in the Layers sidebar, leaving a nice subtle darkening of the iris' outline.

4. To complement the outline, I decided to strengthen the highlights within the iris, as well. I created another new layer at this point with the New Layer icon. I selected the Paintbrush Tool, set the Hardness to 0, and set the foreground color to white by clicking the Switch Between Foreground and Background Colors button near the color selection buttons. I proceeded to paint with this brush on the new layer inside the iris. When I set this layer's Blend Mode to Overlay and lowered the Alpha to 50% in the Layers sidebar, the painting nicely popped out the existing highlights in the iris.

5. If you look at the photo, you'll notice that there's a circular white highlight on the pupil of each eye. I created a new layer and used the Paintbrush Tool, set to 100 Hardness and 13 Size, on that layer to add a big white circle on each of the round highlights. I set this layer's Blend Mode to Overlay, as well. This made the existing highlights stand out even more, giving a brighter all-around appearance to the subject's irises.

6. You also can paint in additional highlight spots on the subject's eyes to enhance the effect even further. I did just that by creating a new layer and using the Paintbrush set to 80% Hardness. I simply painted in a small spot of glare near the bottom right of each iris with white.

7. And finally, to complement the new enhanced eyes even further, I selected the original image layer and darkened and raised the overall contrast of the image. I chose Image > Brightness & Contrast. In the Brightness and Contrast dialog box, I lowered the Brightness setting to -8 and raised the Contrast to 16, and then clicked OK. And that was it, a very simple way to enhance the eyes of the subject in any photograph!

Warhol-izing

Source Image: "amazing beauty portraits" by TriggerPhoto

*S*implifying lines and working with generally flat colors became a trademark in many images created by Andy Warhol. Love his art or hate it, there's no denying his style of taking iconic persons and imagery and simplifying their form still manages to captivate observers daily. In this tutorial, I'm going to show how to take an ordinary portrait of yourself, or a loved one, and make it look as if it were an Andy Warhol... original.

1. The first thing I did after opening the example image of a young woman was to desaturate the entire image by choosing Image > Desaturate. This converted the image to grayscale. There are several ways to simplify the lines within the image. One quick and simple way to do so was to apply a filter. I chose Filters > WebSafe, and it applied a simplifying effect to the picture, giving me the rough outline look that would be a great starting point for this technique.

2. Next, I wanted to emphasize the highlights in the image slightly. So I raised the contrast in the image by selecting Image > Brightness & Contrast menu, raising the Contrast setting to 34, and clicking OK. This turned a lot of the grays within the image into solid whites, creating a more dynamic looking image overall.

3. I then set this layer's Blend Mode to Multiply in the Layers sidebar. This effectively made the white areas transparent. I then created a new layer by clicking the New Layer icon in the Layers sidebar, and then dragged the new layer below the image layer. With the new blank layer selected, I set white as the foreground color by clicking the Restore Colors button and then clicking the Switch Between Foreground and Background Colors button. I selected the Paint Bucket Tool and clicked the new layer to fill it so the transparent areas on the image layer appeared white. I clicked the New Layer icon to create another new layer above the white fill layer, and below my layer with the young woman, for my coloring layer. I clicked the Restore Colors button, and then clicked the Foreground color selection box and chose a yellow gold color using the Select Color dialog box. Using the Paintbrush Tool, I proceeded to paint the woman's hair area on the new layer.

Tip

Remember, this doesn't need to be done perfectly. In fact, slight errors in coloring, going over the lines and such, tends to add to the rough, raw mood typically associated with a Warhol image.

4. I continued this same process throughout the rest of the image, coloring in other areas of the woman's figure and background on the color layer. Using solid colors, I tried to keep the total number of colors used to a minimum to emphasize the simplicity.

5. The background was bothering me, as there were remnants of a sectioned wall remaining. Using the Eraser Tool, I simply erased the distracting background from the layer with the woman. This gave me a nice, solid-colored background.

6. With my entire image colored in, it was safe to flatten the image. So I simply chose Flatten Image from the Options button drop-down list on the Layers sidebar. Next, I selected Image > Canvas Resize and selected new dimensions for my image. I unchecked the Constrain Proportion check box in the Resize Canvas dialog box and entered new canvas dimensions: 1200 for Width and 1600 for Height. I then clicked Apply. I then selected the Transformation Tool, selected the layer with the woman in the Layers sidebar, and resized the image of the woman to fill the top left-hand corner of the canvas. (Change the image zoom to 30% or less with the zoom slider to see what you're doing.) Holding the Shift key while resizing the image enabled me to maintain the original image's proportions. I pressed Enter to apply the new size.

7. I then made three duplicates of this layer (Options button drop-down list > Duplicate Layer), selected each layer in the Layers sidebar, and used the Transformation Tool to assemble them in a 2 x 2 grid as shown. I pressed Enter to apply each transformation.

8. And finally, to apply the various color schemes for each of the other images, I selected each layer separately and chose Image > Hue & Saturation. By sliding the Hue slider and then clicking OK, I applied a different variation to each image. When I was happy with the variations, my image was almost complete. To finish the composition, I selected the Rectangular Selection Tool, made a selection around the entire image but left out any remaining white background remnants. I then chose Image > Crop Selection, and my image was complete! An instant art classic.

Turning a Photo into a Comic Book Panel

Source Image: "Underworld" by Mark Stout

Most of the time, a digital photo artist strives at realism in his or her creations. But in this case, I'm going to do the exact opposite by taking a photo of a man and turning it into an image that looks as if it were pulled right out of the pages of a comic book. For this example, I used a stock image of a man holding a gun for dramatic effect. But for more fun, try this technique on your own personal photos of friends and family, and watch them marvel (pardon the pun) at seeing themselves as the star of their own comic book!

1. In comics, the process is often to sketch the idea, ink the outlines, then color it. In our case, our photograph already serves as the initial sketch, so it's up to us to find a way to ink it. After I opened the original image file in Phoenix, I made a copy of the original photo layer by clicking the Options button drop-down arrow on the Layers sidebar and clicking Duplicate Layer, as I would be needing the original image later on. I wanted to remove all the color on the copied layer, and I did this by selecting Image > Desaturate. Then, to make the photo look as if it were hand drawn in ink, I removed all gray tones so that the image was purely black and white tones. I achieved this look by choosing Image > Brightness & Contrast, raising the Contrast setting to 100, and changing the Brightness to -40. (With the Contrast raised all the way, moving the Brightness slider enables you to adjust how much of the image detail to preserve.) I clicked OK, applying the settings to keep much of the grittiness from the original image.

2. I was happy with the overall look of the effect, but I wanted to delineate the figure from the background a little more. With the foreground color set to black (Restore Colors button), I selected the Paintbrush Tool and set its Size to 4 in the tool's options. I then drew an outline around the figure's face to set him apart from the background. I also drew in stronger defining lines around his nose and under his eyes to strengthen these areas to give it more of a hand-drawn inked appearance.

3. I set the black and white layer's Blend Mode to Overlay. This preserved the black outlines of the image, while the original image layer underneath showed through the white portions of the copied layer. As comics tend to use bright, exaggerated tones, I selected the original image layer in the Layers sidebar. I chose Image > Brightness & Contrast, raised the Contrast to 42 and lowered the Brightness to -12, and clicked OK. This colored the figure with heavily saturated oranges, which I desired.

4. The background was left with a bright yellow look. I wanted to give the background a more contrasted tone so the figure would stand out against it. I copied the original layer (click the Options button drop-down list arrow in the Layers sidebar and click Duplicate Layer). With the new layer copy selected, I chose Image > Hue & Saturation. I slid the Hue slider to the left to -138 to give a purple tone, and clicked OK. This was a nice color to offset the yellows and oranges in the figure's skin.

5. Then it was simply a matter of using the Eraser Tool to erase the purple-toned areas in the figure's face on the new layer to expose the original orange tones from the layer underneath.

6. Next, I imported an image of a halftone pattern using File > Import. As this halftone pattern was a GIF file, I had to specify this when uploading my file by changing the Files of Type option to "gif (*.gif)" on the image uploading prompt. I set this layer's Blend Mode to Overlay in the Layers sidebar. This created the coarse halftone (dot print) appearance generally associated with the four-color printing process for comics.

7. I created a border around the image to make it look even more as if it were a panel from a comic book. I chose Select > Select All to create a selection around the perimeter of the canvas. Then, I chose Select > Modify > Border, entered 10 in the Selection Border text box, and clicked OK to create the 10-pixel selection around the canvas. On a new layer created by clicking the New Layer icon on the Layers sidebar, I filled this selection with black (which should still be set as the foreground color) using the Paint Bucket Tool. I then chose Select > Select None to remove the selection marquee.

8. At this point, we could call the image complete. But for added effect, I wanted to add a paper texture to the image to make it look as if it were ripped right out of a page of an old comic book. I flattened the entire image by clicking the drop-down list arrow for the Options button in the Layers sidebar and then clicking Flatten Layers. I then used File > Import to import an image of paper texture as the top layer.

9. I made two duplicates of the paper texture layer (Options button drop-down list arrow > Duplicate Layer) so I had three to work with. I moved the first paper texture layer below the flattened comic layer in the Layers sidebar; I set the comic layer's Blend Mode to Multiply and lowered the Alpha to 91%. I left the second paper texture layer above the comic layer in the Layers sidebar and set the layer's Blend Mode to Multiply. I then chose Image > Brightness & Contrast, lowered the Brightness to -38, raised the Contrast to 70, and clicked OK. For the third paper texture layer, I also left it positioned above the comic layer in the Layers sidebar and set the layer's Blend Mode to Overlay. I then chose Image > Brightness & Contrast, lowered the Brightness to -61, raised the Contrast to 42, and clicked OK. I further chose Image > Hue & Saturation, lowered the Saturation to -70, and clicked OK. This gave the image a nice paper textured look.

10. Finally, I made a duplicate of the flattened comic layer (Options button drop-down list arrow > Duplicate Layer) and moved it to the top of the list in the Layers sidebar. I set this copied layer's Blend Mode to Overlay and lowered the Alpha to 35%, and the image was complete!

Miniaturizing

Source Image: "Prague in Winter – central market place" by Bennewitz

Another neat effect you can apply to an image is to take an everyday scene and make it appear as if it were a miniature model. The idea is to fool the mind into thinking it's looking at a macro image with very little effort on your part, mainly selective blurring.

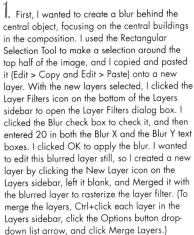

1. First, I wanted to create a blur behind the central object, focusing on the central buildings in the composition. I used the Rectangular Selection Tool to make a selection around the top half of the image, and I copied and pasted it (Edit > Copy and Edit > Paste) onto a new layer. With the new layers selected, I clicked the Layer Filters icon on the bottom of the Layers sidebar to open the Layer Filters dialog box. I clicked the Blur check box to check it, and then entered 20 in both the Blur X and the Blur Y text boxes. I clicked OK to apply the blur. I wanted to edit this blurred layer still, so I created a new layer by clicking the New Layer icon on the Layers sidebar, left it blank, and Merged it with the blurred layer to rasterize the layer filter. (To merge the layers, Ctrl+click each layer in the Layers sidebar, click the Options button drop-down list arrow, and click Merge Layers.)

2. I wanted the central and top buildings in the image to be focused, so I needed to remove the blur surrounding these areas. Using the Eraser Tool set at 85% Hardness, I simply erased on the blurred layer, uncovering the central buildings. Using the Polygonal Selection Tool, I was able to easily make angular selections around the straight edges of the building and remove these segments with Edit > Cut rather than using the Eraser Tool to do all of my extracting.

3. When I blurred the top half of the image in Step 1, it left a dark glow in the sky around my top buildings, which I wanted to remove by painting over it. First, I made a selection around the blurred layer (Select > Selection from Layer). To paint over these areas, I first needed to choose an appropriate hue. With the Eye Dropper Tool selected, I clicked on a surrounding area of the sky to sample the color of the sky. Then, I selected the Paintbrush Tool set at 0 Hardness and painted over these dark glows around the top towers with my sampled sky color to remove them.

4. Noticing a few jagged edges, I went on to clean the edges of the blur layer a bit more by using the Eraser Tool set to 75% Hardness and dragging along the rough edges to soften them up.

5. Next, it was time to apply a blur to the foreground. Blurring both the foreground and background and leaving the center in focus tricks the eye into seeing a depth of field that was non-existent in the original image, creating the macro illusion. As I did earlier with the background, I selected the foreground elements on the original image layer using the Lasso Selection Tool, and copied and pasted this area onto a new layer with Edit > Copy and Edit > Paste.

6. With this new layer selected, I again clicked the Layer Filters icon in the Layers sidebar. I clicked the Blur check box to check it, entered 15 in both the Blur X and Blur Y text boxes, and clicked OK. I clicked the New Layer icon to create a new, blank layer, selected it and the copied foreground layer by Ctrl+clicking each layer in the Layers sidebar, and clicked the Options button drop-down list arrow and then Merge Layers to rasterize the blur effect. Then, using the Eraser Tool set to 0 Hardness and 20% Alpha, I erased the edges of the foreground blur layer to soften the effect around the edges for a cleaner blend.

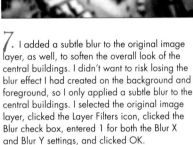

7. I added a subtle blur to the original image layer, as well, to soften the overall look of the central buildings. I didn't want to risk losing the blur effect I had created on the background and foreground, so I only applied a subtle blur to the central buildings. I selected the original image layer, clicked the Layer Filters icon, clicked the Blur check box, entered 1 for both the Blur X and Blur Y settings, and clicked OK.

8. I was happy with the overall look of the image, but I wanted to make the elements look even more like toys. As toys tend to often be deeply saturated in exaggerated colors, I wanted to apply that effect to my image, as well. At this point, I flattened the entire image by clicking the Options button drop-down list arrow in the Layers sidebar and clicking Flatten Layers. I then chose Image > Brightness & Contrast, raised the Contrast setting to 5, and clicked OK. I then chose Image > Hue & Saturation, raised the Saturation setting to 16, and clicked OK.

9. And finally, for an optional effect, I brought the whole thing together by applying a slight green cast over the entire image. I created a new layer by clicking the New Layer icon in the Layers sidebar. I clicked the Foreground color selection box, entered 438F00 in the HEX text box, and clicked OK. I then used the Paint Bucket Tool to fill the layer with the dark green color. Finally, I set the layer's Blend Mode to Overlay in the Layers sidebar, finishing the image!

Note

To flatten your image into one working layer while maintaining all the layers in the document, flatten the layers (Layer > Flatten Layers) to merge the entire image. Select the entire image (Select > Select All), then copy this layer (Edit > Copy). Then, click the Undo button twice to revert the image back into its layered format. Then you can paste the flattened image you copied earlier (Edit > Paste) and it will paste the flattened version of the image onto a new layer, leaving all your previous working layers intact.

Fun with Phoenix

Lemon Car

Source Images: "Classic Car" by B3UK, "Lemon" by Kati Neudert

In this tutorial, I'll be referring to previous tutorials found in the Basic Tutorials section of this book. Combining several of the previous techniques, including Color Replacement, Background Cloning, and Casting Shadows, I'll be turning a red car into a real lemon of an automobile.

1. The first thing was to locate the source images. I found a picture of a cute little red car I figured would work nicely, so I started my composition by opening this image.

2. Then, I needed to find a picture of a lemon with a perspective similar to that of the car. I found this image of a lemon that would suit the car pretty well, so I imported this source image file into my document as well (File > Import).

3. With the lemon layer selected, I chose the Eraser Tool and dragged outside the lemon to extract it from its white background. Then, using the Transformation Tool, I rotated and resized the lemon to align with the size and perspective of the car on its layer. When I was happy with the lemon's placement in the image, I pressed Enter to confirm the transformation.

4. Next, I needed to hide any remnants of the car that the lemon failed to cover. I copied (Edit > Copy) and pasted (Edit > Paste) clean areas of the road from the original layer, and pasted them onto a new layer directly above the original layer. Then, using the Transformation Tool, I moved these segments to cover the exposed car remnants. Then I merged all my clone layers into one by holding down the Ctrl key and selecting all the clone layers on the Layers sidebar. Then I chose Layer > Merge Layers to merge them. (Refer to "Background Cloning" in the Basic Tutorials section for more in-depth information.)

5. And when the cloning was complete, I was left with a clean extracted lemon sitting on the road like this.

6. To make the lemon look like an automobile, it was all a matter of incorporating some of the elements of the original car onto the lemon. So I started with the tires. Working on the original layer, I made a selection around the front right tire with the Lasso Selection Tool and copied and pasted it onto a new layer (Edit > Copy and Edit > Paste). I dragged this tire layer above the lemon on the Layers sidebar. I then used the Transformation Tool to position the tire so it sits along the bottom edge of the lemon.

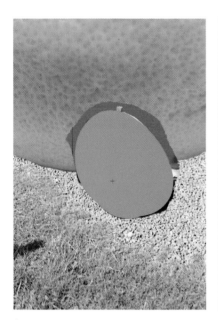

7. To extract the tire cleanly, refer to the "Precision Selection" tutorial from the Basic Tutorials section of this book. I used the same method found in that tutorial to extract the tire cleanly on this layer. I did this by creating a new layer and selecting the Elliptical Shape Tool to create a circle. Then, using the Distortion Tool, I resized the circle to cover the tire and any portions of the image I wanted to remain intact.

8. I then selected the elliptically drawn layer (Select > Selection from Layer), then selected the inverse of the selection (Select > Invert Selection). I hid the layer with the drawn circle and clicked the copied tire layer on the Layers sidebar. With the Eraser Tool, I simply erased around the tires within the selection, leaving the actual tires intact. (Refer to "Precision Selection" in the Basic Tutorials section for more in-depth information.)

9. Next, it was time to incorporate the back tire onto the lemon. After selecting the original layer in the Layers sidebar, I made a selection around the back tire roughly with the Lasso Selection Tool and copied it onto a new layer (Edit > Copy and Edit > Paste). I dragged the copied tire above the lemon layer on the Layers sidebar. I then used the Transformation Tool to resize and position the tire to sit along the back of the lemon and pressed Enter when I was happy with the tire's position on the lemon.

10. I wanted to recolor the red fender above the back tire to a lemony yellow. For this, I selected the Color Replacement Tool. I selected red as my background color, and selected yellow for my foreground color. Then I painted over the rear tire layer with the Color Replacement Tool to simply change the red to yellow. I then used the Eraser Tool to extract the tire cleanly. (Refer to "Color Replacement" in the Basic Tutorials section for more in-depth information.)

11. For the tire on the left side of the car, I made a duplicate of my front driver's side tire on the original layer. I dragged the copied tire below the lemon layer on the Layers sidebar. Using the Transformation Tool, I repositioned the tire to sit below the other side of the lemon car and pressed Enter when I was pleased with the positioning.

12. Next, I copied the windshield from the original layer and pasted it onto a new layer above the lemon layer. Using the Eraser Tool, I extracted the windshield. I then used the Transformation Tool to resize the windshield to fit the lemon and pressed Enter to confirm the resizing.

13. To make it appear as if the windshield were inset into the lemon better, I decided to add a slight shadow on the lemon in a strip above the top of the windshield. I created a new layer (New Layer icon) and dragged it directly below the windshield layer on the Layers sidebar. I selected the Paintbrush Tool and set the Hardness to 10 and set the foreground color to black (Restore Colors button). I painted above the top of the windshield to create a slight shadow to imply depth, then lowered the layer's Alpha to 40% in the Layers sidebar.

14. I repeated the process of copying and pasting elements from the original car layer to add in the side windows, door, and headlight on the car until I was satisfied with the look of the lemon car.

15. And finally, I added a shadow to the bottom of the car just as I did in the "Casting Shadows" tutorial from the Basic Tutorials section. I added in a layer for the shadow below the lemon layer, and then using a black Paintbrush Tool, painted in the shadow. I then lowered the Alpha for the shadow layer to 73% in the Layers sidebar. I added a blue tint to the shadow by creating another shadow layer, this time using a dark blue (#10154C) instead of black, and setting the layer's Blend Mode to Overlay.

Chocolate

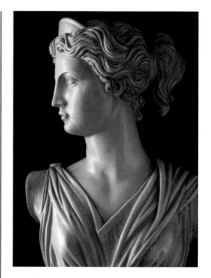

Source Image: "Artemis" by diane39

As with other techniques, there are plenty of different ways to go about creating chocolate. But for those of you who are like me and just don't have the time to harvest cacao seeds in this day and age, I'm going to show how we can create everyone's favorite food right here in Phoenix. The techniques I use in this image can be applied to many different types of images that involve melting or general liquifying and smudging.

1. The first, and most important, step is finding a good source image. Although, realistically, any image would work, I prefer sticking to images like these with very well defined ridges and strong contrasting lights and shadows. This will greatly help in the process and make for a more interesting picture overall.

2. With a source image selected, it was time to have some fun. First, I desaturated the entire image (Image > Desaturate).

3. The fun part for me is creating all the drips, so I decided to do that step next. I looked for any protruding areas first, such as the nose and chin, and laid down the thickest drips there. I selected the Liquify Tool, set the Size to 29, and set the Pressure to 4. I decided to start on the nose first. I dragged the Liquify Tool in a downward motion starting from the tip of the nose directly on the desaturated layer to create the shape and length of the drip.

4. For a more realistic drip, I created a slight blob at the end of the drip. With the Liquify Tool still selected, I dragged the Tool in a small circular motion to create the bulbous end to the drip.

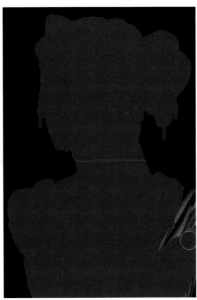

5. I repeated this process throughout the rest of the image, creating drips in and around the ridges of the figure. For a more realistic effect, all the drips shouldn't fall perfectly vertically. Be aware of the contours of your figure, and smudge your drips so that they flow accordingly by dragging the Liquify Tool to flow around the rounded surface of the cheek, etc.

6. Next, it was time to colorize the chocolate. To give the statue a brown tone, I started by creating a new layer (New Layer icon on the Layers sidebar). Then I selected the Paintbrush Tool and set its foreground color to a brown tone by clicking the Foreground color selection box in the tool options, entering 5E2E00 in the HEX dialog box, and clicking OK. I then painted this tone over the entire figure on the new layer.

7. I set this layer's Blend Mode to Hardlight in the Layers sidebar, and it gave the figure a lovely brown hue. Remember, you don't need to get the color perfect on the first shot. You can always go ahead and adjust the Hue and Saturation levels once the figure is covered and you can see exactly how the Hardlight Blend Mode affects the image.

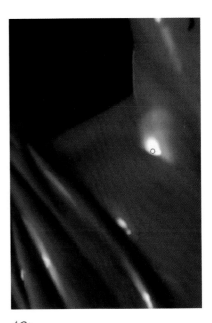

8. At this point, the figure was already look-ing tasty. But I wanted to make the image pop even further. So the next step was increasing the highlights on the figure to make it extra shiny. I created a new layer (New Layer icon) and selected the Paintbrush Tool. I set the Paintbrush Tool's Alpha to 24%, the Hardness to 10, and selected white as the foreground color in the tool's options. I looked for the existing lightest areas on the figure and along the newly created drips and painted over these areas with the Paintbrush. When I set the layer's Blend Mode to Overlay, it nicely enhanced the highlighted areas while maintaining the chocolate's satura-tion. You can do all the highlights on one layer if you're feeling adventurous. I prefer to do the highlights on several layers just as a precaution.

9. I repeated the overall process to enhance the shadows in the figure. I created a new layer (New Layer icon) and changed the Paintbrush Tool's foreground color to black in the tool's options (Restore Colors button). I painted over the existing dark areas of the figure so that when I set the layer's Blend Mode to Overlay as well, it enhanced the shadows of the image and created a nice contrast with the highlights.

10. And finally, I decided to blow out the highlights even further. I created a new layer (New Layer icon) and set the Paintbrush Tool's foreground color back to white. I looked for the brightest points in the image and painted in small overblown highlighted spots in the middle of those key highlighted areas, and the image was complete.

Aliens!

Source Images: "Chocolate" by Aldra, "Anger Management" by FotoIE

They're here! In this tutorial, I'll be showing you how to give a lizard-like appearance to a person by applying a scaly texture to her skin, primarily by using the Overlay Blend Mode. Overlay? More like Reptilian OverLORD Blend Mode!

1. I started with a base image of a female model covered in chocolate because I figured, "Hey, aliens would probably love chocolate, too."

2. First thing I wanted to do was to make the model bald. I imported an image of a bald man into the document (File > Import). Using the Lasso Selection Tool, I made a selection around the man's head, and I copied (Edit > Copy) and pasted (Edit > Paste) it onto a new layer. I then removed the selection marquee (Select > Select None) and hid the bald man layer by clicking its Eye icon in the Layers sidebar.

3. I then selected the Transformation Tool and resized and moved the copied selection to fit the proportion of the woman's head. I pressed Enter to confirm the transformation.

4. Noticing that the head was a little too dark for the rest of the figure, I chose Image > Brightness & Contrast, and raised the Brightness to 59 and lowered the Contrast to -24, then clicked OK to apply the changes. I then selected the Eraser Tool to erase the surrounding elements around the head. I set the Eraser Tool's Hardness to 0 and erased the bottom area of the head layer to blend it into the woman's forehead better.

5. To add further definition to the woman's face, I repeated the process of selecting, copying, pasting, and manipulating segments to cover other facial features, redisplaying and hiding the bald man layer as needed. I selected the portion underneath the man's left eye, and copy and pasted this onto a new layer (Edit > Copy and Edit > Paste). I removed the selection marquee (Select > Select None). Then, I chose Image > Brightness & Contrast, and raised the Brightness of this segment to 44 and lowered the Contrast to -23, and pressed OK to apply the change.

6. With the new layer selected, I used the Distortion Tool to warp the selection to align to the woman's face. I then pressed Enter to confirm the transformation.

7. I repeated the overall process to cover the model's other facial features, such as the eyebrow ridge and nose.

Note

Rather than simply creating an image of a person with scales, I wanted to give the figure less of a human look. I created a very broad distortion of the nose on the figure to create the illusion of an absent nose on the figure, creating a more stereotypically alien look.

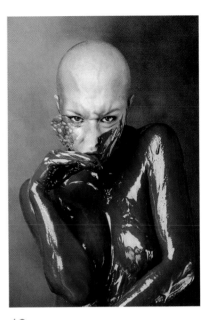

8. Next it was time to add the reptilian texture to the model's skin. I imported a source image of a lizard (File > Import). I made a selection around a portion of the lizard's scales and copied and pasted it onto a new layer (Edit > Copy and Edit > Paste). I then chose Select > Select None to remove the selection marquee and clicked the Eye icon for the lizard layer to hide it.

9. Using the Distortion Tool, I transformed the copied segment to align with the shape of the woman's face, then pressed Enter to apply the distortion.

10. I applied the Overlay Blend Mode to the reptilian texture layer in the Layers sidebar. Doing so textured the woman's skin while maintaining the color of the original skin tone.

11. I repeated the process of copying, pasting, and editing segments from the lizard layer (redisplaying and hiding the lizard layer as needed) to texture the rest of the woman's head. I used the Eraser Tool set to 0 Hardness to soften the edges of the copied segments to blend them into the woman's head more cleanly.

12. Next, I wanted to fill the eyes in black. I created a new layer (New Layer icon) and selected the Paintbrush Tool, with black set as the foreground color (Restore Colors button in the tool's options). I painted over the model's eyes, covering them entirely in black. I then created another layer and changed the Paintbrush Tool's foreground color to white (Switch Between Foreground and Background Colors button in the tool's options) and added a couple highlights by clicking in the middle of each eye to create a white spot. I clicked twice on each eye to create the spot lit effect.

13. Next, I wanted to give the entire figure a greenish tint. I created a new layer (New Layer icon) and dragged it to the top of the list in the Layers sidebar. I selected the Paintbrush Tool and set the foreground color to a dark green color (click the Foreground color selection box, enter 568F35 in the # text box, and click OK). On the new layer, I painted over any exposed areas of the alien's skin.

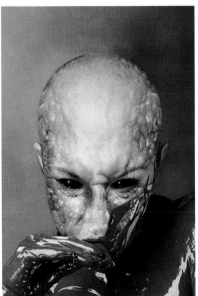

14. I set the green layer's Blend Mode to Overlay, and lowered the layer's Alpha to 55% in the Layers sidebar. This gave the alien's skin a nice green hue throughout, which really enhanced the lizard-like appearance of the figure.

15. For final touches, I added some stronger shadows and highlights to the figure. I created a new layer and dragged it below the green overlay layer in the Layers sidebar. I selected the Paintbrush Tool and set black as the foreground color by clicking the Restore Colors button in the tool's options. Working on the new layer, I painted around the figure's eyes and nose area, etc. I lowered the Alpha of the layer to 75% in the Layers sidebar.

16. I then created another new layer to add some highlights and made sure it was above the shadows layer in the Layers sidebar. I set the Paintbrush Tool's foreground color to white this time (click the Switch Between Foreground and Background Colors button in the tool's options) and painted spots over the figure's forehead to create a more rounded three-dimensional look. The image was complete.

Aging a Person

Source Images: "Newsy series" by Upheaval Design, "senior man" by scorpion56

There are any number of ways to manipulate a photo of a person to make them look older. In this tutorial, I'll be attempting to age an image of a young male by applying segments from a source image of an old man, while still trying to maintain the look and structure of the original boy.

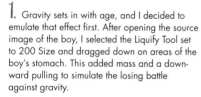

1. Gravity sets in with age, and I decided to emulate that effect first. After opening the source image of the boy, I selected the Liquify Tool set to 200 Size and dragged down on areas of the boy's stomach. This added mass and a downward pulling to simulate the losing battle against gravity.

2. To provide source material to age the figure's skin, I imported the source image of the old man using File > Import. Selecting a suitable source image is crucial in this step, making sure the perspective of the face is similar to that of the original person's, and making sure that the general lighting in the images match as well. I then started by selecting the old man's forehead, and copying (Edit > Copy) and pasting (Edit > Paste) it onto a new layer. I then hid the layer with the old man image by clicking the Eye icon beside it in the Layers sidebar.

3. Using the Distortion Tool, I transformed the copied segment to align with the original boy's head. I pressed Enter on the keyboard when I was happy with the alignment of the segment.

4. I realized that the old man's skin tone was a little too orange compared to the boy's. To fix this, I chose Image > Hue & Saturation, set the Hue to -7 and lowered the Saturation to -30, then clicked OK to apply the color adjustment.

5. I then selected the Eraser Tool and set the Hardness to 0. I erased around the edges of this segment to soften them, thus blending the segment into the boy's original face more cleanly.

6. I repeated the process outlined in Steps 2 through 5 to cover other areas of the boy's face, redisplaying and hiding the layer with as many images as needed. I next selected the old man's right eyebrow with the Lasso Selection Tool and pasted it onto a new layer with Edit > Copy and Edit > Paste.

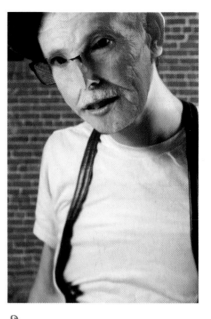

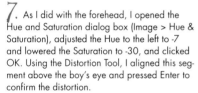

7. As I did with the forehead, I opened the Hue and Saturation dialog box (Image > Hue & Saturation), adjusted the Hue to the left to -7 and lowered the Saturation to -30, and clicked OK. Using the Distortion Tool, I aligned this segment above the boy's eye and pressed Enter to confirm the distortion.

8. I continued this process until most of the boy's face was re-assembled with segments from the old man's face and I was left with something like this.

9. Next, I wanted to lower the saturation in the boy's lips because they looked too bright beside the older skin. I selected the original layer in the Layers sidebar. Using the Lasso Selection Tool, I made a selection around the boy's lips and copied and pasted it onto a new layer with Edit > Copy and Edit > Paste. I chose Image > Hue & Saturation, changed the Hue to 10 and lowered the Saturation to -47, and clicked OK to confirm the change.

10. As I did earlier for the facial features of the figure, I copied the neck from the old man source layer and pasted it onto a new layer using Edit > Copy and Edit > Paste. I then used the Distortion Tool to line up the neck with the boy's. I opened the Hue and Saturation dialog box and adjusted the Hue to the left to -9, lowered the Saturation by -27, and clicked OK to apply the adjustment.

11. I wanted to bring the glasses from the original boy image layer back onto the figure's face. I hid all the layers for the time being (click the Eye icon beside each layer in the Layers sidebar) to see the original layer. Using the Lasso Selection Tool, I made a selection around the boy's glasses in the original layer and pasted this onto a new layer with Edit > Copy and Edit > Paste.

12. I dragged the glasses layer to the top of the list in the Layers sidebar and then redisplayed the other layers by clicking their Eye icon boxes. Using the Eraser Tool set to 90% Hardness, I erased the inside of the glasses to expose the boy's eyes.

13. To add a tint to the glasses, I created a new layer underneath the glasses layer by clicking the New Layer icon on the Layers sidebar and then dragging the layer into position. With the new layer selected, I selected the Paintbrush Tool. In the tool's options, I clicked the Foreground color selection box, entered 403046 in the # text box in the Color Picker dialog box, and then clicked OK to specify a dark muted purple tone. I then painted inside the glasses, over the lens area. I set this layer's Blend Mode to Multiply and lowered its Alpha to 30% on the Layers sidebar to create a slight darker cast on the glasses.

14. And finally, I needed to paint back in shadows for the glasses. I created a new layer underneath the glasses layer and selected the Paintbrush Tool. I set the foreground color to black (click the Restore Colors button in the tool's options) and set the Hardness to 10. I painted underneath the glasses to create simulated shadows for the spectacles.

15. I lowered the layer's Alpha to 67% and selected the Eraser Tool to erase any excess shadows where I may have gone overboard to complete the image.

Animal Hybrids

Source Images: "Squirrel - Lude" by jlola, "Blue-and-yellow Macaw - Ara ararauna" by Global Photographers

Have you ever wondered what it would look like if two of your favorite species of animals mated? Well if you're like me and always longed for the day when you could create your own abominations of the animal kingdom, you're in luck. In this tutorial, I'll be showing you how to create a hybrid of a parrot and a squirrel. The same methods can be applied to create endless combinations of animals. Happy abominating!

1. The first, and most important, step is to locate your source images. Finding images with similar perspective and general lighting is of utmost importance.

2. I started by opening the image of the squirrel, and then I imported the second image of the parrot's head (File > Import). With the parrot layer selected, I chose the Transformation Tool and rotated and resized the parrot head to fit on the squirrel's body, pressing Enter to finish the transformation.

3. Next, I decided to lower the saturation of the image. I chose Image > Hue & Saturation, lowered the Saturation to -20, and clicked OK to confirm the adjustment. Using the Eraser Tool, I erased around the edges of the parrot head to extract it from its original background.

4. The squirrel's ears were still showing from behind the parrot's head. First, I hid the parrot's head layer for the time being by clicking its Eye icon in the Layers sidebar. I selected the Eye Dropper Tool and sampled some color from the background around the squirrel's ear. I then selected the Paintbrush Tool and, working on the squirrel layer, painted over the ear with the sampled color to hide the ear. I then clicked the Eye icon box beside the parrot head layer in the Layers sidebar to redisplay the layer.

5. Next, it was time to add color to the squirrel's body. I wanted to color the squirrel's back in a blue color similar to that on top of the parrot's head. I clicked the New Layer icon in the Layers sidebar and dragged the new layer below the parrot head layer in the Layers sidebar. With the Paintbrush Tool selected, I set a blue tone as the foreground color (click the Foreground color selection box in the tool's options, enter 4096C6 in the # text box, and click OK). I then used the Paintbrush Tool to paint the color on the squirrel's body on the new layer.

6. I then set the color layer's Blend Mode to Overlay in the Layers sidebar. This gave the squirrel's body the bluish tint I desired.

7. I wanted to extend the yellow area on the parrot's head into the body as well, so I created a new layer and also made sure it was below the parrot layer in the Layers sidebar. With the Paintbrush Tool still selected, I changed the foreground color to yellow. On the new layer, I dragged the Paintbrush down starting from the yellow area of the parrot's head, then extending down over the top of his front leg. Then I set this layer's Blend Mode to Overlay in the Layers sidebar.

8. I also wanted to blend some of the black stripes from the parrot's head into the rest of the figure. I created another new layer above the parrot layer and selected the Paintbrush Tool. I set black as the foreground color in the tool's options by clicking the Restore Colors button and painted in stripes by hand where the parrot's white neck met the squirrel's now-yellow fur to blend the head and body together more uniformly. I then set this layer's Alpha to 76% on the Layers sidebar.

9. To make the parrot's neck appear to have more of the texture of fur, I created a new layer with the New Layer icon, being sure to position the layer above the parrot layer in the Layers sidebar. Choosing a small brush size, I then simply drew in small vertical dashes in the white neck area, to the right of the beak. I set this layer's Alpha to 12% on the Layers sidebar to create the textured effect.

10. I wanted to strengthen the shadows in the figure. I created a new layer (New Layer icon) and selected the Paintbrush Tool. I made sure the foreground color was still set to black and lowered the Hardness to 0 in the tool's options. I painted around the figure's limbs and under his belly. I set this layer's Blend Mode to Overlay in the Layers sidebar, darkening the shaded areas even further.

11. And I also wanted to enhance the highlights on the figure. I created another new layer (New Layer icon). With the Paintbrush Tool still selected, I set the foreground color to white in the tool's options and then painted on top of the parrot's head and beak and arms to increase the existing highlights in these areas.

12. And finally, I wanted to sharpen the entire image. First, I flattened all the layers (Layer > Flatten Layers). I duplicated the flattened layer (Layer > Duplicate Layer), then applied the Sharpen filter to it (Filters > Sharpen). Changing the Alpha level of the layer helps me distribute the amount of sharpening I want to add to the image. For this particular image, I set the sharpened layer's Alpha to 84% in the Layers sidebar.

Edible Architecture

Source Images: "Mushroom" by FotoDesign, "Roof Top Traditional Style" by Jacob H., "Sweet Home #2" by Wolverine Enterprises, "Red Roof and Brick Smoke Stack" by Majoros Laszlo, "Smoke" by Hermann Danzmayr.

Throughout fairy tale lore, there've been many tales of fantastical beings inhabiting homes made out of all sorts of edible goods including anything from gingerbread houses to mushroom abodes. In this tutorial, I'm going to bring a fairy tale to life and create a home made from a mushroom. The same methods can be used to apply this effect to any number of objects, edible or not.

1. The first thing I did was to locate the base source image I'd be using for the image. I chose this picture of a mushroom because it was a nice clean image, the surrounding grass made the mushroom appear to have a yard, and the surface of the object was clear enough for me to add a door and windows to make this mushroom look like an actual house.

2. I wanted to add a door to this mushroom first. I located a source image of a cottage with a door similar in perspective to that of my mushroom and imported it with File > Import. I used the Lasso Selection Tool to make a rough selection around the door of the cottage and I copied (Edit > Copy) and pasted (Edit > Paste) it onto a new layer.

3. I then hid the cottage image layer by clicking its Eye icon in the Layers sidebar, as I only needed the copied door. With the door layer selected, I chose the Distortion Tool to warp the segment's perspective to align with the mushroom base. I then pressed Enter to confirm the transformation.

4. To remove the surrounding elements to extract the door by itself cleanly, I used the Eraser Tool and simply dragged around the doorframe to remove the background on the door layer. I also erased some of the bottom of the door to make it appear as if it were behind the grassy area in front of it.

5. To add a shadow for the door, I created a new layer (New Layer icon) and dragged it below the door layer in the Layers sidebar list. I selected the Paintbrush Tool, set the Hardness to 0 and the Alpha to 15%, and set the foreground color to black by clicking the Restore Colors button, all in the tool's options. I then painted the shadow on the mushroom stem along the left side of the door.

6. Noticing that the existing shadows on the mushroom in the original image had a slight brown tone to them, I wanted to mimic the tint in the shadow I just drew in. So I created a new layer above my shadow layer by clicking the New Layer icon on the Layers sidebar and dragging the layer into position. I selected a brown tone (click the Foreground color selection box, enter BA742C in the # text box, and click OK) for the foreground color with the Paintbrush Tool still selected. On the new layer, I painted over the previous shadow in brown. I then set this layer's Blend Mode to Overlay and lowered the Alpha for the layer to 28% in the Layers sidebar. This gave the shadow the brown tint I desired.

7. Next, I wanted to give the doorframe a bit of saturation as well. So I selected the door layer and clicked the New Layer icon to create a new layer above the door layer. On the new layer, I painted over the door frame in the still-selected brown tone using the Paintbrush Tool, and set the layer's Blend Mode to Overlay and lowered the layer's Alpha to 91% in the Layers sidebar.

8. I wanted to add more house-like features onto the mushroom, so I decided to give the place a chimney next. I imported an image of a chimney into the document (File > Import). Using the Lasso Selection Tool, I made a selection around the chimney, and then I copied and pasted it onto a new layer with Edit > Copy and Edit > Paste.

9. I then selected the Transformation Tool and resized and positioned the chimney to sit atop the mushroom roof of the house, then pressed Enter to confirm the move. I selected the Eraser Tool to remove the blue sky surrounding the chimney on its layer. I then erased along the base to make it appear as if the chimney were located on the back slope of the mushroom "roof" in the image.

10. To add smoke to the chimney, I imported a source image of smoke into the document (File > Import). Using the Distortion Tool, I warped the smoke to look as if it were spewing from the top of the chimney. Using the Eraser Tool, I erased out any areas of the smoke that I didn't want in my final image.

11. When I set the smoke layer's Blend Mode to Screen in the Layers sidebar, only the smoke showed through on the image, as the Screen Blend Mode keeps all dark tones invisible, such as the black background of the smoke layer.

12. Next I wanted to add a dormer window to the top of the house. First, I imported an image of a nice window that was along the desired perspective (File > Import). As I did for the door and chimney, I used the Lasso Selection Tool to select the window and then copied and pasted it onto a new layer with Edit > Copy and Edit > Paste. I chose Select > Select None to remove the selection marquee, hid the original window layer by clicking its Eye icon, and reselected the copied window.

13. I selected the Transformation Tool to resize the window to fit the proportions of the rest of the house, then pressed Enter to confirm the transformation. Then I used the Eraser Tool to finish extracting the window from its original surroundings.

14. I wanted to add a shadow for the window. I created a new layer below my window by clicking the New Layer icon and then dragging the new layer below the window layer in the Layers sidebar. I selected the Paintbrush Tool, and in the tool's options set Hardness to 0, Alpha to 15%, and the foreground color to black (Restore Colors button). On the new layer, I darkened the area to the left of the window to create the shadow.

15. I wanted to extend a mushroom type roof to this dormer window as well. So I selected the left edge of the mushroom cap on the original layer and pasted it onto a new layer with Edit > Copy and Edit > Paste. I dragged the new layer with the copied segment above the window layer on the Layers sidebar. I used the Eraser Tool to extract the mushroom top and used the Transformation Tool to drag and resize the segment to sit on top of the window to complete the mushroom house.

Gender Bending

Source Images: "Shine" by Katja De Bruijn, "Biker Portrait" "Strange Bearded Man Smiling" by Michael DeLeon

Have you ever wondered what you'd look like as the opposite gender but just couldn't afford the costly operation? Well, maybe you haven't. But it does make for an interesting picture! In this tutorial, learn how to take a photo of a beautiful woman and turn her into a studly biker dude!

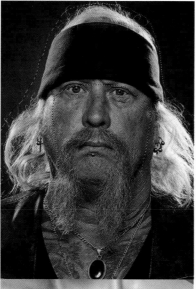

1. First, I wanted to slightly change the woman's facial structure. I enlarged her jaw to give it more of a manly look. To do so, I made a selection around her jaw, copied it (Edit > Copy), and pasted it (Edit > Paste) onto a new layer. I chose Select > Select None to remove the selection marquee. Then, using the Distortion Tool, I pulled the bottom two boxes slightly outwards to create a more square jaw line and pressed Enter to finish the change.

2. Next, I imported source images of a biker and an image of a middle-aged man from which I would be copying elements for the figure. I opened File > Import, and first uploaded the biker image using the Resource Browser dialog box. I followed the same procedure to include the source image of the middle-aged man. I hid the middle-aged man's layer, as I didn't need it at this time. I did want to take the bandana from the biker image and integrate it onto my figure. With the biker's layer selected, I made a selection around his hair and bandana and pasted it onto two new layers with Edit > Copy and then Edit > Paste twice. I selected Select > Select None to remove the selection marquee. I made one of the bandana layers invisible for the time being by clicking its Eye icon in the Layers sidebar. On my visible copy, I selected the Transformation Tool, aligned this selection to situate on the woman's head, and pressed Enter to finish the transformation.

3. Then, I selected the Eraser Tool set to 80% Hardness and erased the edges of this layer so that only the hair and bandana remained extracted.

Note

When you import an image into a document with a smaller canvas size than that of the image you are importing, you'll be prompted to either resize the imported image, resize the canvas to fit your imported image, or crop your imported image to fit the canvas. In my case with this image, I chose Resize Image to fit my source images into my document.

4. I lost a lot of the stray individual hairs around her head during the extracting step. I made my other bandana layer visible by clicking the box for its Eye icon. I set this layer's Blend Mode to Screen so that the light-colored hairs showed up again without obstructing the background. With the screen bandana layer still selected, I chose Image > Brightness & Contrast, lowered the Brightness to -83 and raised the Contrast by 22, and clicked OK. I then dragged this layer below the bandana layer on the Layers sidebar.

5. Next, it was time to rough up and wrinkle the woman's skin. I started by adding wrinkles under the woman's eyes. First, I clicked the eye icon box next to my middle-aged man's layer to make it visible again. I selected the wrinkled area underneath the man's left eye, copied it (Edit > Copy), and pasted it onto a new layer (Edit > Paste). I then hid the man's layer again. Using the Distortion Tool, I aligned the copied segment to fit under the woman's eye, pressing Enter to finish the change. I then set the wrinkle layer's Blend Mode to Multiply. I noticed this created too dark of an effect, so I chose Image > Brightness & Contrast, raised the Brightness to 64 and Contrast to 3, and clicked OK. I then repeated the same process to apply the same effect below the figure's right eye. When both sides were done, I merged both the wrinkle layers of the left and the right eyes into one by holding Ctrl and clicking both wrinkle layers in the Layers sidebar and selecting Layer > Merge Layers. Doing so simplifies the workspace, making an image with many layers much easier to work with.

6. I repeated the process noted in step 5 to furrow the area above her eyebrows and forehead. I copied the segments from the biker image layer and pasted them onto new layers. I used the Transformation Tool to align the copied area. I left the Blend Mode for this layer set to Normal. I did need to adjust the color to match the woman's skin tone, though. I chose Image > Hue & Saturation. I lowered the Hue to -10, raised the Saturation to 12, raised the Brightness to 4, and then clicked OK. I then used a soft Eraser Tool to clean the rough edges to create a smoother blend into the woman's skin.

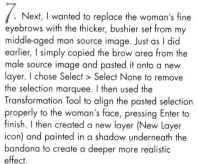

7. Next, I wanted to replace the woman's fine eyebrows with the thicker, bushier set from my middle-aged man source image. Just as I did earlier, I simply copied the brow area from the male source image and pasted it onto a new layer. I chose Select > Select None to remove the selection marquee. I then used the Transformation Tool to align the pasted selection properly to the woman's face, pressing Enter to finish. I then created a new layer (New Layer icon) and painted in a shadow underneath the bandana to create a deeper more realistic effect.

8. I continued the process, taking appropriate segments from the male sources to roughly texturize the woman's nose and cheekbone areas.

9. Next, I wanted to give the woman the mustache from the biker image. I copied and pasted the mustache from the biker image onto a new layer and aligned it with the woman's face using the Transformation Tool. I dragged this layer to the top of the Layers sidebar. I had to use the Eraser Tool set to 0 Hardness to softly blend the mustache onto the woman's face without leaving hard edges to create the illusion it's being dispersed onto her face. I chose Image > Brightness & Contrast, raised the Brightness setting to 8 and the Contrast to 6, and clicked OK.

10. I wanted to add a slight shadow underneath the mustache. I selected the Eye Dropper Tool and selected a reddish skin tone from the shadow under her neck on the original image layer. Then, I created a new layer underneath the mustache layer and drew in a soft shadow using the Paintbrush Tool set at 0 Hardness. When I was happy with the shadow, I merged the shadow with the mustache layer in the Layers sidebar.

11. I copied the vest and chest area from the biker image and pasted them onto new layers. I wanted to apply the new garb onto my woman, but I wanted her to maintain her original physique. So, using the Distortion Tool, I resized the chest and the clothing layers to fit on the woman's original size, pressing Enter to finish the change. Not to obstruct any of the wrinkles and mustache I applied to the woman, I dragged the chest and clothing layers underneath the other layers containing the facial edits on the Layers sidebar.

12. Next, I needed to remove the lipstick from the woman's original lips. I made a selection around the woman's mouth on the original image layer, and copied and pasted it onto a new layer. I chose Image > Hue & Saturation menu, changed the Hue to 12, lowered the Saturation to -57, raised the Brightness to 15, and clicked OK to give the lips a more muted, natural look.

13. Noticing that there were remnants of hair still left on the vest I had added, I decided to lengthen her... er... his hair. I copied a section of the biker's hair and pasted it onto a new layer to create the appearance of longer hair extending down to the figure's shoulders, then did the same for the other side. I applied the Screen Blend Mode to these layers in the Layers sidebar. I then dragged both of these layers to sit on top of my bandana layer in the Layers sidebar.

14. To enhance the image even further, I decided to increase the contrast of the existing highlights and shadows in the picture. I created a new layer for shadows. I selected the Paintbrush set to 0 Hardness,10% Alpha, and set black as my foreground color. I painted around the figure's eyes, nose, and anywhere else shadows already occurred, then set this layer's Blend Mode to Overlay. And I did the same for the highlights, except set the Paintbrush's foreground color to white and created a new layer and painted over the existing highlights on the woman's face. I also set this layer's Blend Mode to Overlay.

15. And finally, I brought the whole image together even further by creating a subtle aqua cast over the entire image. First, I created a new layer (New Layer icon) and, using the Paint Bucket Tool, I filled the entire layer with white. I set this layer's Blend Mode to Overlay, and lowered the layer's Alpha to 12% in the Layers sidebar. This brightened the image slightly overall. I then created a new layer, and filled it entirely with a muted blue tone (HEX #618484 in the Select Color dialog box). I set this layer's Blend Mode to Overlay as well, and lowered the layer's Alpha to 70% to complete the image.

Flying Cars

Source Images: "Rush Hour in New York City" by nicolecioe, "Red Sports Car" by Mark Evans

All throughout our childhood we were promised flying cars in the future. We'd hear about them in school, we'd read about them in works of fiction depicting the future of our civilization, and we'd see them in movies. So we're all left to wonder, where are these flying cars? In this tutorial, I'll show you how to create your own flying car, as we just don't have the time to sit around and wait in this modern age.

1. I started with the scene of a New York traffic jam photographed from above. I also located an image of a sports car and uploaded it to the document (File > Import).

2. Using the Eraser Tool, I erased around the background of the car image to extract the automobile. Then, I selected the Transformation Tool and repositioned and resized the car to make it appear as if it were hovering over the city. I pressed Enter to confirm the move.

3. Next, I wanted to add thrusters to the side of the car. I created these segments from scratch. I first sampled some red from the original car using the Eye Dropper Tool. Then I created a new layer by clicking the New Layer icon. Using the Elliptical Shape Tool, I drew a circle on the new layer. Then I chose the Distortion Tool and arranged it so that the perspective lined up with the angled perspective of the car, finally pressing Enter to confirm the warp.

4. I wanted to cut off the rounded bottom of the thruster. Using the Elliptical Selection Tool, I made a circular selection around the thruster leaving the bottom portion unselected (extending beyond the selection). I then inverted the selection (Select > Invert Selection) and chose Edit > Cut to remove the bottom of the segment.

5. To create the shine on the thruster, I first duplicated the thrust panel layer (Layer > Duplicate Layer) making sure the new layer was above the thruster layer. I changed the color of this duplicated layer to white by choosing Image > Hue & Saturation, lowering the Saturation level to 0 and setting the Brightness to 100, and then clicking OK. Then, using the Distortion Tool, I resized the layer to fit within the thruster. I pressed Enter to confirm the change.

6. I selected the Eraser Tool, set the hardness to 0, and lowered the Alpha to 20%. I slowly erased the bottom of the shine layer to create a gradient highlight on the thrust panel.

7. Next, I wanted to add a shadow along the left side of the thruster panel. I selected the thruster's layer, and made a selection around it (Select > Selection from Layer). I created a new layer (New Layer icon) and made sure that it was selected. I then chose the Paintbrush Tool again and set the foreground color to black (Reset Colors button). I painted over the left side of the thruster on the new layer and changed its Blend Mode to Overlay in the Layers sidebar to darken the front-left portion of the panel.

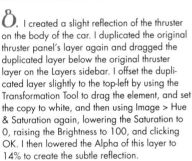

8. I created a slight reflection of the thruster on the body of the car. I duplicated the original thruster panel's layer again and dragged the duplicated layer below the original thruster layer on the Layers sidebar. I offset the duplicated layer slightly to the top-left by using the Transformation Tool to drag the element, and set the copy to white, and then using Image > Hue & Saturation again, lowering the Saturation to 0, raising the Brightness to 100, and clicking OK. I then lowered the Alpha of this layer to 14% to create the subtle reflection.

9. And I also created a shadow to the left of the thruster on the car's body. I did this by first selecting the car layer, then making a selection around it (Select > Selection from Layer). Then I created a new layer and moved it above the reflection layer and below the thruster layer in the Layers sidebar. I selected the Paintbrush Tool. I set the Paintbrush's hardness to 0, and set black as the foreground color. I painted in the area directly to the left of the thruster to create the shadow.

10. I then merged the layers that contained all the elements of the thruster. I clicked each of these layers on the Layers sidebar while holding down Ctrl on the keyboard. Then I merged the layers by clicking Layer > Merge Layers. I duplicated the merged thrust and dragged the duplicated copy to sit along the back tire of the car using the Transformation Tool. I pressed Enter to confirm the move.

11. I wanted to give the car a blue tone, as the entire background seemed to be cast in a slight blue hue. So I created a new layer (New Layer icon) and dragged it to the top of the Layers sidebar. I selected the car layer and made a selection around it (Select > Selection from Layer). Then, I selected the new layer and filled in this area with blue by clicking the Foreground color selection box, entering 5182B7 in the # text box and clicking OK, selecting the Paint Bucket Tool, and clicking in the selection. I then made a selection around each of the thrusters in the same manner and filled these areas in on the same layer. I set the blue fill's layer Blend Mode to Overlay in the Layers sidebar.

12. Next, I wanted to light up the car slightly. I imported a photograph of a neon light (File > Import). Using the Transformation Tool, I positioned the neon light to sit directly on the headlight, then pressed Enter to confirm the move.

13. I set the light's Blend Mode to Screen in the Layers sidebar, then adjusted the brightness. I chose Image > Brightness & Contrast, lowered the Brightness by -35 and raised the Contrast by 29, and clicked OK. I duplicated this layer (Layer > Duplicate Layer) and dragged it to the other headlight on the left, and also applied them to the thruster panels.

14. To add to the effect that the car was actually in this environment, I decided to add reflections of the top of the buildings on the windshield of the car. Hiding any layers that were in the way, I made a selection around some protruding buildings on the original background layer, and I copied and pasted the selection onto a new layer (Edit > Copy and Edit > Paste). I then redisplayed the hidden layers.

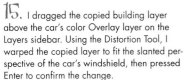

15. I dragged the copied building layer above the car's color Overlay layer on the Layers sidebar. Using the Distortion Tool, I warped the copied layer to fit the slanted perspective of the car's windshield, then pressed Enter to confirm the change.

16. Next, I added a motion blur to the background. I selected the background layer in the Layers sidebar and then clicked the Layer Filters button on the sidebar to open the Layer Filters dialog box. I clicked the Blur check box to check it, changed the Quality to High, and entered 6 in the Blur X text box and 0 in the Blur Y text box. I clicked OK to apply the blur to the layer.

17. Finally, I applied a slight green tint over the entire image to bring it all together. I created a new layer (New Layer icon) and dragged it to the top of the Layers sidebar. I set the foreground color to an aqua green tone (click the Foreground color selection box, enter 9CD4A5 in the # text box, and click OK). I set the layer's Blend Mode to Overlay and lowered the Alpha to 47% in the Layers sidebar, and my image was complete.

Toiletbot

Source Images: "Men's Room" by Bitfire, Inc., "WC Pan" by Webwise Studios, "Disabled Toilet" by Show Me Scents, "Toilet in a hotel room" by Ljupco Smokovski, "Bathroom" by annthphoto, "Brain control 2" by Andreas G., "Empty Toilet Roll" by David G. Freund

Many people have a fear of using public restrooms. I, for one, refuse to use one under any circumstances. You never know what sort of evils lurk within the bowels of the public bathroom. In this tutorial, I'm going to show how to create a real monster using items found around the bathroom. I'll be showing how spending the time to find suitable source images can greatly cut down on the actual work time.

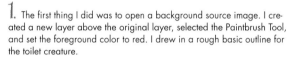

1. The first thing I did was to open a background source image. I created a new layer above the original layer, selected the Paintbrush Tool, and set the foreground color to red. I drew in a rough basic outline for the toilet creature.

2. The next step, and possibly the step which took the longest, was to hunt down all the source images needed to assemble the creature. I looked for images of toilets and sinks from different angles that would fit within the general outlines of the segments I roughly sketched in. I then uploaded all my source images to the document (File > Import). I then hid all the source layers until I needed them by clicking the Eye icon beside each one.

3. Then it came time to assemble the figure. I started with the body. I unhid one of the toilet source image layers, the one I figured would fit best within the sketch of the body. I selected the Lasso Selection Tool, and then I made a rough selection around the toilet and copied and pasted it onto a new layer (Edit > Copy and Edit > Paste). I then re-hid the toilet source layer by clicking its Eye icon box in the Layers sidebar.

4. Then, I selected the Transformation Tool and resized and positioned the toilet to fit along the guidelines. I pressed Enter to confirm the change.

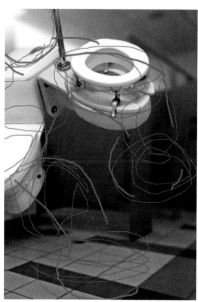

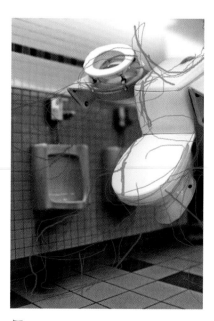

5. I selected the Eraser Tool and used it to erase the background around the toilet, leaving it cleanly extracted.

6. I repeated the process outlined in Steps 3 through 5 to begin the shoulder segment of my creature. The trick to locating the appropriate source images of elements for the various segments is to compare the perspective and angle of the elements to the area you want to copy the piece onto.

7. As the shoulder on the figure's right side was along the same perspective of the left shoulder, I simply duplicated the layer holding the toilet I had used for the left shoulder (Layer > Duplicate Layer) and dragged this layer below the body segment on the Layers sidebar. I then used the Transformation Tool to drag the toilet segment to the right shoulder area of the figure and pressed Enter when I was happy with the placement.

8. I then chose to use the source image of the sink to complete the figure's right arm. It had a long slender shape, which fit well with the original guideline sketch.

9. I selected the sink layer from the Layers sidebar and used the Transformation Tool to align the sink to fit under the figure's shoulder, then pressed Enter to confirm the move.

10. For the figure's left hand, I used the image of the toilet roll hook, as it made for an interesting-looking hand for the creature.

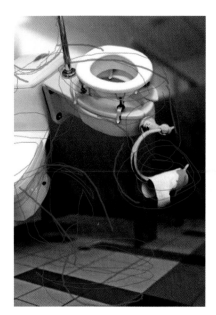

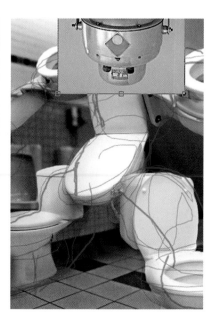

11. As I did with the other elements, I simply extracted the toilet roll hook and moved it onto the end of the figure's left shoulder with the Transformation Tool to create the illusion that this was indeed the creature's hand.

12. For the creature's head, I found a source image of an interesting piece of machinery. I took the time to look for an image of this piece of machine that resembled a figure's face instead of trying to create a face for the figure from scratch. This is a good example of how taking the time to look for appropriate source images greatly helps reduce the actual time it takes to make the image.

13. I flipped the image vertically (Edit > Transform > Flip Vertical). Then I used the Transformation Tool to resize and position the head to sit on top of the figure where the head would naturally go. Then I pressed Enter to confirm the transformation. Next, I chose the Eraser Tool with the Hardness set to 90 and Size set to 25 and erased around the head to remove the background surrounding the head.

14. I wanted to give the head a blue tint, as the rest of the image seemed to have a slight blue cast. So I created a new layer (New Layer icon) over the layer with the head on it, and selected the Paintbrush Tool. I set the Paintbrush Tool's Hardness to 0, and set the foreground color to a light blue and painted over the entire head. I later set this layer's Blend Mode to Overlay and lowered the layer's Alpha to 66% in the Layers sidebar to apply the tint to the head.

15. I finished assembling the figure by adding its legs, repeating the process used to create the figure's body and arms. When I was happy with the composition of the figure, I added shadows in between each of the segments. I created a new layer on top of the Layers sidebar and selected the Paintbrush Tool. I set the Hardness to 0 and set the foreground color to black and lowered the Alpha to 12%. I then painted in between each of the segments to delineate them and add a sense of depth.

16. And finally, I wanted to create a slight reflection of the figure on the tiled floor. I set the Paintbrush Tool's foreground color to white (click Restore Colors and then Switch Between Foreground and Background Colors). I created a new layer (New Layer icon) and dragged it directly above the original background layer. On the new layer I painted in a subtle shadow leading directly from the figure's right foot to create the illusion of the reflection on the floor, and the image was done.

Inanimate Objects

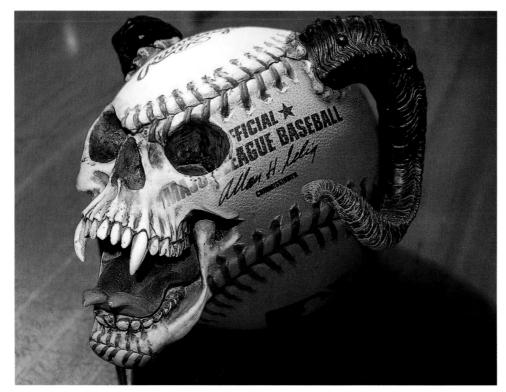

Source Images: "Baseball" by Robert Badgley, "Skull" by Cy Campbell aka cycoze

In the past, I often wondered if my toys came to life when I turned out the lights at night. This irrational phobia always kept me up at night imagining all my possessions springing to life and attacking me while I slept. But enough about last week. In this tutorial, I'm going to address my fears head-on by creating one of the demons of my mind. After all, a creation can't turn on his creator, can he? I'm assuming he can't, anyways.

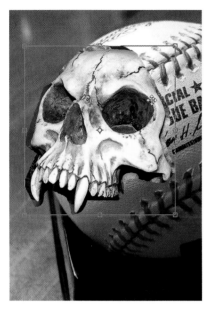

1. I started my document with the base image of a baseball. I then imported the image of a skull into the document with File > Import, which placed the second image on a new layer. Using the Lasso Selection Tool, I selected the front facial portion of the skull and copied and pasted this segment onto a new layer with Edit > Copy and Edit > Paste. I then clicked the Eye icon beside the skull layer in the Layers sidebar to hide the skull layer and reselected the pasted layer in the Layers sidebar. I chose Select > Select None to remove the selection marquee. Using the Transformation Tool, I resized and moved the face segment of the skull to align with the leftmost edge of the baseball, pressing Enter to finish the transformation.

2. With the pasted face layer still selected, I chose Image > Brightness & Contrast, raised the Brightness by 6 and lowered the Contrast by -2, and clicked OK to suit the lighting of the original baseball image a little better. Then, using the Eraser Tool, I removed the remnants of original background from the skull face layer. I then set the Eraser Tool's hardness to 0 and softened the edges where the face met the baseball to create a smoother blend.

3. I repeated the process from steps 1 and 2, redisplaying and hiding the skull layer as needed, to copy and paste the lower jaw of the skull onto a new layer and then blend it into the baseball as well.

4. I repeated the process again for the closer horn on the skull. I copied and pasted the horn section onto a new layer. I noticed a crack on the skull in front of the right horn (the skull's left) and found it to align with the seam of the baseball well. So I used the Transformation Tool to align the crack to the seam.

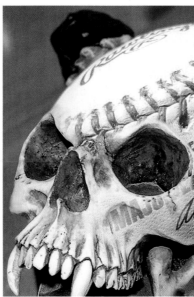

5. Using the Eraser Tool, I removed the surrounding elements to finish extracting the horn. I carefully erased the areas to expose the stitching of the baseball, yet made sure to keep the crack from the skull layer.

6. Next, I added the farther horn from the skull image layer. As I did with the previous segments, I redisplayed that layer, copied and pasted this area onto a new layer, and hid the skull layer. I used the Eraser Tool to extract the horn cleanly. I added a slight blur to this layer as it appears farther away in the image. I clicked the Layer Filters icon in the Layers sidebar and clicked the Blur check box. I entered 3 in both the Blur X and Blur Y text boxes, set the Quality to High, and clicked OK.

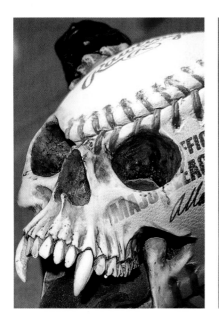

7. The next step was to clean the overall blending of the skull sections into the baseball. For example, I didn't like how the stitching of the baseball was covered by the skull's face on the brow area between the eye sockets. So, I used the Eraser Tool to expose some of the stitches that went missing on the brow.

8. I noticed the lower jaw looked a little too bright. I wanted to add a shadow to the lower portion of the jaw around the bottom. With the lower jaw layer selected, I chose Select > Selection from Layer to draw a selection marquee around the lower jaw. Then, I created a new layer (New Layer icon on the Layers sidebar) and painted an undershadow along the lower portion of the jaw using the Paintbrush Tool set to black foreground color, 0 Hardness, and a low 10% Alpha. I then chose Select > Select None to remove the selection marquee.

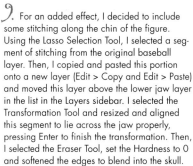

9. For an added effect, I decided to include some stitching along the chin of the figure. Using the Lasso Selection Tool, I selected a segment of stitching from the original baseball layer. Then, I copied and pasted this portion onto a new layer (Edit > Copy and Edit > Paste) and moved this layer above the lower jaw layer in the list in the Layers sidebar. I selected the Transformation Tool and resized and aligned this segment to lie across the jaw properly, pressing Enter to finish the transformation. Then, I selected the Eraser Tool, set the Hardness to 0 and softened the edges to blend into the skull.

10. And for the finishing touches, I added shadows for additional elements. I wanted to include a shadow on the area where the front horn meets the baseball, as well as where the horn casts a shadow on the side of the baseball. I created a new layer above the horn's layer. Then, I selected the Eye Dropper Tool, selected the original baseball layer, and clicked to select a dark reddish tone to get an accurate color for the shadow. Reselecting the new shadow layer, I then used a soft Paintbrush Tool and painted in a shadow under the area where the horn joins the baseball on the new layer. I repeated this process to add a shadow along the side of the baseball on a new layer, dragging this layer below the horn layer on the Layers sidebar. I set the layer's Blend Mode to Multiply on the Layers sidebar.

11. Finally, I enhanced the existing shadows around the cracks of the skull as well. I created a new layer, moved it to the top of the list of layers in the Layers sidebar, and painted in the desired shadow areas with black. I then set the Blend Mode for all three shadow layers to Multiply and this created a more seamless blend between the elements.

Unzipped

Source Images:
"Vic's Cat" by
Oleksiy Petrenko,
"Zipper" by mvp64

As the title of this book states, there's more than one way to skin a cat. But I personally find it most convenient (and least messy) to do it with a zipper! In this tutorial, I'm gonna show how I pulled off the unzipping effect of the cover image to give this kitty a fresh new start on life.

1. I started by opening the image of the cat in Phoenix. Using the Lasso Selection Tool, I drew a selection around the top half (cat's right) of the face and I copied (Edit > Copy) and pasted (Edit > Paste) this selection onto a new layer.

2. Working on the new layer, I selected the Distortion Tool and skewed this pasted segment to line up to the cat's face on an angle. When I was happy with the placement of the segment, I pressed Enter to confirm the transformation. This began the process of "opening" up the figure's head.

3. I returned to the original image layer and repeated the process from Steps 1 and 2 on the opposite side of the cat's face to open up the cat's head on both sides.

4. I then selected the Eraser Tool set to 85 Hardness and cleaned the edges on the pasted layers for both the top and bottom halves of the cat's head. I also used the Eraser Tool to erase the cat's eyes from the pasted segments.

5. At this point, I decided to change the color of the inner cat to help differentiate between the two. Selecting the original layer in the Layers sidebar, I made a selection around the cat's entire face and neck using the Lasso Selection Tool, and then copied and pasted this selection onto a new layer (Edit > Copy and Edit > Paste). I made sure the new layer was listed below the layers with the pasted face halves in the list in the Layers sidebar. Then, using the Transformation Tool, I dragged the copied cat slightly to the right to create more of an offset from the face halves, pressing Enter to confirm the move.

6. I wanted to give the inner kitten a gray tone. With the inner cat's head layer selected, I made a selection around the eyes and nose of the cat with the Lasso Selection Tool. (Shift+Drag to make the second and third selections.)

7. I then inverted the selection (Select > Invert Selection), because I wanted to remove the color from everything but the kitten's eyes and nose. To turn the kitten gray, I chose Image > Hue & Saturation. I then lowered the Saturation to -80 and clicked OK to confirm the adjustment.

8. The next step was to add some basic shadows on the cat's face. I created a new layer by clicking the New Layer icon on the Layers sidebar and made sure it was positioned just above the inner cat layer on the Layers sidebar. I then took a soft black Paintbrush Tool set to 15% Alpha in the tool's options and painted over the edges and crevices on the new layer to enhance the shadows. I set this Layer's Blend mode to Overlay in the Layers sidebar to give the inner kitty a little more pop.

9. With the Paintbrush Tool still selected, I created a new layer and darkened the shadows directly below the edges of the face halves.

10. I wanted to give the inner kitty a slight hint of color for realism. I created a new layer (New Layer icon) just above the inner cat layer, and selected the Paintbrush Tool and chose a tan color (HEX c09e01 selected using the Foreground color selection box) and 20% Alpha in the tool's options. I then painted over the cat's ears on the new layer. I set this layer's Blend Mode to Overlay and lowered the layer's Alpha to 55% in the Layers sidebar. You can adjust the Alpha to your desired setting depending on how much color you applied when painting the figure.

11. I noticed the whiskers from the original image layer were still showing. So I clicked the original layer in the Layers sidebar (temporarily hiding other layers first as needed), then with the Lasso Selection Tool I made a selection around a clean segment of the floor. I copied and pasted this segment onto a new layer just above the original layer, used the Transformation Tool to move the segment to cover the exposed whiskers, and pressed OK.

12. To attach whiskers back onto the halved segment of the face, I selected the original layer again (temporarily hiding other layers as needed) and using the Lasso Selection Tool, I made a selection around the original cat's whiskers. I copied and pasted this selection onto a new layer, then dragged this layer to lay above the cat's halved face layer on the Layers sidebar. First, I desaturated the layer (Image > Desaturate), then I adjusted the contrast. I chose Image > Brightness & Contrast, lowered the Brightness to -70 and raised the Contrast to 70, and clicked OK. Using the Transformation Tool, I then dragged this selection to align with the existing whisker remnants on the cat's halved face and pressed Enter. Finally, I set the layer's Blend Mode to Screen in the Layers sidebar.

13. Next, it was time to add the zipper. I imported a file with an image of a zipper (File > Import). I selected the zipper's slider first with the Lasso Selection Tool and copied it onto a new layer with Edit > Copy and Edit > Paste.

14. Using the Transformation Tool, I rotated and resized the zipper pull and placed it so that it appeared over the person's finger. I pressed Enter to confirm the move.

15. I did the same thing for the actual teeth of the zipper, taking small segments at a time and placing them around the edge of the outer cat's face, with emphasis on "small segments." Especially when you're following along the more curvy paths and using limited zipper sources, though it may seem tedious, keeping your segments small and numerous will leave you with complete control over these challenging areas.

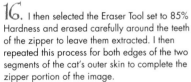

16. I then selected the Eraser Tool set to 85% Hardness and erased carefully around the teeth of the zipper to leave them extracted. I then repeated this process for both edges of the two segments of the cat's outer skin to complete the zipper portion of the image.

17. To place the finger back into the image over the zipper's slider, I hid layers as needed and selected the original layer again. I used the Lasso Selection Tool to select the fingertip and pasted it onto a new layer with Edit > Copy and Edit > Paste. I dragged this layer above the zipper pull layer in the Layers sidebar. I used the Eraser Tool to erase around the finger to expose the zipper pull underneath as needed.

18. I wanted to create a slight shadow underneath the finger. I created a new layer underneath the finger (New Layer icon) and selected the Paintbrush Tool. I selected a dark brown tone as my foreground color (click the Foreground color selection box in the tool's options, enter 6A4D04 in the HEX text of the Select Color dialog box, and click OK). I set the Paintbrush Tool's Hardness to 0 and painted in the shadow directly below the finger to set some depth to the section, and the image was complete.

Fire!

Source Images: "Fire Eater 2" by Srabin, "Fire" by SCM Studios

In this tutorial, I'll show how to take an image of fire and reshape the flames to create any figure imaginable. I couldn't resist attempting to create a Phoenix in Aviary's Phoenix. It was just too deliciously literal!

1. The first thing I did after uploading the initial fire breather photo was to create a new layer directly under the fire breather layer by clicking the New Layer icon on the Layers sidebar and then dragging the new layer below the fire breather layer in the Layers sidebar list. I set the foreground color to black by clicking the Restore Colors button, and then used the Paint Bucket Tool to fill the new layer with black. I reselected the fire breather layer in the Layers sidebar, used the Transformation Tool to drag the fire breather lower on the canvas to give me room at the top to create a fiery figure, and then pressed Enter to finish the transformation.

2. I wanted to increase the contrast on the fire breather image to darken the edges of the photo to blend in with the black background fill layer I created. I chose Image > Brightness & Contrast, lowered the Brightness to -13 and raised the Contrast to 9, and then clicked OK.

3. Next, it was time to define the outline of the figure I would be turning into fire. So, I created a new layer by clicking the New Layer icon, selected a red foreground color (Foreground color selection box) and the Paintbrush Tool, and roughly drew in the silhouette of the bird I wanted to create. I planned to use this outline as a rough guide for compositing the fiery Phoenix.

4. To assemble the figure, I needed to take apart portions of the existing flames and apply them to form the figure I outlined. I did this in many different parts, starting by selecting a small portion of the existing flames on the original image layer, copying it and pasting it onto a new layer, and choosing Select > Select None to remove the selection marquee. I then used the Transformation Tool to resize and rotate the copied portions to fit within the outline.

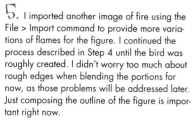

5. I imported another image of fire using the File > Import command to provide more variations of flames for the figure. I continued the process described in Step 4 until the bird was roughly created. I didn't worry too much about rough edges when blending the portions for now, as those problems will be addressed later. Just composing the outline of the figure is important right now.

6. Adding bright white highlights in the middle of fire creates a nice dramatic appearance. So I created a new layer (New Layer icon) and dragged it to the top of the list of layers in the fiery composition, selected the Paintbrush Tool and a white foreground color in the tool's options, and painted the middle of the Phoenix figure. I set the layer's Blend Mode to Overlay in the Layers sidebar to saturate the highlights.

7. Now it came time to smooth the blends between fire segments. I selected all the layers with segments of fire used to assemble the Phoenix by Ctrl+clicking each layer in the Layers sidebar, and merged them into one layer by clicking the Options button drop-down list arrow and clicking Merge Layers. I selected the Liquify Tool and dragged the tool across the rough edges to blend them together. I also dragged across the edges of the fire to create the appearance of wild flames.

8. I wanted to paint in some reddish smoke behind the newly assembled Phoenix. I created a new layer by clicking the New Layer icon, and dragged it below the fire layer in the Layers sidebar. I reselected the fire breather layer, selected the Eye Dropper Tool, clicked on the layer to sample the red color around the original flames, reselected the new layer, and painted in a similar smoky highlight effect behind the Phoenix using the Paintbrush Tool set to 0 Hardness.

9. For added detail, I decided to give my Phoenix an eye. I copied a triangular segment from the original flames on the fire breather layer and pasted it onto a new layer with Edit > Copy and Edit > Paste. I dragged this new layer to the top of the list in the Layers sidebar. Using the Transformation Tool, I dragged this pasted eye segment up to the head area of my Phoenix and rotated it so it resembled an eye, pressing Enter to finish the transformation. Then, using a soft Eraser Tool, I erased the edges to blend it into the Phoenix' head.

10. And finally, I created one more new layer at the top of the Layers sidebar (New Layer icon) and filled the entire thing with a Radial Gradient with white in the center radiating to a gray. (Click the Gradient Fill tool, choose Radial from the Gradient Type drop-down list in the tool's options, and drag diagonally from the center of the image.) I set this layer's Blend Mode to Overlay in the Layers sidebar. This added a nice subtle lighting effect by blowing out the highlights in the center of the image and darkening the corners and edges, creating a vignette effect.

Water

We've all seen marvelous ice sculptures before. It's an incredibly difficult and unforgiving medium to work in, as the window of opportunity to work on any particular piece is hindered by multiple factors including temperature and gravity. Since we aren't limited by such forces of nature in the digital world, let's take it one step further and create a sculpture… out of water! In this tutorial, I'm going to do just that and take a splash of water and sculpt it into a dolphin.

Source Image: "Ice" by Irina Tischenko

1. I started with the image of the splashing water in a glass. I made a duplicate copy of the original layer and then clicked the Eye icon beside the duplicate layer in the Layers sidebar to hide the layer for now. I then resized the original image on its layer to about one quarter of its original size using the Transformation Tool, dragged the selection to the lower-right corner of the canvas, and pressed Enter to confirm the transformation.

2. The next step was planning out the shape of the splash. I decided to go with the figure of a dolphin, but the possibilities here are limitless. But I find creating an image of an animal or object with a very distinct silhouette greatly helps the recognition factor of the image. I created a new layer and roughly drew in the dolphin shape with the Paintbrush Tool set to a contrasting red color.

3. After I was happy with the general outline of the figure, it was time to start assembling it. First, I clicked the Eye icon box next to the duplicate of the original glass image to unhide that layer. On this layer, I selected a segment of the water splash by using the Lasso Selection Tool. I then copied and pasted this splash onto a new layer using Edit > Copy and Edit > Paste.

4. I hid the duplicate glass layer again for now. Using the Transformation Tool, I rotated the copied splash segment to align with the bottom tail area of the dolphin, then pressed Enter to confirm the transformation. I set the layer's Blend Mode to Multiply in the Layers sidebar. I selected the Eraser Tool and erased portions of the splash that may have strewn past the outline too much. Straying from your guidelines a little is okay, but go too far and you risk losing shape recognition for the figure.

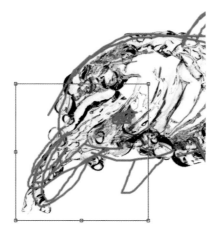

5. I repeated the process from steps 3 and 4 to fill in the top outline of the figure. I set each splash segment layer's Blend Mode to Multiply in the Layers sidebar. This way, when I assembled the figure, the segments weren't obstructed with remnants of the white background found on your pasted splash segments, and only the water will be seen. Another good practice is to periodically hide the guideline layer to see how the figure stands on its own without it, redisplaying the guideline layer as needed.

6. To create the beak of the dolphin, I used the same process as for the dolphin's body. I had to be sure to find an appropriate piece in the water glass image to use for the beak, so I chose the pointiest segment of the water's splash that I could find. I copied and pasted this segment onto a new layer (Edit > Copy and Edit > Paste) just as I did for the rest of the body. I set the layer's Blend Mode to Multiply, as well. I used the Transformation Tool to rotate and align this piece to sit directly where I drew in the beak in the guideline and pressed Enter to confirm this transformation.

7. I repeated the process of copying segments of water from the duplicate of the original layer to assemble the bottom of the dolphin figure. I tried to vary the sections of water as much possible to avoid having an obvious "cloned" effect on the splashes.

8. Just as for the beak, I had to find a segment in the glass of water image that most resembled the triangular shape of the dorsal fin. I copied an appropriate section of the splash onto a new layer (Edit > Copy and Edit > Paste), aligned it to the dorsal fin area using the Transformation Tool, and set the layer's Blend Mode to Multiply. I also dragged this layer above the other splash layers in the Layers sidebar. Where the dorsal fin portion overlapped the dolphins' back, the area appeared to be a little jumbled. So I selected the splash layer which the dorsal fin was obstructing and used the Eraser Tool to erase out the areas directly under the dorsal fin to clean up the area.

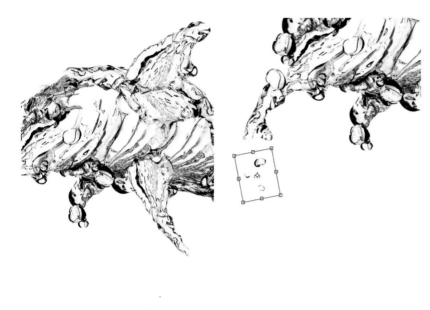

9. I repeated the same process as for the dorsal fin to assemble the figure's flippers. At this point, I also added a droplet on the figure's head area to create a semblance of an eye. I did this by selecting one of the larger drops from the original image and copying (Edit > Copy) and pasting (Edit > Paste) it onto a new layer above my water layers. Then I dragged it into position using the Transformation Tool and pressed Enter to confirm the move. I then set this layer's Blend Mode to Multiply on the Layers sidebar. Then, I created a new layer directly below this eye layer and selected the Paintbrush Tool with white set as my foreground color to paint within the perimeter of the eye.

10. To enhance the splashing effect even further, I decided to include some stray water droplets around the figure. I unhid the duplicate glass of water layer again and selected a few of the airborne water droplets. I copied this selection and pasted it onto a new layer (Edit > Copy and Edit > Paste) and hid the glass of water layer again. With the Transformation Tool, I moved the pasted droplets to fall under the dolphin's beak. I repeated this process to create droplets of water floating around the figure's dorsal fin and flippers.

11. And finally, to make the figure pop even more, I decided to strengthen the outline of the figure. I created a new layer (New Layer icon) and dragged it to the very top of the list in the Layers sidebar. I selected the Paintbrush with the Hardness set to 10 and painted around the silhouette of the figure with black set as the foreground color.

12. I set this outline layer's Blend Mode to Overlay and lowered the Alpha to 70% in the Layers sidebar. This darkened the edge of the figure, creating a more prominent silhouette of the dolphin.

S-s-smokin'

Source Images: "Male portrait 5" by Valentin Casarsa, "Dancing Girl,"
"Smoke" by pixelfactory

In this tutorial, I'm going to create one smokin' woman using a few source images and simple tools. So follow along, and I'll try to share a few secrets into some of the magic, without the smoke and mirrors. Well, maybe a little smoke.

1. With the general idea already in my mind, I needed to find a suitable background image of a smoker. The image I found turned out perfect because of the line of direction of the main figure's vision. He's looking directly where I planned to place a smoky woman, creating unity among our elements.

2. The first step was to remove most of the smoke from the original image, as I would be creating other smoke later on. I started by creating a new layer (New Layer icon on the Layers sidebar). Reselecting the original layer, I selected the Clone Stamp Tool and Shift+ clicked a clean area of the background to sample it. Then I reselected the new layer and painted over the smoke covered areas with the selected sample. It didn't need to be perfect at this point, as most of it would be covered by the end anyways.

3. Next, I imported a high contrast image of a model (File > Import). Not only do the natural stark shadows and highlights of this image look good, but hey, the contrast will do half the work for us in the long run. First, I flipped the image of the woman horizontally (Edit > Transform > Flip Horizontal).Using the Transformation Tool, I resized and moved the figure to where I wanted the smoke to flow and pressed Enter when I was pleased with the figure's placement.

4. I then set this layer's Blend Mode to Screen and lowered the Alpha to 82% in the Layers sidebar. This Blend Mode only allows the light areas of the image to be visible, thus hiding the black background of the image already creating a semi-ghostly appearance.

5. Now that we have our basic composition in place, it's time to make the figure look more like smoke. Using the Liquify Tool, I smudged the edges of the figure and pulled out trails to draw a smoky effect. I did that until I was left with a wispy looking figure.

6. Our lady could always be more smokin'. And what's more smokin' than, well, smoke? I imported a source image of smoke into the document next using File > Import. Using the Lasso Selection Tool, I selected some of the smoke on the new layer and then copied and pasted the segment onto a new layer using Edit > Copy and Edit > Paste. I then clicked the Eye icon beside the imported smoke layer to hide the layer and chose Select > Select None to remove the selection marquee.

7. Using the Transformation Tool, I moved the copied smoke segment to cover one of the brighter areas of the woman's figure and pressed Enter to finish the transformation. I then set the layer's Blend Mode to Screen in the Layers sidebar.

8. I repeated this process to cover the rest of the figure, redisplaying and hiding the layer with the imported smoke image as needed. I took a larger segment of the smoke and pasted it on the upper portion of the image with the Transformation Tool and pressed Enter to confirm the move. I lowered the Alpha of this layer to 12%. This created a bit of a smoky mist in the air congested by the cigarette.

9. Now we're getting somewhere! But I still wanted to expose a few of the highlights of the smoke a bit more. Just to give it that extra pop. I did this by creating a new layer for highlights (New Layer icon in the Layers sidebar). Then I selected the Paintbrush Tool and set the foreground color to white and Hardness set to 0 in the tool's options. On the new layer, I used the Paintbrush Tool to paint over the brightest areas of the figure.

10. I then set this layer's Blend Mode to Overlay. This bumped up the highlights in the smoke, creating a more dramatic appearance.

11. I then created a new layer and set the foreground color to a light blue by clicking the Foreground color selection box, entering 49ABFF in the HEX text box of the Select Color dialog box, and clicking OK. I selected the Paint Bucket Tool and clicked the new layer to fill the entire layer with the light blue. I set the layer's Alpha to 28% in the Layers sidebar.

12. I set the blue fill layer's Blend Mode to Overlay in the Layers sidebar, as well. This placed a slight blue cast over the entire image, bringing the image together and also adding a somber mood, which I liked.

13. And finally, I wanted to saturate the smoke just a little further. I created another new layer (New Layer icon) and selected the Paintbrush Tool. I set the Paintbrush Tool's foreground color to a blue tone (click the Foreground color selection box, enter 38AFF0 in the HEX text box, and click OK), set the Hardness to 0, and lowered the Alpha to 50% in the tool's options. On the new layer, I roughly painted over the smoky figure with the blue tone.

14. I set this final layer's Blend Mode to Overlay and lowered its Alpha to 50% in the Layers sidebar. This gave the smoke a nice subtle blue hue, which enhanced the mood of the image, and my composition was complete.

Chrome

Source Images: "Picking an Apple" by Elena Elisseeva, "Field" by Lise Gagne

Creating the appearance of chrome is tricky business. Often times, people just assume a mirrored surface is gray and try to work around that. In this tutorial, I'll show how to pull off a convincing chrome effect simply by using portions of images to create the reflective look directly on an apple.

1. I started with the image of an apple. I chose this image because I liked the fingers surrounding the apple, which would allow me to create suitable reflections enhancing the chrome effect.

2. Next, I uploaded an image of a field with File > Import. This image would serve as the base of my chrome apple.

3. I selected the Transformation Tool and dragged the field layer to cover the apple, pressing Enter to confirm the move. I then selected the Eraser Tool and erased the edges of the field layer to leave an apple shaped portion of the field covering the fruit on the original layer.

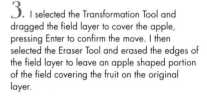

4. I then chose Select > Selection from Layer with the field layer still selected, and then I clicked the original apple layer in the Layers sidebar. I copied (Edit > Copy) and pasted (Edit > Paste) this selection onto a new layer, and dragged the newly copied layer above the field layer on the Layers sidebar. I chose Image > Desaturate, leaving a grayscale apple layer on top of the field layer.

5. I set this layer's Blend Mode to Overlay, and lowered the layer's Alpha to 46% in the Layers sidebar. This applied some of the original apple's highlights and shadows to the new apple.

6. Next, I wanted to enhance the shadows around the apple to enhance the depth. With the apple selection still selected, I created a new layer. I selected the Paintbrush Tool and set the foreground color to black (Restore Colors button), set the Hardness to 0, and lowered the Alpha to 12%. On the new layer, I lightly painted around the edges of the apple to darken them and create the deeper sense of depth.

7. The essence of chrome is in its reflections. I started by attempting to create a reflection for the person's thumb. After selecting the original layer in the Layers sidebar, I chose the Lasso Selection Tool and created a rough selection around the figure's thumb. I copied and pasted the thumb onto a new layer (Edit > Copy and Edit > Paste).

8. I selected Edit > Transform > Flip Horizontal to flip my copied thumb, creating a mirror image of the original. I pressed Enter to confirm the transformation.

9. I dragged the thumb reflection layer above the field layer, but below the shadow and overlay layers, on the Layers sidebar. With the Eraser Tool selected, I erased around the thumb in the thumb reflection layer to extract it from its background.

10. I repeated the process to add reflections for the finger on the right, and two leaves above the apple. I wanted the palm of the figure's hand reflected on the bottom of the apple as well. With the Lasso Selection Tool selected, I made a selection around a portion of the figure's palm on the original layer and copied it onto a new layer with Edit > Copy and Edit > Paste. Using the Transformation Tool, I dragged the palm into position along the bottom of the apple.

11. I then dragged this layer above the field layer on the Layers sidebar. Using the Eraser Tool, I cleaned the edges of the layer to create the palm's reflection on the apple. I then used the Eraser Tool set at 0 Hardness and softened the edges of the thumb and finger reflection layers to blend these into the palm reflection.

12. When I was happy with the reflections, it was time to create a surface shine on the chrome apple. I made a selection around the apple again by choosing Select > Selection from Layer with the field layer selected. Then, I created a new layer (New Layer icon) and dragged it to the very top of the Layers sidebar. I selected the Gradient Fill Tool and dragged from top to bottom to create a gradient over the apple.

13. Using the Transformation Tool, I resized the gradient shine smaller to fit within the apple, but not completely covering it. I chose Image > Brightness & Contrast, lowered the Brightness by -93 and raised the Contrast by 16, then clicked OK. I set this layer's Blend Mode to Screen, and lowered the layer's Alpha to 52%. This gave me the shine I desired on the apple.

14. And finally, I wanted to blow out a couple highlights near the top of the apple. I created a new layer (New Layer icon) and dragged it to the top of the Layers sidebar. I selected the Paintbrush Tool. I set the foreground color to white (Switch Between Foreground and Background Colors button), and lowered the Paintbrush Hardness to 0. I then painted in a couple of highlight spots near the top-left part of the apple to blow out this area a little more, completing the image.

Stone

Source Images: "makeup and beauty treatment" by nitorphoto, "High quality marble" by scorpion26

In this tutorial, I'll turn a photograph of a person into a memorial statue. But I'm going to take it one step further and show a second effect, making the model in my image appear as if she were a statue to begin with, and a make-up artist is painting flesh right onto the stone.

1. I only wanted the left side of the model's face (viewer's right) turned to stone. Using the Lasso Selection Tool, I selected half of her face and her neck and copied this segment onto a new layer with Edit > Copy and Edit > Paste. I then selected Image > Desaturate to remove all color from the copied layer. This will be the base of the statue portion of the image. I then chose Select >Select None to remove the selection marquee.

2. I wanted to remove the iris and pupil from the eye on this portion of the figure. Using the Eye Dropper Tool, I sampled a gray tone from the desaturated portion of the face to set a gray foreground color. I selected the Paintbrush Tool with the Hardness set to 10 and the Alpha set to 30%. I painted the gray foreground color over the pupil and iris directly on the desaturated layer.

3. Next, I wanted to add stone texture to the figure's face. To do so, I imported an image with marble texture onto a new layer on the document using File > Import. I selected the desaturated face layer in the Layers sidebar and chose Select > Selection from Layer. With this area selected, I reselected the marble texture layer in the Layers sidebar and copied this selected area onto a new layer. I then set the newest layer's Blend Mode to Multiply to create the marble texture effect on the woman's face and clicked the Eye icon beside the imported marble image layer in the Layers sidebar to hide that layer. I chose Select > Select None to remove the selection marquee.

4. I wanted to make it look as if the skin was being painted over the marble textured side of the woman's face, so I needed to make the appearance of paint strokes on the edge where the skin meets the marble. To do this, I first made a duplicate copy of the original layer by selecting it in the Layers sidebar, clicking the Options button drop-down list arrow, and clicking Duplicate Layer. I dragged the new layer copy to the top of the list in the Layers sidebar.

5. Then, I applied a Layer Mask to this duplicate layer (Layer > Mask Layer). Initially, doing so hides the entire layer. By drawing on the Mask Layer, I'm able to draw in and uncover the hidden layer wherever I choose. I selected the Shape Brush Tool, chose a splattered brush shape in the tool's options, and drew along the edges of the stone area to give it the paint stroke appearance. If I made an error, I simply selected the Eraser Tool and dragged over any undesirable areas on the Mask Layer, just as I would on any normal layer.

6. I continued this process until I was happy with the look and amount of paint texture I had applied to the figure.

7. At this point, it was time to add some subtle shadows. I selected the desaturated face layer. I chose Image > Brightness & Contrast, lowered the Brightness to -16, and clicked OK. I also enhanced the shadows around the face. I created a new layer (New Layer icon) and dragged it under the marble texture layer. I selected the Paintbrush Tool set to 0 Hardness and 10% Alpha, and set the foreground color to black in the tool's options. Working on the new layer, I painted over the existing shadows on the areas around the stone figure's eyes, nose, lips, neck, cheekbone, and anywhere else shadows already appeared. I then set this layer's Blend Mode to Overlay in the Layers sidebar. I then created another new layer and carefully painted a subtle shadow under the edges of the skin where it met the stone.

8. To add even more interest to the image, I added some cracks to the stone texture of the face. I selected the desaturated face layer in the Layers sidebar again. I selected the Liquify Tool and set the Pressure to 3 and the Size to 14 in the tool's options. I created the cracks in the face by starting with a darkened area of the face, for example inside the mouth, dragging the tool in a haphazard manner to create the rough, imperfect cracks on the face.

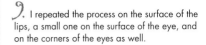

9. I repeated the process on the surface of the lips, a small one on the surface of the eye, and on the corners of the eyes as well.

10. I noticed some of the cracks became more dispersed than I wanted, or appeared more faint than desired. To darken the cracks, I simply created a new layer over the desaturated face layer and painted over the cracks in black with the Paintbrush Tool to strengthen any cracks that needed it.

11. Next, I sharpened the image overall to further boost the marble texture on the figure. To do so, I first flattened the image (Layer > Flatten Layers). I then duplicated the layer so I had two flattened copies to work with. On the top copy, I applied the Sharpen filter (Filter > Sharpen). This sharpened the image a lot more than I desired. Playing with the Alpha slider on the Layers sidebar enabled me to distribute the Sharpen effect to my liking. I lowered the Alpha of this layer to 15% for a subtle boost in sharpening.

Note

Sometimes, I want to merge all my layers into one, while maintaining all the working layers at the same time in case I want to go back to them later. To create both the flattened and unflattened layers in one document, first I flattened the entire image (Layer > Flatten Layers). Then I chose Select > Select All to make a selection around the entire canvas, then I copied it (Edit > Copy) onto my clipboard. Next, I clicked the Undo button twice to bring me back to my fully layered image. Next, I chose Edit > Paste, and this pasted my copied flattened layer into my working document on a new layer. I was now free to edit on my flatened layer while all my working layers remained intact underneath.

12. And finally, to bring the whole thing together, I created a new layer at the top of the Layers sidebar (New Layer icon). I filled the entire layer with a light brown tone (click the Foreground color selection box, enter C59F6D in the HEX text box, click OK, select the Paint Bucket Tool, and click the layer). I set the layer's Blend Mode to Overlay and lowered the Alpha to 25% in the Layers sidebar, which gave the whole image a slight tan overcast, unifying the whole image a little further.

Canvas Earth

Source Images: "On the top of world" by Oleg Prikhodko, "Age Profile" by Duncan Walker

*f*rom Italy shaped like a boot, to Slovenia being shaped like a chicken, we see that God (or insert deity of your choice) has an artistic side to him (or her, if you prefer). In this tutorial, we're going to prove this fact by taking a naturally formed mountain and reshaping it in the guise of an old man's face.

1. I started with a source image of a mountain side. I liked the shape of this image and figured it would be suitable to graft the man's face onto.

2. Next, I uploaded the image of the side profile of a man's face (File > Import). I flipped the face horizontally (Edit > Transform > Flip Horizontal) to match the direction of the mountain. This will be the guide I use in building the mountain face.

3. I lowered the Alpha setting for the face layer to 50% on the Layers sidebar and selected the Transformation Tool. I dragged the face to sit along the side of the mountain and pressed Enter when I was happy with the face's position in the composition.

4. I reset the face layer's Alpha to 100%. I then removed the background around the face on its layer. As the background was basically a single colored space, I simply selected the Magic Wand Tool and clicked the background to select it, and then cut out the background portion (Edit > Cut).

5. Next, it was all a matter of finding suitable portions from the original mountain layer to fit in the various sections of the man's face. I started with the nose. There was a piece protruding out from the side of the mountain that resembled the shape of a nose upside down. I clicked the layer in the Layers sidebar, and then I made a selection around this segment using the Lasso Selection Tool and copied (Edit > Copy) and pasted (Edit > Paste) it onto a new layer. Then I dragged the layer over the face layer on the Layers sidebar.

6. I then flipped this piece vertically (Edit >Transform > Flip Vertical). I selected the face layer and lowered the Alpha of the layer to 50%. Using the Transformation Tool, I dragged and resized the copied layer to align with the old man's nose. Then I pressed Enter when I was pleased with the positioning of the segment.

7. Using the Eraser Tool set to 50 Hardness, I erased around the segment to leave just the area of the nose and upper lip remaining.

8. Next, I wanted to add the lower mouth section to the figure. Going back to the original mountain layer, I made a selection around a portion of the mountain with the Lasso Selection Tool and copied and pasted it onto a new layer (Edit > Copy and Edit > Paste). Using the Transformation Tool, I dragged and rotated this segment to fit under the upper lip in my previous layer to create the appearance of the figure's lower mouth, pressing Enter to finish the transform. I then used the Eraser Tool to erase the areas extending beyond the old man layer.

9. I repeated the process to add an eye to the figure. I found a section of the mountain with a heavy shadow, which had the appearance of the deep in-set eye of the old man. I selected it on the original layer, copied and pasted, moved and rotated, and then fine-tuned with the Eraser Tool.

10. To add the man's forehead to the image, I needed to find a wide, clear portion of the mountain to use. Reselecting the original layer, I selected the surface of the mountain using the Lasso Selection Tool and copied it onto a new layer (Edit > Copy and Edit > Paste).

11. Using the Transformation Tool, I rotated the piece to line up with the man's forehead. Then I pressed Enter to confirm this move.

12. I then added aging lines to the side of the man's head to create the fish-eye look. I selected a crack in the mountain on the original layer, and repeated the previous process to apply it to the man's face.

13. I repeated this process several times to compile the rest of the man's face. When I finished assembling my figure's main facial features, I was left with something like this. As you can see, the facial features are now recognizable, but I wanted to enhance the general look of the entire head a little better.

14. To do so, I superimposed the layer of the old man directly onto the face of the mountain. I selected the old man layer, set it back to 100% Alpha, and changed the Blend Mode to Hardlight in the Layers sidebar. I needed to adjust the darkness of the layer a bit more. I chose Image > Brightness & Contrast and lowered the Brightness by -19 and raised the Contrast by 29. I clicked OK to confirm the adjustment.

15. Using the Eraser Tool set at 0 Hardness, I erased the overblown white section along the left side of the face. I duplicated this layer (Layer > Duplicate Layer) and set the copied layer's Blend Mode to Add and its Alpha to 75% in the Layers sidebar.

16. All that was now left was enhancing the highlights and shadows. First, I created a new layer for the highlights. Using the Paintbrush Tool with white set as my foreground color (click Restore Colors and then click Switch Between Foreground and Background Colors) and the Hardness set to 0, I painted along the figure's nose, cheekbone, over the eyelid, and over the lips to accentuate these areas. I then set this layer's Blend Mode to Overlay.

17. And finally, I added shadows to the figure's face. I created another new layer for the shadows. I changed the foreground color to black (Restore Colors button). With the Paintbrush Tool still selected, I painted over the figure's eye, around the nose, and any other areas that had depth and creases. This enhanced the already existing shadows, completing the image.

Robot Frog

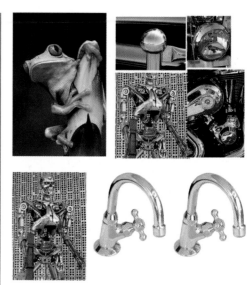

Half robot, half frog. In this tutorial, I'm basically emphasizing the importance of spending that extra time in the planning stage for your composite images: finding the most suitable source images and even sketching out the basic compositions before the actual image creation stage. After all, why create more work for yourself, such as putting some copied content in the wrong place, when you don't need to?

Source Images: "Red-eyed Tree Frog Peeping Around Plant" by Mark Kostich, "Terminator" by Athewma, "Motorcycle Chrome" by tillsonburg, "Motorcycle Chrome" by Linda Bucklin, "well polished knob" by Wired Gallery and Frame, "Rubinetto" by Afonso Lima

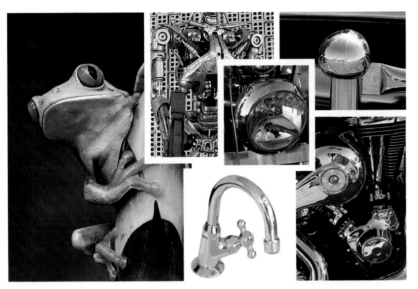

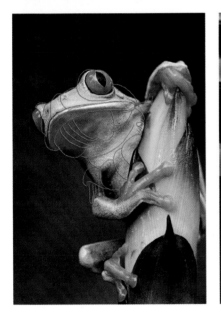

1. So the first step was to gather source images. First, I started with an image of a frog. Any animal will do for this type of project, but I prefer to stick with animals with an easily identifiable figure. Once you go on to cover the figure in metal, you want the underlying creature to still read clearly regardless of the material it's constructed from. I gathered images with various chrome, engine, and robotic parts. While doing this, I kept on the lookout for pieces that had a relatively similar tone in reflection to them. Of course, you can apply the necessary changes with non-uniform source images, but it's always easier to spend the time now in the initial source hunt stage instead of trying to fix source images later. I began the composition by opening the image of the frog in Phoenix. Then I imported the other source images into the file (File > Import). I hid all but the frog layer by clicking the Eye icon beside each layer to hide in the Layers sidebar.

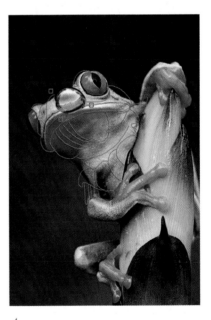

2. It was time to start drawing out a blueprint for the mode of attack on this image. Still in the planning stage, I spent a little time sketching out the basic outlines of where I wanted to apply chrome in the image. I created a new layer by clicking the New Layer icon on the Layers sidebar. Using the Paintbrush Tool set with a contrasting red selected as the foreground color (use the Foreground color selection box in the tool's options to select the color), I drew guidelines for the areas where I wanted to add chrome segments.

3. So now armed with a ground plan and source images, it was all a matter of following the outline. First, I unhid the chrome source layers to look for appropriate areas to use. Using the Lasso Selection Tool, I roughly selected a small segment from one of the chrome source images, copied it (Edit > Copy), and pasted it (Edit > Paste) onto a new layer. I clicked the Eye icon beside the source image layer in the Layers sidebar to hide it again. I also chose Select > Select None to remove the selection marquee from the pasted chrome segment.

4. Then it was all a matter of skewing the pieces to fit the guidelines as best I could. First, I selected the Transformation Tool to place the segment roughly in place, and pressed Enter to confirm the move. Then, using the Distortion Tool, I resized the copied segment to fit into one of the outlined segments on the rough sketch created in Step 2, then pressed Enter to confirm the transformation.

5. I repeated the process outlined in Steps 3 and 4 to create copied segments to cover the majority of the figure. I was careful to select segments in the source images that were roughly in the shape of the sketched segments. As an aside, I like to start with the pieces furthest from the camera, then work my way forward. This makes sure that the segments that appear closest to the camera are higher up in the list in the Layers sidebar.

6. For the frog's mouth, I needed a wider piece of chrome. I decided to copy a segment from an image of a faucet source image for this part, because the top of the faucet in the image offers an area with a longer arched piece that would fit the shape of the mouth relatively well. So again, I just extracted the pipe by selecting and then copying and pasting it, and used the Transformation and Distortion Tools to form the pasted segment around the mouth area.

7. There, now the frog was covered in chrome. But I noticed a few remnants of the original background remained visible on the edges. Using the Clone Stamp Tool, I sampled a clean area of the background (Shift + Click) and just painted over the unwanted areas around the chrome directly on the original frog layer.

8. Now that I was satisfied with the look of the basic figure, it was time to add a few shadows to this guy. I started by selecting one of the chrome layers. Then I created a new layer directly above this one. On this new layer, I used a soft, black Paintbrush Tool, and painted in shadows on the lower areas of the chrome segment, following the contours of the piece.

9. I repeated the process described in Step 8 to create new layers sandwiched in between the chrome layers and painted shadows on the new layers until I was satisfied with the look of the figure.

10. And to further accentuate the shadows, I added a few slight highlights to the top edges of the chrome pieces. I inserted a new highlight layer at the top of the Layers sidebar (New Layer icon), selected the Paintbrush Tool, and set it to a small size and white foreground color in the tool's options. On the new layers, I then painted the edges and existing highlighted areas for emphasis.

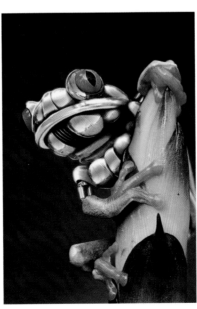

11. I wanted to add a slight hint of the plant reflecting onto the frog as well. I created a new layer, selected the Paintbrush Tool, selected green as the foreground color in the tool's options, and painted along the edge where the frog meets the plant. I then set this layer's Blend Mode to Overlay in the Layers sidebar to give a slight green cast on this area.

12. And finally, I created a final new layer at the top of the Layers sidebar, clicked the Foreground color selection box, entered CB9A00 in the HEX text box of the Select Color dialog box, and clicked OK, and I then used the Paintbrush Tool to fill the new layer with the brown color. I then set this layer's Blend Mode to Overlay and lowered the Alpha of the layer to 30% in the Layers sidebar. This brought the image together by casting a slight, uniform yellow tone to the whole image.

Animal Dress-Up

Source Images: "Attitude" by Sloane Court Photography, "Tabby kitten playing" by Eagle Eye Imaging , "Roaarr!!!" by Andrea Simonato

As much of an atrocity as it may be, you can't deny the adorableness of dressing up your pets! Well, maybe you can, but I'm going to do it anyway. In this tutorial, I'll be taking a photo of a kitty, and turning him into one rocked out feline.

1. First, I started off with the base image. I chose an image of a youngster with a guitar, as this would give me an interesting pose with attitude that I desired.

2. Next, I imported the image of the roaring kitten (File > Import). Using the Lasso Selection Tool, I made a rough selection around the cat's head, then copied (Edit > Copy) and pasted (Edit > Paste) the selection onto a new layer. I chose Select > Select None to remove the selection marquee.

3. I hid the kitten source layer by clicking its Eye icon in the Layers sidebar. With the copied kitten face layer selected in the Layers sidebar, I chose Edit > Transform > Flip Horizontally to flip the kitten's face. I then selected the Transformation Tool to move, resize, and rotate the kitten's head to fit closer proportionately to the original figure's body, and then pressed Enter when I was happy with the size.

4. Next it was time to remove the unwanted areas around the cat's head. Using the Eraser Tool set at 10 Hardness, I erased around the cat's head, leaving a feather edge due to the softness of the Eraser Tool.

5. The top of the original boy's head was exposed at the top, so I wanted to remove that area. I hid the copied kitten face layer by clicking its Eye icon in the Layers sidebar. I selected the original layer, then using the Lasso Selection Tool to select a clean portion of the background, I copied and pasted it onto a new layer (Edit > Copy and Edit > Paste). I used the Transformation Tool to drag this selection over the exposed part of the boy's head to hide it, pressing Enter to finish the change. I then clicked the box for the kitten face layer's Eye icon to redisplay the layer.

6. I wanted to edit the fur around the cat's head better so it wasn't just a soft blur. I selected the kitten face layer and then zoomed in. I selected the Eraser Tool and set the Hardness to 50 and the Size to 2 and I carefully erased in an inward motion from the outside of the cat's head towards the center to create the fur effect around the figure. I zoomed back out when I was satisfied with the changes.

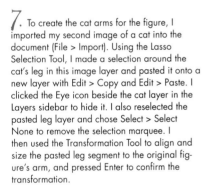

7. To create the cat arms for the figure, I imported my second image of a cat into the document (File > Import). Using the Lasso Selection Tool, I made a selection around the cat's leg in this image layer and pasted it onto a new layer with Edit > Copy and Edit > Paste. I clicked the Eye icon beside the cat layer in the Layers sidebar to hide it. I also reselected the pasted leg layer and chose Select > Select None to remove the selection marquee. I then used the Transformation Tool to align and size the pasted leg segment to the original figure's arm, and pressed Enter to confirm the transformation.

8. As I did with the cat's face earlier, I erased the surrounding elements around the cat's arm, then emphasized the furry edges with the small Eraser Tool again. I was careful to clean up the area where the cat's leg met the edge of the sleeve of the T-shirt.

9. I noticed some remnants of the boy's hand were still showing through. I hid the cat leg layer for the time being. I selected the original layer and clicked the New Layer icon in the Layers sidebar to create a new layer above the original layer in the Layers sidebar. Using the Eye Dropper Tool, I clicked an area on the guitar near the boy's hand to sample that color. Then, working on the new layer, I selected the Paintbrush Tool and painted over the boy's hand with the sampled foreground color to hide it. I then redisplayed the cat leg layer by clicking the box for its Eye icon in the Layers sidebar.

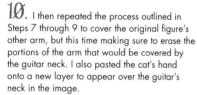

10. I then repeated the process outlined in Steps 7 through 9 to cover the original figure's other arm, but this time making sure to erase the portions of the arm that would be covered by the guitar neck. I also pasted the cat's hand onto a new layer to appear over the guitar's neck in the image.

11. Next it was time to add shadows. I created a new layer underneath the arm layers by selecting the layer in the Layers sidebar and clicking the New Layer icon. On this layer, I selected the Paintbrush Tool with black set as the foreground color and 0 Hardness in the tool's options, and painted a shadow along the bottom edge of the arm. I lowered this layer's Alpha to 80%, but you could adjust to your liking depending on how strongly you painted in the shadows to begin with. I created another layer and applied the same technique under the cat's head to create some depth there as well.

12. And to create a shadow underneath each of the sleeve edges, I used the same process. But this time, I created a new layer above the cat's arm layer and painted in the area appearing directly under the sleeves with the Paintbrush Tool.

13. I wanted to bring the whisker ends that were lost during the face swap back onto the cat's face. I created a new layer, then took the Paintbrush Tool, set white as the foreground color (click the Switch Between Foreground and Background Colors button), set the Size to 3 in the tool's options, and carefully drew in whiskers. Using the Eraser Tool, I was able to taper off the edges so that the whiskers came to a point for more realism. I continued this process until I was happy with the number of protruding whiskers.

14. For a few final touches, I wanted to create a slight vignette effect over the entire image. I created a new layer (New Layer icon) and dragged it to the top of the list in the Layers sidebar. I selected the Gradient Fill Tool, set the Mode to Radial in the tool's options, and dragged it diagonally from the cat's face to a lower corner to get a spotlight effect over the cat as seen above. I then set this layer's Blend Mode to Overlay and Alpha to 22% in the Layers sidebar.

15. And finally, I created a new layer (New Layer icon), filled it with a pink tone with the Paint Bucket Tool, then set this layer's Blend Mode to Overlay and changed the Alpha to 14%. I created another new layer, but this time filled it with a dark green color and set the Blend Mode to Overlay and the Alpha to 11%. These color overlay layers gave the entire image a more uniform tone and helped to bring the entire image together.

Creating an MP3 Player

It seems every banner advertisement online is offering free MP3 players these days. But the truth is, nobody is giving away free MP3 players. So why not create one of your very own? In this tutorial, I'll be showing you how to create your own MP3 player from scratch in Aviary.

Source Image: "Happy Holidays" by Meowza Katz

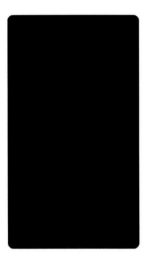 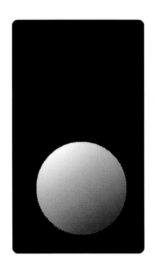 

1. I started by creating a new image (File > New Document) with a white canvas set at 1200px X 1600px. The first step in creating the player was to draw the general outline of the player. I selected the Rectangular Shape Tool, set the Corner Rounding value to 30, and set the foreground color to black (Restore Colors button) in the tool's options. I created a new layer (Layer > New Layer) and drew a rectangular shape as the base for the player. You may need to zoom out of the image to see the entire canvas, making it easier to draw in your rectangle to the desired size. I left some white space on the bottom to add my reflective shadow in later on.

2. I wanted to create a menu rocker button for the MP3 player. I selected the Elliptical Selection Tool and created a circular selection on my player. I held down the Ctrl key on the keyboard while dragging the Tool to constraint the proportions to a circle. I created a new layer (New Layer icon), selected the Gradient Fill Tool, and dragged diagonally from the top left toward the bottom right to create a gradient in the selected circular area. I then chose Select > Select None to remove the selection marquee.

3. To create a center button in the middle of the rocker, I created another new layer above the rocker layer by clicking the New Layer icon. With the Ellptical Selection Tool selected, I created a circular selection in the middle of the rocker button on the new layer by pressing Ctrl while dragging and filled it with black using the Paint Bucket Tool.

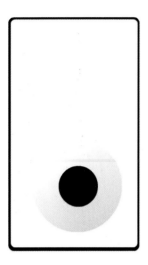

4. Next, I wanted to cast a shine on the player for that sleek, modern look. I created a new layer with the New Layer icon and dragged the new layer above the base layer and below the rocker button layers on the Layers sidebar. I selected the Rectangular Shape Tool, set the Corner Rounding to 25 and set the foreground color to white (Switch Between Foreground and Background Colors button) in the tool's options. I dragged the Tool within the confines of the base layer but slightly smaller.

5. I wanted to apply a gradient to the shine so I chose Select > Selection from Layer to draw a selection around the newly drawn shape. Then, I selected the Gradient Fill Tool and dragged in a diagonal direction starting from the top-left corner to the bottom-right corner to create the gradient.

6. Then, I deselected the layer (Select > Select None). I selected the Polygonal Selection Tool and clicked points around the areas I wanted to remove from the shine layer, leaving a diagonal shine on the top right portion of the player. Then, I chose Edit > Cut to remove the unwanted areas from the image. I chose Select > Select None, and lowered the Alpha of this layer to 43% in the Layers sidebar.

7. To create the window on the player, I created another new layer with the New Layer icon and dragged the layer to the top of the list in the Layers sidebar. I chose the Rectangular Shape Tool and set the Corner Rounding value to 30. With black set as my foreground color (click the Restore Colors button in the tool's options), I dragged to create the rectangular window shape right over the reflection on the new layer, creating the base for the window.

8. I wanted to create a gray border around the window to give it more of an inset 3D appearance. So I made a selection around the entire window (Select > Selection from Layer), then set a 5 pixel border selection around it (Select > Modify > Border, enter 5 in the text box, and click OK). With the border selected, I set my foreground color to a gray tone (click the Foreground color selection box, enter A6A6A6 in the # text box, and click OK) and filled in the border selection with the Paint Bucket Tool by clicking anywhere within the selection. You may need to zoom in to the image closer in order to see the interior of the selection to target the Paint Bucket click. I then chose Select > Select None to remove the selection marquee.

9. Next, I wanted to make the icons for the menu pad. I selected the Text Tool and clicked on the top portion of the menu rocker button to add a Text layer. I set the Text Tool's color to a light gray by clicking the Color box in the tool's options, entering CCCCCC in the text box at the top of the palette that opens, and pressing Enter. I also set the Size to 32 and left the font set to Arial in the tool's options. I typed "MENU" to add the top menu rocker button choice. Then, I selected the Transformation Tool to drag the text into the exact position I wanted, then pressed Enter to confirm the move.

10. To create the play, rewind, and fast forward icons, I started with a triangle. Using the Polygonal Selection Tool, I clicked the three corners of the triangle to make a triangular selection. Then, I created a new layer and filled the selection on that layer with light gray using the Paint Bucket Tool. I chose Select > Select None to remove the selection marquee.

11. Then I selected the Transformation Tool, reduced the size of the triangle and moved it into position on the right side of the menu rocker button, and pressed Enter when I was happy with the size and position. I duplicated this layer (Layer > Duplicate Layer) and used the Transformation Tool to move the second triangle beside the previous triangle. Again, it helps to zoom in 200% or more in order to work with the small triangles much easier. Then I created one more layer and drew a small rectangle along the side of the rightmost triangle to complete my fast forward/skip icon. I then Ctrl+ clicked the two triangle and rectangle layers in the Layers sidebar and merged them (Layer > Merge Layers) onto one single layer.

12. I duplicated the fast forward button (Layer > Duplicate Layer) and flipped it horizontally for my rewind button (Edit > Transform > Flip Horizontal). Then, I selected the Transformation Tool and dragged the copied icon to the left side of the menu rocker button. To make the play/pause icon, I again made a duplicate copy of the fast forward button, but this time I erased one of the triangles and added one more rectangle to the right side instead. Then, with the Transformation Tool, I moved the play/pause icon to the bottom of the rocker button.

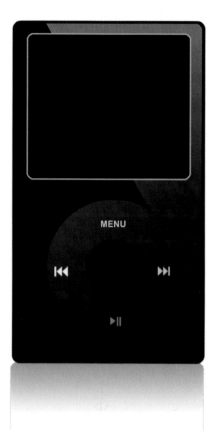

13. To enhance the modern look, I wanted to apply a surface reflection for the player. I duplicated the base layer, and then dragged it below the original base layer on the Layers sidebar. I made a selection around the copied layer (Select > Selection from Layer) and selected the Gradient Fill Tool. I set a light gradient to the image that disperses as it draws further from the player. To do so, I simply dragged the Gradient Tool from bottom to top in the selection to create this appearance, and I raised the Brightness (Image > Brightness & Contrast) by 50. The amount of Brightness you apply will depend on how heavy you apply your gradient, and how much surface reflection you want based on personal preference. Then, I selected the Transformation Tool and dragged the reflection to sit underneath the MP3 player on the canvas, then pressed Enter to confirm the move.

14. And finally, I wanted to include an image on my player's window. I imported a festive painting of Aviary's birds into my document (File > Import) for decoration. I then used the Transformation Tool to resize it and position it within the confines of the window and my player was complete.

Anatomy Scramble

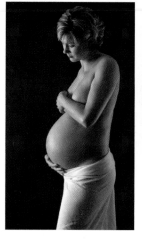

$\mathcal{S}$urgery gone wrong. It sounds like a new special coming soon to cable television. In this tutorial, I'm going to create a "surgical error," taking a photograph of a pregnant woman and grafting a man's head onto her belly. I never thought I'd say that sentence in my life.

Source Images: "Portrait of Motherhood" by Digital Savant LLC, "Sunglasses and Scream" by Nuno Silva.

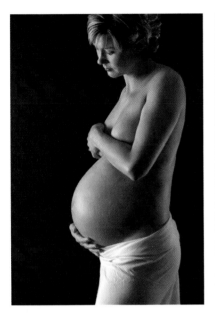

1. I started by loading an image of a pregnant woman. There was plenty of space on the woman's stomach, as well as negative space in the background, which would work perfectly for the composition I had in mind.

2. Next was to find an image of a face that I could graft onto the woman's stomach. I found an image of a screaming face that would look amusing to blend into the pregnant woman's anatomy, so I uploaded this image into the document (File > Import).

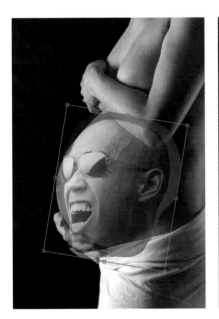

3. I moved the face to position on the area of the woman's stomach. First, I set the Alpha of the screaming face layer to 50% in the Layers sidebar. This made it easier to see exactly where I was moving the face to. I selected the Transformation Tool and dragged and resized the face to fit along the woman's stomach. I rotated the face to fit the confines of the woman's stomach, as well, then pressed Enter to confirm the transformation.

4. Using the Eraser Tool set to 0 Hardness, I erased the surrounding elements of the face on its layer to blend it into the skin of the woman. I then reset the Alpha for the face layer to 100% on the Layers sidebar.

5. I noticed that the saturation level in the screaming face source was lower than that of the woman's layer, so it was a simple matter of raising the saturation on the screaming face. With the face layer selected, I chose Image > Hue & Saturation. I raised the Saturation by 16 and raised the Brightness by 4. I then clicked OK to confirm the adjustment.

6. I needed to then eliminate the portion of the woman's abdomen that was exposed past the screaming face by copying a segment of the background and using the segment to cover the woman's stomach. After selecting the original layer with the woman in the Layers sidebar, I selected the Lasso Selection Tool and made a selection around part of the background. I then copied (Edit > Copy) and pasted (Edit > Paste) this selection onto a new layer.

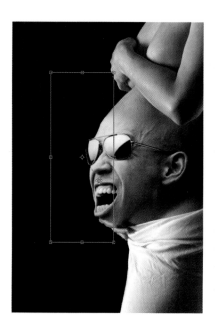

7. Using the Transformation Tool, I dragged this copied segment over the woman's belly to the left of the face. Using the Eraser Tool set to 0 Hardness, I then softened the edges around the segment to blend it into the rest of the background.

8. The copied segment covered part of the woman's hand. I wanted the woman's hand exposed, so it appears as if she's holding the screaming face. So I selected the original layer again and using the Lasso Selection Tool, I made a selection around the upper portion of the woman's hand and copied and pasted it onto a new layer (Edit > Copy and Edit > Paste). I then dragged this layer above the face layer on the Layers sidebar.

9. Working on the copied hand layer, I used the Eraser Tool to expose the screaming face's lower lip area. I wanted to have the screaming man's bottom lip overlapping the woman's hand very clearly, so I copied the lip from the original screaming face layer and pasted it onto a new layer as well. Then I dragged this layer above the woman's hand layer on the Layers sidebar.

10. Using the Transformation Tool, I dragged the copied lip layer to situate it back on the screaming face and hanging off of the woman's hand. Then I pressed Enter to confirm the move.

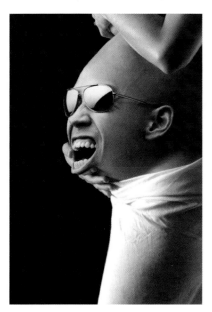 

11. I selected the Eraser Tool and erased around the edges of the copied lip on its layer to extract it cleanly, creating the illusion of it being above the hand. I then created a new layer (New Layer icon) and dragged it below the lip layer on the Layers sidebar.

12. Finally, I added a slight blue tint to the entire image to bring the whole thing together. I created a new layer (New Layer icon) and dragged it to the top of the Layers sidebar, selected a light blue foreground color (click the Foreground color selection box, enter 89AFB0 in the # text box, and click OK), and then filled the layer using the Paint Bucket Tool. I set this layer's Blend Mode to Overlay and lowered the Alpha to 83% in the Layers sidebar, and the image was complete.

Creating a Sea Monster

Of all the undiscovered creatures that have fascinated cryptozoologists and the public alike, few have garnered as much attention as the Loch Ness Monster. From the days of the famed "Surgeon's photo" from 1934, people have been continually making false claims of evidence of Nessie for over 70 years. But a grainy black and white photo just doesn't hold up in this modern age of photography. So in this tutorial, we're going to update the old photographs of the Loch Ness Monster and make our very own image of Nessie to perpetuate this hoax even further!

Source Images: "Orta san giulio" by E_B_E, "Epic Dinosaur" by Daniel Bendjy, "Dinosaur Face" by Dave Skinner.

1. I started with an image of a lake. I then imported an image of a plastic dinosaur figurine (File > Import).

2. I wanted to start by creating the creature's head and neck emerging from the waters. I selected the Lasso Selection Tool and made a rough selection around the dinosaur's neck and copied (Edit > Copy) and pasted (Edit > Paste) it onto a new layer. Chose Select > Select None to remove the selection marquee.

3. I hid the original dinosaur layer for the time being by clicking its Eye icon in the Layers sidebar. With the copied layer selected, I used the Transformation Tool to rotate and resize the dinosaur's neck to make it appear as if it were coming out of the water. I pressed Enter to confirm the transformation. Then I simply used the Eraser Tool to erase around the dinosaur neck, extracting it from its orange background.

4. Next, I imported a second source of a dinosaur figurine's head (File > Import). I liked the clarity and detail in this source image much better than the head from the first dinosaur source.

5. Using the Eraser Tool, I erased the elements surrounding the dinosaur's head on the newly imported layer. Then, I selected the Transformation Tool and resized and aligned the dinosaur head to sit on the top of the original dinosaur's neck, pressing Enter when I was happy with the placement. I used the Eraser Tool to remove any excess portions of the dinosaur's neck from the first dinosaur layer, which remained exposed past the newly added face.

6. I wanted the neck of the creature to match the green tint of the figure's head. I selected the creature's neck layer and chose Image > Hue & Saturation. I slid the Hue slider to the right to 56 to give the neck a green tone and clicked OK. I then merged the head and the neck layers. To do this, I held down the Ctrl key as I clicked each of these layers on the Layers sidebar and chose Layer > Merge Layers when I had them both selected.

7. Next, I added humps protruding from the water behind the monster's neck to suggest the size of a large creature in the water. I made the first dinosaur source layer visible again by clicking the box for its Eye icon in the Layers sidebar. I chose the Lasso Selection Tool and made a selection around the figure's hump and copied it onto a new layer (Edit > Copy and Edit > Paste). I then rehid the source layer and chose Select > Select None to remove the selection marquee.

8. Using the Eraser Tool, I erased around the hump, leaving it extracted on the copied layer. I selected the Transformation Tool and dragged the hump to sit behind the creature's head and appear as if it were protruding from the water, then pressed Enter when I was pleased with its placement on the surface.

9. I added a second hump as described in Steps 7 and 8, and repeated the process to include the dinosaur's tail appearing from the water, as well.

10. Next, I wanted to create reflections in the water. I duplicated the creature's head layer (Layer > Duplicate Layer) and dragged the duplicated layer under the original head layer on the Layers sidebar. I then mirrored the duplicated layer by selecting Edit > Transform > Flip Vertical and dragged it below the original head on the canvas using the Transformation Tool. I pressed Enter to confirm the move.

Aviary

More Than One Way to Skin a Cat: Create Eye-Popping Effects Using Aviary

11. Using the Eraser Tool with the Hardness set to 0, I faded the reflection near the bottom by dragging the tool across the bottom to subtly erase it.

12. I added highlights to the figure next. As the light was hitting the figure from behind, I decided to add a backlit effect to the creature. With the creature's head layer selected, I made a selection around the entire segment (Select > Selection from Layer). I created a new layer (New Layer icon), made sure it was selected, and then selected the Paintbrush Tool. I selected white as the foreground color, set the Hardness to 0, and set the Alpha to 50%. I then painted along the right edge of the creature's head and neck to create the highlight.

13. To further enhance the highlight, I created another layer for highlights. With the Paintbrush Tool still selected, I raised the Hardness to 50 and raised the Alpha to 100%. I then drew a thin line along the right edge of the figure's neck to create the stark line of highlight. I then chose Select > Select None to remove the selection marquee.

14. I repeated the process across the creature's humps and tail to add highlights to the entire figure.

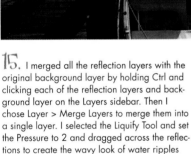

15. I merged all the reflection layers with the original background layer by holding Ctrl and clicking each of the reflection layers and background layer on the Layers sidebar. Then I chose Layer > Merge Layers to merge them into a single layer. I selected the Liquify Tool and set the Pressure to 2 and dragged across the reflections to create the wavy look of water ripples across the reflections.

16. I wanted to add a yellow tint to the highlights across the figure's highlights. I created a new layer (New Layer icon) and dragged it above the highlight layers on the Layers sidebar. I selected the Paintbrush Tool and set the foreground to a dark yellow color (click the Foreground color selection box, enter BB965B in the # text box, and click OK), and set the Hardness to 0. I painted over the highlights on the new layer and set the layer's Blend Mode to Overlay.

17. And finally, I gave the entire image a slight yellow tint. I set my foreground color to a muted tan color (#AD9F88). Then, I created a new layer and dragged it to the top of the list on the Layers sidebar. I filled the entire layer with the foreground color using the Paint Bucket Tool. I set the layer's Blend Mode to Overlay and the image was done.

Cyborg

As a young child, I was fascinated with science fiction, especially the idea of robots. I'd spend days with my friends gathering cardboard boxes in futile attempts to craft our own cyborgs to do our bidding. Now, with the power of Phoenix, I'm able to travel back to my childhood days and build the mechanical friend I have always wanted. In this tutorial, I'll show you just how I went about creating my very own cyborg.

Source Image: "Young pretty woman receiving face massage" by Yuri Arcurs

1. I started with an interesting source image of a woman receiving a facial massage. I wanted to manipulate the image to make it appear as if the hands were removing the woman's face.

2. First, I wanted to separate the hands and face from the rest of the image. I made a copy of the original layer (Layer > Duplicate Layer). I selected the Eraser Tool, and erased everything but the hands and the face on the duplicated layer.

Note

I created a new layer in between my original and duplicated layers, and filled the layer in with green using the Paint Bucket Tool to cover the original layer for the time being. This enabled me to see what portions of the image were being erased and which parts remained, which would have been difficult to decipher had I tried to work on the duplicated layer with the same original image on a layer directly below it. When I was finished, I deleted the green layer by clicking it in the Layers sidebar and then clicking the Drop Layers (trashcan) icon in the sidebar.

3. I selected the Transformation Tool and dragged the duplicated layer higher up on the canvas to offset it against the original image. I then pressed Enter to confirm the move.

4. I wanted to get rid of the hands and lips on the original layer. First, I made a duplicate of my original layer (Layer > Duplicate Layer). I selected the Eye Dropper Tool and clicked on the background area beside the hands on the duplicated layer. Then, I selected the Paintbrush Tool with the Hardness set to 0 and painted over the hands with the sampled color directly on the original layer. I repeated this process to remove the lips by sampling the woman's skin color around her face and painting over the lips. Obviously, the more work I put in during this stage the better, but it didn't need to be perfect, as I'd be applying a strong blur to this layer eventually.

5. Next, I created a seam running down the figure's face to add to the manufactured effect. I created a new layer (New Layer icon) and dragged it above the duplicated face layer on the Layers sidebar. Using the Elliptical Shape Tool, I drew very narrow shapes down the center of the face to create the base for the seam.

6. I set the seam layer's Blend Mode to Overlay. I wanted to add a bevel to this layer to make it look more three-dimensional. I clicked the Layer Filters icon on the bottom of the Layers sidebar to bring up the list of filter options. I checked the Bevel check box to apply the Bevel. I changed the Quality to High, increased the Strength to 8, changed the Angle to 128, and set the Distance to 4. I then clicked OK. This applied a highlight across the right side of the seam, giving the line more depth.

7. The mask layer was still lacking the artificial look I desired. So I decided to simulate a plastic effect by creating a shiny look over the entire surface of the mask. I clicked the New Layer icon to create a new layer above the line layer in the Layers sidebar. Starting with the left cheekbone, I simply took the Elliptical Shape Tool with white set as the foreground color (click Restore Colors and then click Switch Between Foreground and Background Colors) and drew a circle over the figure's cheek.

8. With the Distortion Tool selected, I warped the circle to a skewed oval shape to bend along the woman's cheekbone. I pressed Enter to confirm the transformation when I was pleased with the general shape of the shine.

9. I wanted to fade the shine near the bottom. So I selected the Eraser Tool and set the tool's Size to 136 and the Alpha to 20% and clicked on the bottom of the shine to give the appearance of the shine gradually fading. I duplicated this layer (Layer > Duplicate Layer) and flipped the duplicated shine (Edit > Transform > Flip Horizontal). Then, I selected the Transformation Tool and dragged the duplicated shine over to the right cheekbone to create a mirror image of the one on the left cheek. I pressed Enter when I was pleased with the shine's placement on the cheek.

10. I wanted to create further shines on the face to really give the appearance the face was constructed of plastic. Next, I decided to put a big shine on the forehead. I created a new layer (New Layer icon) and selected the Elliptical Shape Tool and white as my foreground color. Working on the new layer, I drew a big circle on the center of the face to begin.

11. Again, I selected the Eraser Tool and tapered off the shine across the bottom of the circle. I also erased out any portions of the shine that were obtruding on the woman's facial features.

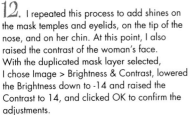

12. I repeated this process to add shines on the mask temples and eyelids, on the tip of the nose, and on her chin. At this point, I also raised the contrast of the woman's face. With the duplicated mask layer selected, I chose Image > Brightness & Contrast, lowered the Brightness down to -14 and raised the Contrast to 14, and clicked OK to confirm the adjustments.

13. I further enhanced the appearance of an artificial mask by creating rivets on the sides of the woman's face. This was easily done by first creating a new layer and drawing a dark brown circle using the Elliptical Shape Tool. Then, using the Distortion Tool, I reshaped the circle to appear as if it were a hole on the side of the woman's face, and pressed Enter when I was happy with the shape and placement of the circle.

14. Then I made a selection around the hole (Select > Selection from Layer). I selected the Paintbrush Tool and changed the foreground color to a lighter tan color (click the foreground color selection box in the tool's options, enter 8E7160 in the # text box, and click OK). Using the Paintbrush Tool, I drew along the left inner edge of the rivet directly on its layer. I duplicated this layer (Layer > Duplicate Layer) and flipped the duplicate horizontally (Edit > Transform > Flip Horizontal). Then I dragged the duplicated copy to the right side of the woman's face.

15. Next, I applied a blur to the original image to create the illusion that the hands and the mask are set closer to the camera. I selected the original layer and clicked the Layer Filters icon on the Layers sidebar. I selected the Blur check box and adjusted the Blur options. I changed the Quality to High, and set the Blur X and Blur Y settings to a strength of 10. I clicked OK to confirm the adjustment.

16. I wanted to create reflections of the figure's thumbs on the woman's face. I created a new layer by clicking the New Layer icon and painted these in manually using the Paintbrush Tool with white set as the foreground color.

17. And finally, I applied a blue tint over the entire image to create a cold, sterile environment over the entire image. I created a new layer and dragged it to the top of the Layers sidebar list. I set the foreground color to a dark aqua by clicking the Foreground color selection box, entering 688F88 in the # text box, and clicking OK. I selected the Paint Bucket Tool and clicked the new layer to fill it. I then set this layer's Blend Mode to Overlay and lowered the Alpha to 70% in the Layers sidebar. The cyborg image was complete.

Dragons

Source Images: "Portrait of a Lizard" by SpanicPhoto, "Hungry Croc" by Luka Esenko, "Rhino" by Clivia, "Goat" by Art-Y, "Fruit Bat in Flight" by 945-ontwerp, "Hands With Keys" by Focusing on People

Dragons have appeared in some form in the folklore of almost every culture worldwide. But the way they're portrayed in traditional stories varies greatly from culture to culture. They often hold spiritual significance in religion and represent primal forces of nature. And also, they just look pretty darned cool. In this tutorial, we'll be taking parts of several different animals and compositing them together to create our very own dragon.

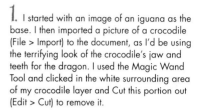

1. I started with an image of an iguana as the base. I then imported a picture of a crocodile (File > Import) to the document, as I'd be using the terrifying look of the crocodile's jaw and teeth for the dragon. I used the Magic Wand Tool and clicked in the white surrounding area of my crocodile layer and Cut this portion out (Edit > Cut) to remove it.

2. To assemble the mouth, I first started with the top jaw. I used the Lasso Selection Tool to select the top half of the crocodile's mouth and I copied (Edit > Copy) and pasted (Edit > Paste) this segment onto a new layer, then made the imported crocodile layer invisible for now by clicking its Eye icon in the Layers sidebar. I also chose Select > Select None to remove the selection marquee. Making sure that the layer with the copied jaw was selected in the Layers sidebar, I selected the Transformation Tool and resized and repositioned the top half of the crocodile mouth to situate on the iguana's mouth and pressed Enter to confirm the move. To remove the white background area around the crocodile teeth, I selected the Magic Wand Tool, clicked in the white area, then chose Edit > Cut to remove the white background portion from this layer.

3. I repeated this process to situate the lower jaw to the iguana as well, redisplaying and hiding the crocodile layer as needed. Part of the iguana's head was visible in between the jaws. To remove the exposed portion of the iguana's face, I created a new layer below the crocodile jaw layer and above the original layer. I selected the Paintbrush Tool with white set as my foreground color and painted over the exposed areas of the iguana to cover it.

4. Next, I merged the two jaw layers together by Ctrl+clicking each layer on the Layers sidebar and choosing Layer > Merge Layers. I then chose Image > Hue & Saturation, adjusted the Hue by -12 to achieve a more yellow tone to the jaw as was apparent in the iguana's face, raised the Saturation level by 10, and clicked OK to confirm the adjustment.

5. I wanted to apply the color from the iguana's face to the jaw further. So I first made a selection around the jaw layer (Select > Selection from Layer) and created a new layer (New Layer icon) above the jaw layer. I selected the Eye Dropper Tool and clicked on a portion of the iguana's face to sample the mustard yellow tone from its skin (HEX #D8BF52). Then, I selected the Paint Bucket Tool and filled the selected area with this tone, and set the layer's Blend Mode to Overlay in the Layers sidebar. I then lowered the Alpha of the layer to 48% and I was left with the jaw blending into the rest of the face more cleanly.

6. It was time to give the dragon some horns! I imported an image of a rhinoceros to my document (File > Import). I selected the Lasso Selection Tool and made a selection around the horns of the rhinoceros, then I copied and pasted this segment onto a new layer (Edit > Copy and Edit > Paste). I chose Select > Select None to remove the selection marquee, clicked the Eye icon beside the full rhino layer in the Layers sidebar to hide the layer, and then reselected the pasted horn layer.

7. I flipped the horn segment horizontally (Edit > Transform > Flip Horizontal), as the rhino was looking in the opposite direction than the iguana. I used the Magic Wand Tool and selected the white background surrounding the horns and removed this area (Edit > Cut). I chose Select > Select None to remove the selection marquee. Then, I selected the Transformation Tool and used it to position and size the horns on the dragon's face, pressing Enter to confirm the transformation. Finally, using the Eraser Tool set to 0 Hardness, I softened the bottom edge of the horns to blend it into the iguana's face more smoothly.

8. I also wanted to add horns to the top of the dragon's head. I imported another source image to my document (File > Import), this time that of a goat. I selected the horns and ear with the Lasso Selection Tool and pasted the selection onto a new layer with Edit > Copy and Edit > Paste. I then removed the selection marquee and hid the original goat layer. I used the Magic Wand Tool and selected the white background surrounding the horns and removed this area (Edit > Cut). I chose Select > Select None to remove the selection marquee. Then, I selected the Transformation Tool and used it to position and size the horns on the top of the dragon's head, pressing Enter to confirm the transformation.

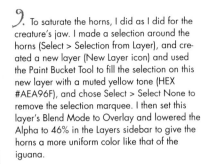

9. To saturate the horns, I did as I did for the creature's jaw. I made a selection around the horns (Select > Selection from Layer), and created a new layer (New Layer icon) and used the Paint Bucket Tool to fill the selection on this new layer with a muted yellow tone (HEX #AEA96F), and chose Select > Select None to remove the selection marquee. I then set this layer's Blend Mode to Overlay and lowered the Alpha to 46% in the Layers sidebar to give the horns a more uniform color like that of the iguana.

10. The face of the dragon was now complete. To create a more playful atmosphere for this creature, I decided to set the dragon on a human hand. I imported an image of a person's hand into my document with File > Import. I was prompted to resize my imported image due to the fact it was larger than my original canvas size. I selected Resize Image and the image was automatically resized to fit within the working canvas size. Using the Transformation Tool, I dragged the hand to the lower portion of the canvas in an appropriate position to hold the dragon and pressed Enter to confirm the move.

11. I selected the Eraser Tool, and erased the sky background on the hand layer. I also erased sections of the hand that were overlapping the iguana's arms to create the appearance that the iguana's "hands" were overlapping the human hand.

12. I needed to create the appearance of shadows under the dragon's arms next. I selected the human hand layer, and made a selection around the hand (Select > Selection from Layer). I then created a new layer (New Layer icon on the Layers sidebar) to hold the shadows. With the selection still around the human hand, I selected the Paintbrush Tool and selected black as the foreground color by clicking the Restore Colors button in the tool's options. I set the Hardness of the Paintbrush to 0, set the Alpha to 12%, and began painting in shadows underneath the iguana's hands on the human's skin. I then duplicated this layer (Layer > Duplicate Layer), and set the Blend Mode to Overlay for one of these shadow layers.

13. I then raised the contrast of the human's hand. I selected the hand layer by clicking it in the Layers sidebar. I chose Image > Brightness & Contrast, raised the Contrast to 10, and then clicked OK to confirm this adjustment.

14. To further make the creature appear like a dragon, I then decided to add wings. I imported a source image of a bat into the document using File > Import. Using the Lasso Selection Tool, I made a selection around the bat's wings and pasted it onto a new layer with Edit > Copy and Edit > Paste.

15. I dragged the wings using the Transformation Tool so that they appeared to be positioned on the dragon's back, then pressed the Enter key to confirm the move. Using the Eraser Tool, I removed the background from the bat wings layer, and erased the portions that were covering the rest of the dragon to make it appear as if the wings emerged from the back of the figure.

16. I added shadows on the wings next. I made a selection around the wings by selecting the wings layer and selecting Select > Selection from Layer. I chose the Paintbrush Tool, made sure black was still selected as the foreground color, set the Hardness to 0, and set the Alpha to 15%. I created a new layer, then dragged the Paintbrush to create the shadows around the base of the wings closest to the dragon figure. I duplicated my shadow layer (Layer > Duplicate Layer), and set the Blend Mode of my copied layer to Overlay. I then selected my original shadow layer and set the layer's Alpha to 75% on the Layers sidebar. You may end up needing to use different layer Alpha settings than mine depending on how strong you painted in the shadows to begin with.

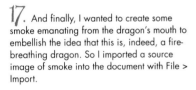

17. And finally, I wanted to create some smoke emanating from the dragon's mouth to embellish the idea that this is, indeed, a fire-breathing dragon. So I imported a source image of smoke into the document with File > Import.

18. I set this layer's Blend Mode to Screen, then used the Transformation Tool to resize and position the smoke to appear as if it were spewing from the dragon's mouth, and the image was complete.

19. And finally, I created two new layers at the very top of the Layers sidebar. I filled one of the layers completely with a dark yellow color (#8E8554) and the other with a dark blue (#69799A) using the Paint Bucket Tool. I set both of these layers Blend Modes to Overlay, giving a uniform color cast over the entire image.

Index

A

accentuating highlights, 62
adding
  borders, 12, 134–139, 147, 151
  colors, 79, 172, 216
  contrast, 141, 314
  damaging effects, 162
  definition, 204
  depth, 63
  dimension to images, 19
  effects, 9
  elements, 157
  glare, 96
  glowing, 66, 169
  gradient lighting, 143
  highlights, 26, 67, 254, 281, 302
  images, 78
  make-up effects, 167
  moons, 89
  objects, 34, 227
  Radial Gradient, 169
  reflections, 234, 281, 301
  ripples, 83
  saturation, 97
  selections, 85
  shadows, 34, 59, 159, 223, 228, 270, 277, 314
  shine, 308
  smoke, 222, 255
  space, 49
  stars, 89

  text, 5
  textures, 161, 217, 269
  tint, 206, 213, 303
  tone, 63, 234
  windows, 222
  wrinkles, 226
Adjust Levels dialog box, 149
aging
  people, 208–212
  photographs, 160–163
aliens, 202–207
aligning
  layers, 23
  objects, 108, 221
  reflections, 50
Alpha settings
  modifying, 25
  reducing, 41
anatomy scramble, 294–297
angles, modifying, 81
animals
  dress-up, 282–287
  hybrids, 214–217
applying
  colors, 312
  glowing, 31
  gradients, 290
  Layer Mask, 33
  layers, 6–9
  tint, 235, 309
  varying color schemes, 181
  vignette effects, 151
  yellow tints, 161

architecture, edible, 218–223
areas
  copying, 87
  darkening, 93
  enhancing, 158
  extending, 216
  moving, 3
  removing, 33, 39, 284
  shaded areas, creating, 46

B

Background Colors button, 93, 207
backgrounds
  behind glass, 94–97
  blurring, 53
  cleaning, 280
  cloning, 28–31
  colors, 4
  deleting, 21, 99, 180
  hiding, 69
basis for shadows, creating, 21
black and white, converting to, 182
black borders, creating, 159
blemishes, removing, 165
blending, 108
  colors, 171
  gradient colors, 4
  Overlay Blend Mode, 46
  smoothing, 254
blend modes, formatting, 25
blue colors, snowy days, 73

blueprints, drawing, 279
blurring
  images, 187, 309
  motion, 52–55, 235
  objects, 35
  snowy days, 74
borders
  adding, 12, 134–139, 147, 151
  comic book panels, 184
  creating, 159, 291
  selecting, 158
brightening images, 73
Brightness and Contrast dialog box, 8, 85
brushes, Shape Brush Tool, 4
burning, dodge & burn, 140–143
buttons, creating, 289

C

canvas earth, 272–277
cars, flying, 230–235
casting
  glowing, 45
  shadows, 16–19, 31, 197
  shine, 290
channels, Green, 38
chocolate, 198–201
chrome, 264–267
cleaning
  backgrounds, 280
  edges, 8, 13, 37
Clone Stamp Tool, 5, 261
cloning
  backgrounds, 28–31
  foregrounds, 30
close (X) button, 21
clouds, in the, 90–93
clowns, 122–125
Color Picker dialog box, 23, 85
Color Replacement Tool, 39
colors
  adding, 79, 172, 216
  applying, 161, 312
  Background Colors button, 93, 207
  backgrounds, 4
  blending, 171
  comic book panels, 182–185
  fading, 22
  foregrounds, 4
  foregrounds, modifying, 75

foregrounds, selecting, 23
hair, 167, 170–173
increasing, 150
inverting, 159
line art, 126–129
modifying, 37
Paint Bucket Tool, 4
Pick Color button, 153
replacing, 36–39
Restore Colors button, 158, 253
saturation, 47
Select Color dialog box, 5, 281
selecting, 3
shadows, 150
skin, modifying, 60–63
two-color borders, 135
comic book panels, 182–185
compositional cropping, 144–147
Constrain Proportion check box, 146
contrast
  adding, 314
  darkening, 141
  increasing, 229, 253
copying, 206
  areas, 87
  hue, 22
  images, Warhol-izing, 178–181
  layers, 11, 232, 257
  objects, 75
  segments, 258, 280
  selections, 37
  tint, 220
  with Transformation Tools, 29
creating. See formatting
cropping, 144–147
cross processing, 148–151
cutting, 12. See also moving
cyborgs, 304–309

D

damaging effects, adding, 162
darkening
  areas, 93
  colors, 61
  contrast, 141
  day to night images, 84–89
  images, 77
  objects, 23
  reflections, 82
  shadows, 109

day to night, 84–89
deepening shadows, 26
defining outlines, 253
definition to objects, adding, 204
deleting. See also cropping
  areas, 33, 39, 284
  backgrounds, 21, 99
  elements, 220
  selection marquees, 25
  smoke, 261
depth
  adding, 63
  enhancing, 69
  points of, 49
desaturation
  images, 70, 179
  selective, 152–155
deselecting layers, 290
dialog boxes
  Adjust Levels, 149
  Brightness and Contrast, 8, 85
  Color Picker, 23, 85
  Hue and Saturation, 142, 211
  Layer Filters, 87
  Layers Filter, 13
  Level Adjustment, 38
  Resize Canvas, 180
  Select Color, 5
dimension to images, adding, 19
disabling background layers, 53
displacement, 114–117
displaying toolbars, 17
distorting elements, 5
Distortion Tool, 3, 58, 103, 117, 247
  shadows, matching, 22
documents, creating, 7
dodge & burn, 140–143
dragging. See also moving
  freehand selections, 3
  layers, 235
  Liquify Tool, 5
  objects, 3
  Rectangle Selection tool, 3
  Rectangular Shape Tool, 4
  Smudge Tool, 5
dragons, 310–315
drawing. See also comic book panels
  blueprints, 279
  lightning, 65
  outlines, 175

drips, creating, 199. *See also* liquifying
Drop Layer, 9
dulling reflections, 82
duplicating. *See also* copying
  images, Warhol-izing, 178–181
  layers, 83, 161
  shapes, 17

E

edges
  cleaning, 8, 13, 37
  jagged, removing, 19
edible architecture, 218–223
editing, 206
  images, 284
  layers, 8
effects
  adding, 9
  blurring. *See* blurring
  damaging, adding, 162
  lighting, 44–47
  make-up, adding, 167
  splashing, 259
  vignette, applying, 151
elements
  adding, 157
  distorting, 5
  extracting, 17
  removing, 220
Elliptical Selection Tool, 3, 88
Elliptical Shape Tool, 41, 88, 231
enhancing
  areas, 158
  composition, 147
  depth, 69
  eyes, 174–177
  gradient light, 67
  highlights, 217, 277
  lighting, 45
  retouching, 164–169
  saturation, 132–133
  shadows, 245, 266, 277
Eraser Tool, 4, 117, 232
  backgrounds, applying on, 17
  reflections, 49
erasing. *See also* deleting
  backgrounds, 180
  layers, 71
exporting images, 9
exposing highlights, 262
extending areas, 216

extracting elements, 17
Eye Dropper Tool, 39, 231
eyes, enhancing, 174–177

f

face swaps, 106–109
fading
  colors, 22
  objects, 66
  reflections, 51
  shine, 307
feathered borders, 136
Feather feature, 172
filling
  Gradient Fill tool, 255
  layers, 315
  objects, 206
filters, Layers Filter dialog box, 13
fire, 252–255
flattening
  images, 77, 151, 189
  layers, 63
flipping. *See also* moving
  layers, 50
  segments, 312
floating borders, 137
floods, 80–83
flying cars, 230–235
foggy days, 68–71
fonts, selecting, 5
foregrounds
  cloning, 30
  colors, 4
  colors, modifying, 39, 70, 75
  colors, selecting, 23
formatting
  blend modes, 25
  borders, 159, 291
  buttons, 289
  layers, 9, 13
  lightning, 64–67
  new documents, 7
  new images, 289
  reflections, 233, 301
  selections, 18
  shadows, 13
  shadows, basis for, 21
  smoke, 315
  windows, 291
freehand selections, 3

G

gender bending, 224–229
ghosts, 28–31
glare
  adding, 96
  saturation, adding, 97
glass, behind, 94–97
7glowing, 87
  adding, 66, 169
  applying, 31
  casting, 45
gradient colors, 4
Gradient Fill Tool, 85, 255
gradient lighting
  adding, 143
  applying, 290
  enhancing, 67
Gradient Tool, 45
  shadows, 18
graffiti, 102–105
grayscale images, transforming, 153
Green channel, 38
grunge borders, 139

H

hair
  colors, 170–173
  lightening, 167
halftone patterns, 184
handles, 3
Hardlight Blend Mode, 200
hazy effects, 71, 73. *See also* foggy
    days
HEX text box, 263, 281
hiding
  backgrounds, 69
  layers, 30, 61, 86, 262
  shadows, 23
  toolbars, 17
highlights
  accentuating, 62
  adding, 26, 67, 254, 281, 302
  enhancing, 217, 277
  exposing, 262
  eyes, 176
  painting, 177
hue
  copying, 22
  modifying, 37

Hue and Saturation dialog box, 142, 211
hybrids, animal, 214–217

I

images
adding, 78
aging, 160–163
aliens, 202–207
anatomy scramble, 294–297
animal dress-up, 282–287
animal hybrids, 214–217
backgrounds, cloning, 28–31
behind glass, 94–97
blurring, 187, 309
borders, 134–139
brightening, 73
canvas earth, 272–277
chocolate, 198–201
chrome, 264–267
in the clouds, 90–93
clowns, 122–125
colors, hair, 170–173
colors, line art, 126–129
colors, modifying skin, 60–63
colors, replacing, 36–39
colors, selecting, 3
comic book panels, 182–185
compositional cropping, 144–147
cross processing, 148–151
cyborgs, 304–309
darkening, 77
day to night, 84–89
desaturation, 70, 179
dimension, adding to, 19
dodge & burn, 140–143
dragons, 310–315
edible architecture, 218–223
editing, 284
effects, lighting, 44–47
enhancing eyes, 174–177
exporting, 9
face swaps, 106–109
fire, 252–255
flattening, 77, 151, 189
floods, 80–83
flying cars, 230–235
foggy days, 68–71
gender bending, 224–229
graffiti, 102–105

importing, 7, 21, 57, 63, 101–105, 225
inanimate objects, 242–245
layers, masks, 32–35
lemon car, 192–197
lighting, matching, 24–27
lightning, creating, 64–67
liquify-displacement, 114–117
liquify-melting, 110–112
liquify-texturing, 118–121
merging, 63
miniaturizing, 186–189
motion, blurring, 52–55
moving, 58, 283
MP3 players, creating, 288–293
multiple, combining, 6. *See also* layers
people, aging, 208–212
perspective, 56–59
positioning, 7
precision selection, 40–43
rainy days, 76–79
recoloring, 39
resizing, 196, 225, 283
retouching, 164–169
robot frog, 278–281
rotating, 147
saturation, enhancing, 132–133
sea monsters, 298–303
selecting, 10–13
selective desaturation, 152–155
selective inversion, 156–159
shadows, casting, 16–19
shadows, matching, 20–23
sharpening, 217, 271
smoke, 260–263
snowy days, 72–75
softening, 92
stone, 268–271
surfaces, reflections, 48–51
tattoo art, 98–101
toiletbot, 236–241
tools, 2
unzipped, 246–251
Warhol-izing, 178–181
water, 256–259
weathering, 163
**importing images, 7, 21, 57, 63,
101–105, 225**
inanimate objects, 242–245
increasing. *See also* **adding**
colors, 150
contrast, 253

ink, 182. *See also* comic book panels
inserting. *See* adding
in the clouds tutorial, 90–93
inverting
colors, 159
selections, 156–159, 231, 248
isolating objects, 11

J

jagged edges, removing, 19

L

Lasso Selection Tool, 3, 83, 266
Lasso Tool, 11
Layer Filters dialog box, 87
layers
copying, 11, 232, 257
creating, 13
deselection, 290
dragging, 235
duplicating, 83, 161
editing, 8
erasing, 71
filling, 315
flattening, 63
flipping, 50
formatting, 9
hiding, 30, 61, 86, 262
masks, 8, 306
merging, 30, 42, 54, 74, 82, 233, 271,
311
moving, 3, 9
naming, 7
New Layer button, 47
overview of, 6–9
pasting, 243
positioning, 23
selections, 22
superimposing, 276
viewing, 54
Layers Filter dialog box, 13
lemon car, 192–197
Level Adjustment dialog box, 38
levels
Adjust Levels dialog box, 149
Alpha settings, reducing, 41
modifying, 38
lightening objects, 142, 167. *See also*
darkening; dodge & burn

lighting
day to night, 84–89
effects, 44–47
enhancing, 45
gradient, adding, 143
matching, 24–27
reflections, 51
lightning, creating, 64–67
line art colors, 126–129
liquifying. *See also* **Liquify Tool**
displacement, 114–117
melting, 110–112
textures, 118–121
Liquify Tool, 5, 79, 92, 199
lists, Quality drop-down, 86
lowering saturation, 161, 211

M

Magic Wand Tool, 3, 21, 99
make-up effects, adding, 167
marble texture, 269
marquee selections, removing, 25
mascara, applying, 168
masks, layers, 8, 306
matching
lighting, 24–27
shadows, 20–23
sharpness, 109
tones, 25
melting, 110–112
menus, View, 17
merging
images, 63
layers, 30, 42, 54, 74, 82, 233, 271, 311
reflections, 303
miniaturizing, 186–189
modifying
Adjust Levels dialog box, 149
Alpha settings, 25
angles, 81
colors, 37
colors, foregrounds, 75
hue, 37
levels, 38
saturation, 22
Tolerance settings, 3
tone, 109
toolbars, 17
monotone images, 71

motion
blurring, 52–55, 235
snowy days, 74
moving
images, 58, 283
layers, 3, 9
objects, 100
selections, 51
MP3 players, creating, 288–293
multiple-color borders, 135
multiple images, combining, 6. *See also* **layers**
Multiply Blend Mode, 95, 101, 117

N

naming layers, 7
navigating, 1
tools, 2–5
new documents, creating, 7
new images, creating, 289
New Layer button, 47
new layers, formatting, 9

O

objects
adding, 34, 227
aligning, 108
blurring, 35
copying, 75
cutting, 12
darkening, 23
dragging, 3
fading, 66
filling, 206
inanimate, 242–245
isolating, 11
painting, 35
positioning, 221
recoloring, 173, 196
removing, 53
replacing, 227
resizing, 33, 267
rotating, 100
skewing, 79, 279
Options button, 254
outlines. *See also* **shapes**
defining, 253
drawing, 175
overlapping shadows, 27
Overlay Blend Mode, 46, 105

P

Paintbrush Tool, 4, 89, 97
shadows, applying to, 19
Paint Bucket Tool, 4, 97
painting
foreground images, 70
highlights, 177
objects, 35
shadows, 26
pasting, 206. *See also* **moving**
layers, 243
objects, 11
people, aging, 208–212
perspective, 56–59
warping, 3
photographs. *See* images; tutorials
Pick Color button, 153
planning
blueprints, 279
shapes, 257
points of depth, 49
Polygonal Selection Tool, 81, 86
positioning
images, 7
layers, 23
objects, 221
reflections, 50, 82
precision selection, 40–43
previewing selections, 38
processing, cross, 148–151

Q

Quality drop-down list, 86

R

Radial Gradient, adding, 169
rainy days, 76–79
ranges, modifying color tolerance, 3
re-adding un-blurred objects, 54. *See also* **adding**
rearranging layers, 9
recoloring
images, 39
objects, 173, 196
Rectangular Selection Tool, 3, 12, 86
Rectangular Shape Tool, 4
reducing Alpha settings, 41

reflections, 27
  adding, 59, 234, 281
  angles, modifying, 81
  chrome. *See* chrome
  creating, 77, 233, 301
  lighting, 51
  merging, 303
  positioning, 82
  surfaces, 48–51
removing. *See also* **cropping; erasing**
  areas, 33, 39, 284
  backgrounds, 21, 99
  blemishes, 165
  elements, 220
  jagged edges, 19
  objects, 53
  selection marquees, 25
  smoke, 261
replacing
  colors, 36–39
  objects, 227
Resize Canvas dialog box, 180
resizing, 3
  images, 196, 225, 283
  objects, 33, 267
Restore Colors button, 141, 158, 253
retouching images, 164–169
reversing
  images, 58
  selections, 49
ripples, adding, 83
robot frog, 278–281
rotating. *See also* **moving**
  images, 147
  objects, 100
roughing up surfaces, 226

S

saturation, 313
  adding, 97
  colors, 47
  enhancing, 132–133
  Hue and Saturation dialog box, 211
  lowering, 161
  modifying, 22
  selective desaturation, 152–155
sea monsters, 298–303

segments
  copying, 258, 280
  flipping, 312
Select Color dialog box, 5, 281
Selection Border text box, 158
selections
  adding, 85
  colors, 3
  copying, 37
  creating, 18
  fonts, 5
  images, 10–13
  inverting, 231, 248
  Lasso Selection Tool, 266
  layers, 22
  marquees, removing, 25
  moving, 51
  objects, freehand, 3
  precision, 40–43
  previewing, 38
  Rectangular Selection Tool, 12
  reversing, 49
  tools, 2
selective desaturation, 152–155
selective inversion, 156–159
shaded areas, creating, 46
shadows
  adding, 26, 34, 59, 159, 223, 228, 270, 277, 314
  casting, 16–19, 31, 197
  colors, 150
  darkening, 109
  deepening, 26
  enhancing, 245, 266, 277
  formatting, 13
  hiding, 23
  matching, 20–23
  overlapping, 27
  painting, 26
Shape Brush Tool, 4, 171
shapes
  duplicating, 17
  planning, 257
sharpening
  images, 217, 271
  matching, 109
shine
  adding, 308
  casting, 290
  fading, 307

simple borders, 135
skewing
  objects, 79, 279
  shadows, 18
skin, 60–63, 226. *See also* **surfaces**
smoke, 260–263
  adding, 222, 255
  creating, 315
  removing, 261
smoothing
  blending, 254
  surfaces, 165
Smudge Tool, 5
snowy days, 72–75
softening images, 92
space, adding, 49
splashing effects, 259. *See also* **water**
stars, adding, 89
stone, 268–271
superimposing layers, 276
surfaces
  chrome, 267
  reflections, 48–51
  roughing up, 226
  smoothing, 165
  stone. *See* stone
Switch Between Foreground button, 207

T

tattoo art, 98–101
Text tool, 5
texture. *See also* **surfaces**
  adding, 161, 217, 269
  comic book panels, 185
  liquifying, 118–121
  viewing, 103
thick borders, 135
tint
  adding, 206, 213, 303
  applying, 235, 309
  copying, 220
toiletbot, 236–241
Tolerance settings, modifying, 3
tone
  adding, 63, 234
  matching, 25
  modifying, 109

tools
   Clone Stamp Tool, 5, 261
   Color Replacement Tool, 39
   Distortion Tool, 3, 22, 58, 103, 117
   Elliptical Selection Tool, 3, 88
   Elliptical Shape Tool, 41, 88, 231
   Eraser Tool, 4, 49, 117, 232
   Eye Dropper Tool, 39, 231
   Gradient Fill Tool, 85, 255
   Gradient Tool, 18, 45
   Lasso Selection Tool, 3, 83, 266
   Lasso Tool, 11
   Liquify Tool, 5, 79, 92, 199
   Magic Wand Tool, 3, 21, 99
   Paintbrush Tool, 4, 19, 89, 97
   Paint Bucket Tool, 4, 97
   Polygonal Selection Tool, 81, 86
   Rectangular Selection Tool, 3, 12, 86
   Rectangular Shape Tool, 4
   selecting, 2
   Shape Brush Tool, 4, 171
   Smudge Tool, 5
   Text, 5
Transformation Tool, 3, 29, 193
trimming reflections, 81
tutorials
   aging photos, 160–163
   aliens, 202–207
   anatomy scramble, 294–297
   animal dress-up, 282–287
   animal hybrids, 214–217
   backgrounds, cloning, 28–31
   behind glass, 94–97
   borders, 134–139
   canvas earth, 272–277
   chocolate, 198–201
   chrome, 264–267
   in the clouds, 90–93
   clowns, 122–125
   colors, hair, 170–173
   colors, line art, 126–129
   colors, modifying skin, 60–63
   colors, replacing, 36–39
   comic book panels, 182–185
   compositional cropping, 144–147
   cross processing, 148–151
   cyborgs, 304–309

   day to night, 84–89
   dodge & burn, 140–143
   dragons, 310–315
   edible architecture, 218–223
   effects, lighting, 44–47
   enhancing eyes, 174–177
   face swaps, 106–109
   fire, 252–255
   floods, 80–83
   flying cars, 230–235
   foggy days, 68–71
   gender bending, 224–229
   graffiti, 102–105
   inanimate objects, 242–245
   layers, masks, 32–35
   lemon car, 192–197
   lighting, matching, 24–27
   lightning, creating, 64–67
   liquify-displacement, 114–117
   liquify-melting, 110–112
   liquify-texturing, 118–121
   miniaturizing, 186–189
   motion, blurring, 52–55
   MP3 players, creating, 288–293
   people, aging, 208–212
   perspective, 56–59
   precision selection, 40–43
   rainy days, 76–79
   retouching photos, 164–169
   robot frog, 278–281
   saturation, enhancing, 132–133
   sea monsters, 298–303
   selective desaturation, 152–155
   selective inversion, 156–159
   shadows, casting, 16–19
   shadows, matching, 20–23
   smoke, 260–263
   snowy days, 72–75
   stone, 268–271
   surfaces, reflections, 48–51
   tattoo art, 98–101
   toiletbot, 236–241
   unzipped, 246–251
   Warhol-izing, 178–181
   water, 256–259
two-color borders, 135

U
unzipped, 246–251

V
vertical motion blur effects, 55
viewing
   layers, 54
   texture, 103
   toolbars, 17
View menu, 17
vignette effects
   applying, 151
   borders, 138

W
Warhol-izing images, 178–181
warping perspective, 3
water, 256–259
weathering images, 163
windows
   adding, 222
   creating, 291
wrinkles
   adding, 226
   removing, 165

Y
yellow tints, applying, 161

Z
zooming, 17

License Agreement/Notice of Limited Warranty

By opening the sealed disc container in this book, you agree to the following terms and conditions. If, upon reading the following license agreement and notice of limited warranty, you cannot agree to the terms and conditions set forth, return the unused book with unopened disc to the place where you purchased it for a refund.

License:

The enclosed software is copyrighted by the copyright holder(s) indicated on the software disc. You are licensed to copy the software onto a single computer for use by a single user and to a backup disc. You may not reproduce, make copies, or distribute copies or rent or lease the software in whole or in part, except with written permission of the copyright holder(s). You may transfer the enclosed disc only together with this license, and only if you destroy all other copies of the software and the transferee agrees to the terms of the license. You may not decompile, reverse assemble, or reverse engineer the software.

Notice of Limited Warranty:

The enclosed disc is warranted by Course Technology to be free of physical defects in materials and workmanship for a period of sixty (60) days from end user's purchase of the book/disc combination. During the sixty-day term of the limited warranty, Course Technology will provide a replacement disc upon the return of a defective disc.

Limited Liability:

THE SOLE REMEDY FOR BREACH OF THIS LIMITED WARRANTY SHALL CONSIST ENTIRELY OF REPLACEMENT OF THE DEFECTIVE DISC. IN NO EVENT SHALL COURSE TECHNOLOGY OR THE AUTHOR BE LIABLE FOR ANY OTHER DAMAGES, INCLUDING LOSS OR CORRUPTION OF DATA, CHANGES IN THE FUNCTIONAL CHARACTERISTICS OF THE HARDWARE OR OPERATING SYSTEM, DELETERIOUS INTERACTION WITH OTHER SOFTWARE, OR ANY OTHER SPECIAL, INCIDENTAL, OR CONSEQUENTIAL DAMAGES THAT MAY ARISE, EVEN IF COURSE TECHNOLOGY AND/OR THE AUTHOR HAS PREVIOUSLY BEEN NOTIFIED THAT THE POSSIBILITY OF SUCH DAMAGES EXISTS.

Disclaimer of Warranties:

COURSE TECHNOLOGY AND THE AUTHOR SPECIFICALLY DISCLAIM ANY AND ALL OTHER WARRANTIES, EITHER EXPRESS OR IMPLIED, INCLUDING WARRANTIES OF MERCHANTABILITY, SUITABILITY TO A PARTICULAR TASK OR PURPOSE, OR FREEDOM FROM ERRORS. SOME STATES DO NOT ALLOW FOR EXCLUSION OF IMPLIED WARRANTIES OR LIMITATION OF INCIDENTAL OR CONSEQUENTIAL DAMAGES, SO THESE LIMITATIONS MIGHT NOT APPLY TO YOU.

Other:

This Agreement is governed by the laws of the State of Massachusetts without regard to choice of law principles. The United Convention of Contracts for the International Sale of Goods is specifically disclaimed. This Agreement constitutes the entire agreement between you and Course Technology regarding use of the software.